IMAGES
of America

FORT MYERS

FORT MYERS—YOU ARE MY HOME!

FLOWERING FLORIDA; ocean-edged, lake-dotted and sunshine-soaked; breezed and fanned with water-cooled winds, fresh from their playground o'er Gulf and Ocean; with no mountain range to halt and hold rain-laden clouds, humidity is gone—banished, it seems, by the foresight of Nature's intention. Eons ago was a dirge chanted at the funeral of chill and cheerless weather.

Four hundred miles further south than San Diego and yet no farther east than Cleveland, snuggling next the edge of Caloosahatchee's rippling waters; a short ride from the opalescence of the Gulf, is my home—Fort Myers. Nearby lie the beaches that are your setting, sloping borders of a shell-sand fringe—pounded to powder by the ceaseless waves of centuries of Time.

O'erhead a deep blue heaven, specked with fluffy clouds driven by the never-failing winds of the semi-tropic trades; an ethereal arch, as a roof for my home, dipping to the west to sink into the myriad colored waters of the gulf—to the east ending in the vast Beyond of the great Atlantic.

A gem-city, rich in a thousand ways—fascinating to the eye; peopled with men and women, home-builders and home-keepers, by the manner of their birth; clean, well planned and managed, graced with Nature's greatest gifts of soil, air, water and vegetation. A thriving, bustling place, wrapt in the healthy fever of rapidly acquired wealth, yet ever awake to the needs of a safe and sane future. Surrounded by marvelous back country—in places muck—the rotted fall of vegetable growth of centuries; muck equal to that of the fertile valley of the Nile.

Road-barred, you have been for years, to the eager, pleasure-seeking pilgrim of America—but now within reach; now shall the northern hordes worn by weary winters and battles of big business, seek out the glories of which they've heard—to revel in them. Rumor of your worth and beauty spreads fast among people of wealth and leisure. Thousands have come, hundreds have stayed and other thousands left but to return again. God hid you within what once was an impassable terrain that the achievement of your finding might be the greater.

But Man came—sturdy leather-handed pioneers with purpose; they came and saw a future, built homes and reared families; hewing and filling, grading the long smooth ribbons of road that have opened the treasure trove to the eager eyes of a waiting world. And the world has come in throngs—and will continue coming—settling here to delight in your glories—to grow still further with you. Some will spend the fortunes won in the stress and battle of business in other parts. Still others farming the rich loamy lands, shall take from out the soft soil-pad that tops your base of rock and coral the wealth of thriving crops.

Your future is assured, your value known. And by the manner of your building you shall be judged. And, soundly built and sanely planned, you shall rise ever higher into your own place in the sun. Fort Myers, where Nature's work is finished, but where Man's has just begun—you are My Home!

Flowery prose characterized land boom ads of the 1920s. The above example appeared in a promotional booklet prepared by the city's Chamber of Commerce.

On the cover: Picnickers have boarded the steamboat *Corona* and prepare to leave Fort Myers c. 1915. Since time immemorial the wide and beautiful Caloosahatchee River has linked Fort Myers to the outside world.

IMAGES
of America

FORT MYERS

Gregg Turner and Stan Mulford

ARCADIA
PUBLISHING

ISBN 978-0-7385-0667-8

Published by Arcadia Publishing
Charleston, South Carolina

Printed in the United States of America

Library of Congress Catalog Card Number: 00-110538

For all general information contact Arcadia Publishing at:
Telephone 843-853-2070
Fax 843-853-0044
E-mail sales@arcadiapublishing.com
For customer service and orders:
Toll-Free 1-888-313-2665

Visit us on the Internet at www.arcadiapublishing.com

Images herein, unless otherwise noted, are courtesy of the Fort Myers Historical Museum, Sara Nell Gran, and the Lee County Black Historical Society, Inc.

Proceeds of this book benefit the Fort Myers Historical Museum Foundation, Inc.

CONTENTS

ACKNOWLEDGMENTS

The authors take much pleasure in acknowledging the following individuals and organizations. Their professional and responsive support made this book possible.

Joan Morris, Florida State Photo Archives; Cynthia Wise, Florida State Library; Manny Arocho, Photo Archives Librarian, Tampa-Hillsborough County Public Library System; Mildred Santiago, Fort Myers Historical Museum; Jeanne Hickam and Mike Mulligan, the Railroad Museum of South Florida; Daisy Benjamin and Nina Denson Rogers, Lee County Black Historical Society; Marjorie Johnson; Sara Nell Gran; Sherrie Stokes; Jo Talbird; and Thomas D. Jones.

To one and all we extend our sincerest appreciation!

—G.T. and S.M.

INTRODUCTION

"There is only one Fort Myers, and ninety million people are going to find it out."
—inventor Thomas Edison

The city of Fort Myers, Florida, is charmingly situated on the wide and beautiful Caloosahatchee, some 15 miles up river from the Gulf of Mexico. Tropical flowers and shrubbery help form the city's landscape, and many of its streets are lined with royal palms. The community itself is located almost due south of Cleveland, Ohio, and, interestingly, some 400 miles farther south than San Diego, California.

The "City of Palms" began life as a military setting, at a time when over 50 such outposts were scattered throughout the territory of Florida during the Second Seminole War (1835–1842). To know something about that war and why Fort Myers was established, we need to retreat a few centuries in time to the arrival of the Spaniards.

Seeking gold and rejuvenating waters since Columbus first visited Hispaniola in 1492, explorer Juan Ponce de Leon ventured further west in 1513 and discovered a "new" land during the Spanish Feast of Flowers (Pascua Florida). "Florida" thus became a Spanish acquisition. Back then there were about 40,000 Native Americans living on land that their ancestors had occupied for some 12,000 years. Tribal in-fighting was not uncommon, and many were highly skilled in combat. To the Spanish intruders they proved quite unfriendly.

Several years would pass before the pen-pushers of Madrid finally validated Ponce's claim. Later, in 1521, Ponce left Puerto Rico with all the paraphernalia to colonize his new land. A landing attempt was made on the west coast of Florida, perhaps near the Caloosahatchee ("River of the Calusa"), where Ponce encountered one of the most savage of tribes. Badly wounded, he and his group retreated to Cuba where he shortly passed on to a greater reward.

Years later Pedro Menendez de Aviles, captain general of the Spanish treasure fleets, was assigned the task of removing any rivals in Florida plus converting the Native Americans to Catholicism. He had far greater success with the former than with the latter. Menendez himself is best remembered as having established, in 1565, the first European settlement in what became the United States of America. St. Augustine, with its protective fort, helped guard the sea lanes for Spanish ships carrying gold and silver from Mexico and Peru. The Spanish also founded Pensacola, on the western edge of the Panhandle. These two settings, plus a middle establishment at St. Marks, were the only permanent communities the Spaniards made during their lengthy occupancy.

When not converting Native Americans, the Spaniards took many of the indigenous tribesmen as slaves, two ambitions that fueled nearly 200 years of hostilities. Constant warfare and the devastating effects of European diseases (syphilis, yellow fever, influenza, and smallpox) decimated the native tribes of Florida. By the middle of the 18th century only a few Native Americans remained.

With Florida practically empty and the Spanish empire slowly crumbling, certain Native-American tribes of Georgia and Alabama began moving into Florida to escape the encroachment of English settlers and the politics of the Creek Nation. Most of the tribes spoke their own language, and collectively they became known as Seminoles, from the Oconee word meaning "runaway" or "wild."

A critical problem among the Seminoles, and between the Native Americans and English settlers, was the issue of African-American slaves. Many often slipped away or were stolen from their owners, and in Spanish Florida escaped slaves could not be legally hunted or returned. Many, in fact, willingly became Native-American slaves—life was not as harsh and intermarriage was not uncommon.

With the usual disregard for minor legalities, a number of freebooters and blithe spirits began to occupy the fertile lands of the Panhandle, and attempts were made to drive the Seminoles off the land and capture the slaves. The Native Americans, of course, fiercely resisted and countered with vigorous defense measures, including the use of firearms, all of which greatly disturbed the white settlers.

In 1818, President Monroe sent Gen. Andrew Jackson into Spanish-held Florida with an army of almost 2,000 men. Jackson destroyed a fort that was built by former slaves (for defense) and hung several English traders for furnishing firearms to the Native Americans. The invasion shocked Madrid, which could really only do one thing: sell Florida for a nominal sum. After America acquired Florida in 1821, settlers flocked to the Panhandle, where the soil proved ideal for corn, cotton, and tobacco. This left the Native Americans with no choice but to flee south, and their farming life of ages past gave way to a nomadic hunting culture.

To further heighten the hostilities, Pres. Andrew Jackson signed the Indian Removal Act in 1830. Jackson and others were determined to get rid of the tribes, pay for lands taken, and deport them to reservations west of the Mississippi. But the Native Americans refused to go, and they fought back in guerrilla style. Five years later, Maj. Francis Dade and over 100 of his men on a march from Fort Brooke to Fort King were killed by Native Americans. By orders of the President, the Second Seminole War began.

This second of three Seminole wars raged all across southern Florida, especially along the Caloosahatchee and Lake Okeechobee. Small army depots (called forts) sprang up along the river, such as Fort Thompson, Fort Adams, Fort Denaud, and one at the river's mouth named Fort Dulany. After three-and-a-half years of hit and run fighting, many of the Native Americans became exhausted. In fact nearly 3,000 men, women, and children eventually surrendered and were sent to Indian Country in Oklahoma. Those that remained were ready to talk peace but not deportation.

The curtain now went up on Maj. Gen. Alexander Macomb, commander in chief of the army. Macomb came to Florida to iron out differences with several Native-American chiefs in 1839. As an inducement, Macomb offered them a huge reservation—all land west of Lake Okeechobee from the headwaters of the Peas (Peace) River to the southern tip of Florida. Even a substantial trading post would be erected on the Caloosahatchee, which coursed through the dedicated lands. How much of the oral treaty the chiefs really understood will never be known, but they agreed to move their people within 60 days.

And this is where our story really begins.

One

The Fort

The treaty proferred by General Macomb in 1839 certainly seemed inviting. In exchange for peace, Florida's remaining Native Americans would be allowed to live unmolested on a huge allotment of land in South Florida, where they could grow crops, hunt, and fish. Further, a well-stocked trading post would be built for them on the Caloosahatchee. Unfortunately, Macomb failed to mention that the reservation was only a stop-gap measure—and that one day mass deportation to the West was inevitable.

Nevertheless, several Native-American chiefs accepted the oral treaty and soon the migration to the reserve began. In early July, Lt. Col. William Selby Harney sailed up the Caloosahatchee in search of a trading post location. The Caloosahatchee itself sliced through the reservation, and flowed lazily from Lake Flirt for 40 miles west to the Gulf waters at Punta Rassa. The tribes would be able to reach the river post by canoe, or in conjunction with its many tributaries or canals that had been originally dug by the ancient Calusa tribe. Footpaths, too, crisscrossed the reserve lands.

Colonel Harney selected a trading post site in modern-day Cape Coral. Once encamped, he and 26 soldiers went to work building a large log cabin for the three civilian traders who would do business with their new clients. Two black men who had lived with the Seminoles accompanied Harney and acted as interpreters.

As construction of the post unfolded, curious natives canoed across the river from modern-day Fort Myers to watch the progress, including one of the Seminole's most ferocious warriors, Chief Billy Bowlegs. The Native Americans talked to the soldiers as well as the future storekeepers and interpreters, but their visits suddenly ceased.

By now, the tribes had learned that the Macomb "treaty" was a temporary measure. Quickly a war council was called, and chiefs throughout the reservation angrily denounced the army general with forked tongue. Duly aroused, a delegation of warriors (including Bowlegs) silently crossed the Caloosahatchee near dawn on July 24, 1839. Slowly they crept toward Harney's camp, which lacked sentries.

The ensuing attack was a complete and total surprise. The Native-American warriors shrieked through the trading post grounds and killed soldiers on the spot—many in their bunks. Eighteen men perished that morning along with the three traders and the river pilot. Harney and eight soldiers managed to escape; they swam to their boats and left for Punta Rassa. The Second Seminole War had just been reignited!

News of the bloody Harney Point Massacre shocked Floridians; cries went up for the army to take action, and that they did.

Zachary Taylor, promoted from colonel to brigadier general for his part in the Battle of Okeechobee, now re-established supply forts along the length of the Caloosahatchee, including Fort Dulany at the river's mouth. By controlling this important waterway, Taylor's troops could systematically spread out and penetrate the Native-American settlements in the forbidding Everglades. Villages were eventually burned, crops destroyed, and many Native American men, women, and children were captured. It was during this period that Colonel Harney, of massacre fame, got his revenge. Harney rooted out one of the chiefs that raided his Caloosahatchee camp, Chakaika, who was hung along with a half-dozen of his warriors.

Taylor's forces hunted and hounded the Native Americans from every quarter. Even bloodhounds were brought in from Cuba! No less than 53 military posts were established in Florida, which were linked by a system of wagon roads. The goal was to deprive the Native Americans of food, camp, and rest.

As 1841 drew to a close there were probably a thousand Native Americans left in all of Florida. Some Floridians now felt there was no reason to continue the bloody hostilities, but government money continued to flow into the war machine. After all, army volunteers and civilian employees received attractive cash payments, as did plantation owners, who were collecting fat fees for their hired-out slave labor.

Penetrating the Big Cypress Swamp and the Everglades made the Caloosahatchee an important base of operations. As noted, Fort Dulany was re-established at Punta Rassa in the summer of 1841, but shortly after its buildings were constructed a hurricane destroyed the setting. Its commander, Captain McKavitt, was then ordered to build a new fort in a safer location. McKavitt went up the Caloosahatchee some 15 miles and found a relatively high hammock of land with palm, pine, and oak trees. A fresh water creek was discovered nearby and the location was amazingly free of mosquitoes. Thus, a new supply station was built that November and named Fort Harvie, in memory of a lieutenant who had died of malaria.

Fort Harvie was short lived and was abandoned in March of 1842, shortly after the Second Seminole War ended. Several hundred Native Americans now remained in South Florida, and they continued to live in the territory that was promised to them back in 1839. Eventually they burned Fort Harvie to the ground and the post was forgotten.

The next eight years were relatively peaceful times in the region until five drunken Native Americans killed a trader named Whiddon at his post on the Peace River. Even though the guilty Native Americans were punished, cries again went up for total Native American removal. To achieve that end, the war department decided, in 1850, to build a new fort on the Caloosahatchee.

On St. Valentine's Day, Maj. Gen. David Twiggs ordered a Major Ridgely of the 4th Artillery to "proceed up the Calusa River and select a suitable place for the establishment of a post . . . and to throw up such light works as may secure his stores and remove from the Indians any temptation to which his isolated position may give rise. The post will be called Fort Myers."

Major Ridgely sailed up the Caloosahatchee and spotted an inviting clearing on a large hammock with palm, pine, and oak trees. A fresh water creek was nearby, and the area was amazingly free of mosquitoes. Ridgely may have known that this very spot was where Fort Harvie stood eight years before. He probably also knew why General Twiggs wanted the new post to be called Fort Myers. Most forts were named after soldiers who have died in the line of duty or performed valorous deeds. Fort Myers was named after Brevet Lt. Col. Abraham Charles Myers, a soldier who was deeply in love with the general's daughter.

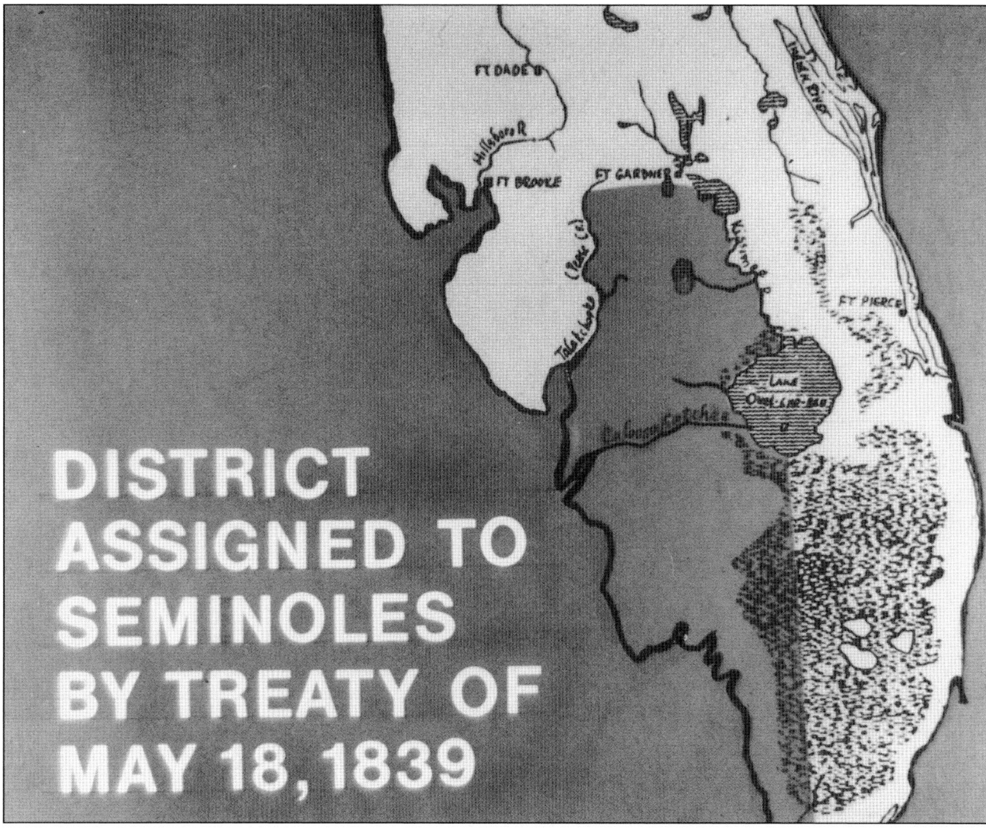

The map's shaded area depicts the huge territory offered to Florida's remaining Native Americans in 1839, an inducement to end a four-year-old war. They reluctantly accepted, thinking the Indian Removal campaign was over and they could live in peace. That summer several hundred Seminoles and other tribes moved into the Caloosahatchee area, but the military failed to mention it was a temporary measure and that deportation to the West was inevitable.

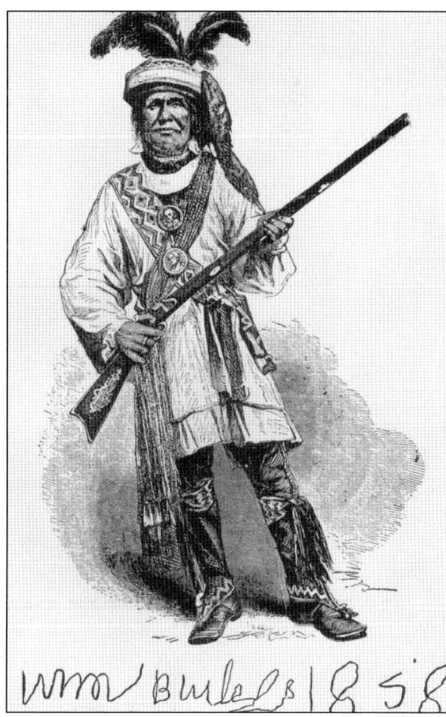

Seminole Chief Holata Micco inherited the name of a French ancestor named Bealieu. In time, though, the Native-American tongue mangled the pronunciation to the English equivalent of "Bowlegs," even though there was nothing wrong with Billy's legs! In fact the chief proved to be one of the most ferocious warriors the military ever encountered. (Courtesy of Florida State Photo Archives.)

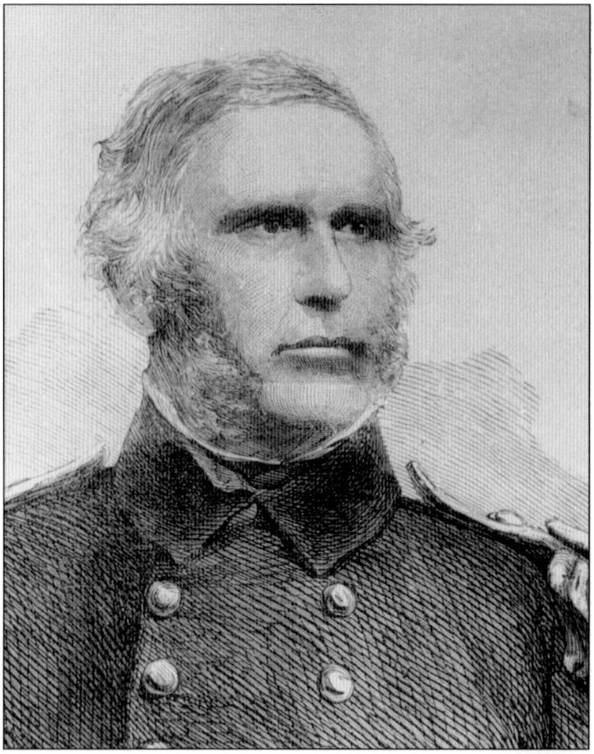

Lt. Col. William Harney's failure to post sentries that fateful night of July 24, 1839, resulted in the loss of many men and re-ignited the Second Seminole War. Nevertheless, Harney would acquit himself with valor in the ensuing Indian Wars as well as the Mexican War of 1846–1848. On the eve of the Civil War (1861), he was one of only four United States officers ranked as general.

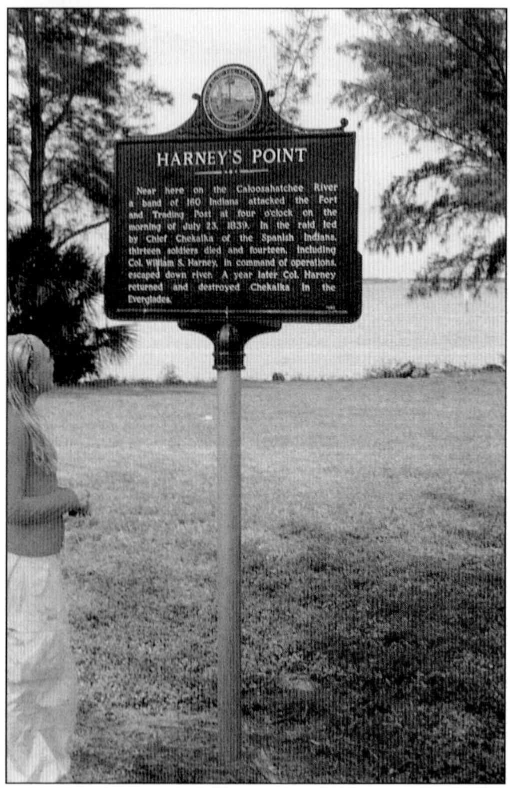

When news of the "Harney Point Massacre" hit the newspapers, the tranquil parcel seen here became forever known as Harney's Point. In 1958 it became part of the new city of Cape Coral. Years later a bridge across the Caloosahatchee was begun from the Point, and today most motorists fly past the marker with no inkling they are treading on history.

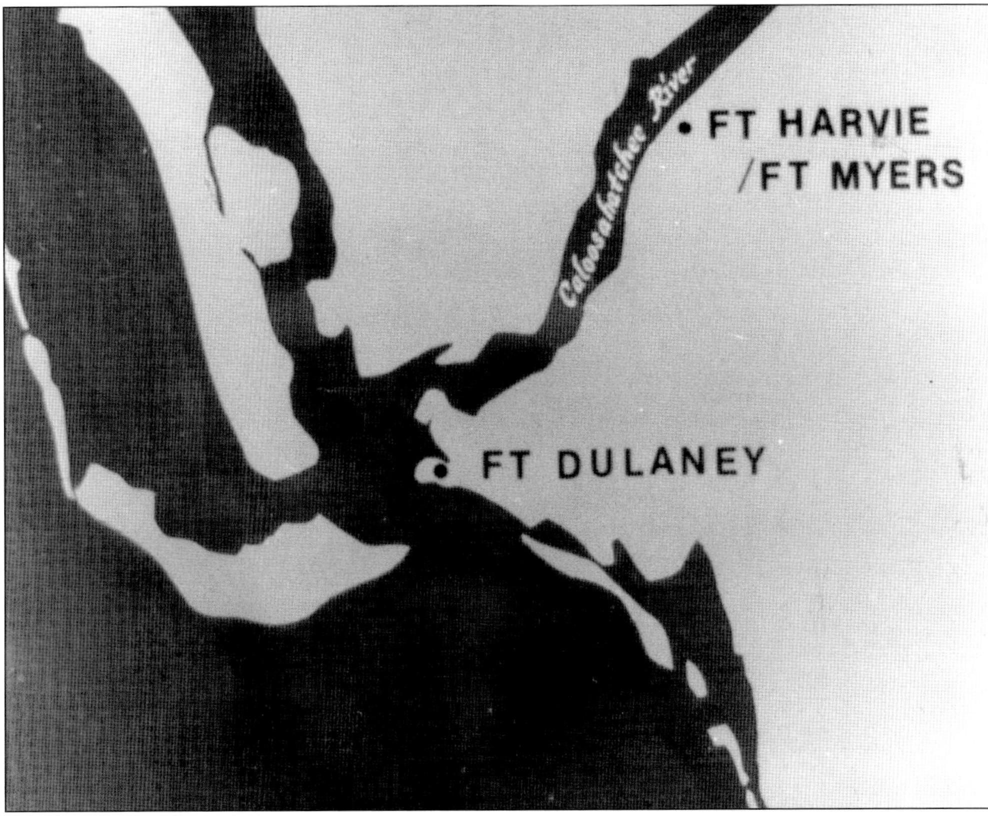

Fort Dulany, near the mouth of the Caloosahatchee, was a supply base during the Indian wars. It was destroyed by a hurricane in October 1841, whereupon soldiers built a safer facility 15 miles up river and named it after Lt. James Harvie. Within four months the structure was abandoned as the war ended. Native Americans celebrated by burning Fort Harvie and it was soon forgotten.

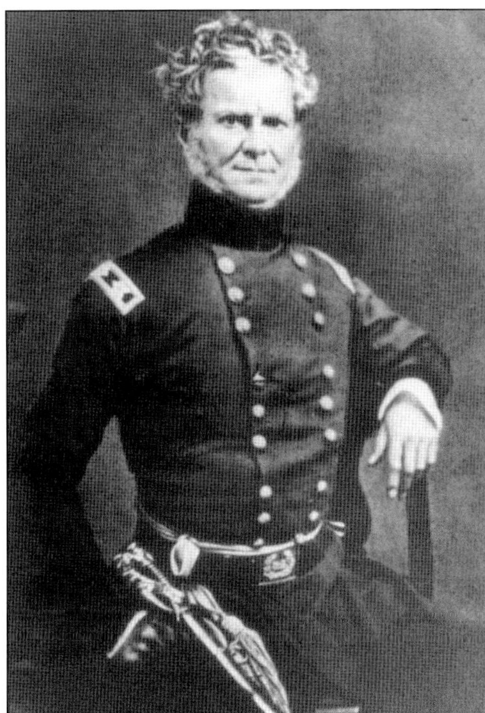

Eight years after the Second Seminole War ended, the government was still keen on removing Native Americans from the peninsula. To pursue that end, Gen. David Twiggs (seen here), commanding army officer in Florida, wrote an order on February 14, 1850, instructing a Major Ridgely to proceed up the Caloosahatchee and establish a new fort. The site Ridgely selected was the old forest clearing of Fort Harvie.

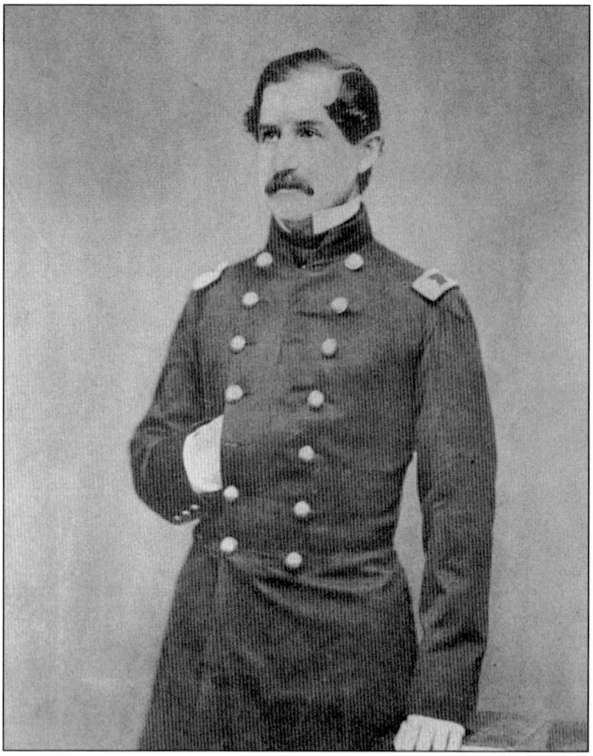

General Twiggs named the new Caloosahatchee facility Fort Myers. Forts were usually named for soldiers who had performed deeds of valor, and Lt. Col. Abraham Charles Myers (West Point '34) had performed valorously in the Mexican War and other fields; however, the honor was really bestowed upon the General's chief quartermaster for one reason—he was in love!

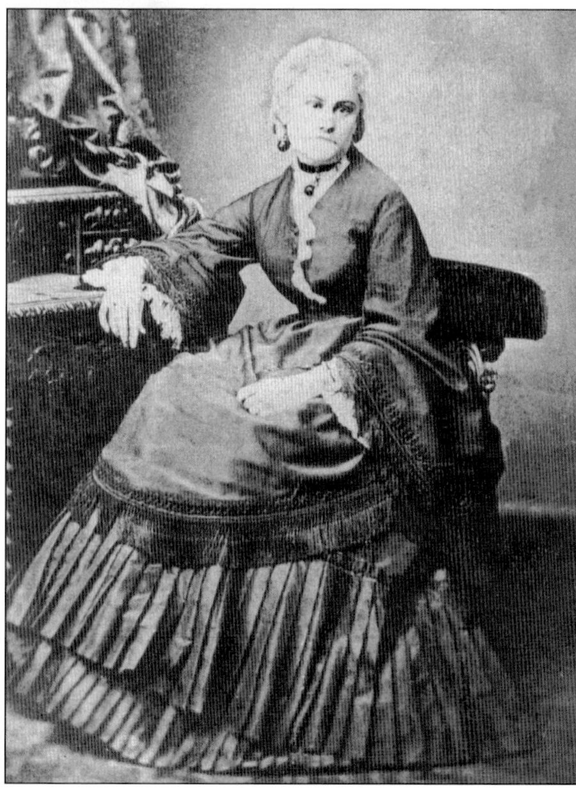

Shown in this photograph as a mature mother of four, Marion Twiggs Myers is not as fetching as she was in 1850, when she became engaged to her father's chief quartermaster. She was betrothed to Lt. Col. Abraham Myers at age 13, married at 16, and of course rejoiced when her father named a fort after her beau.

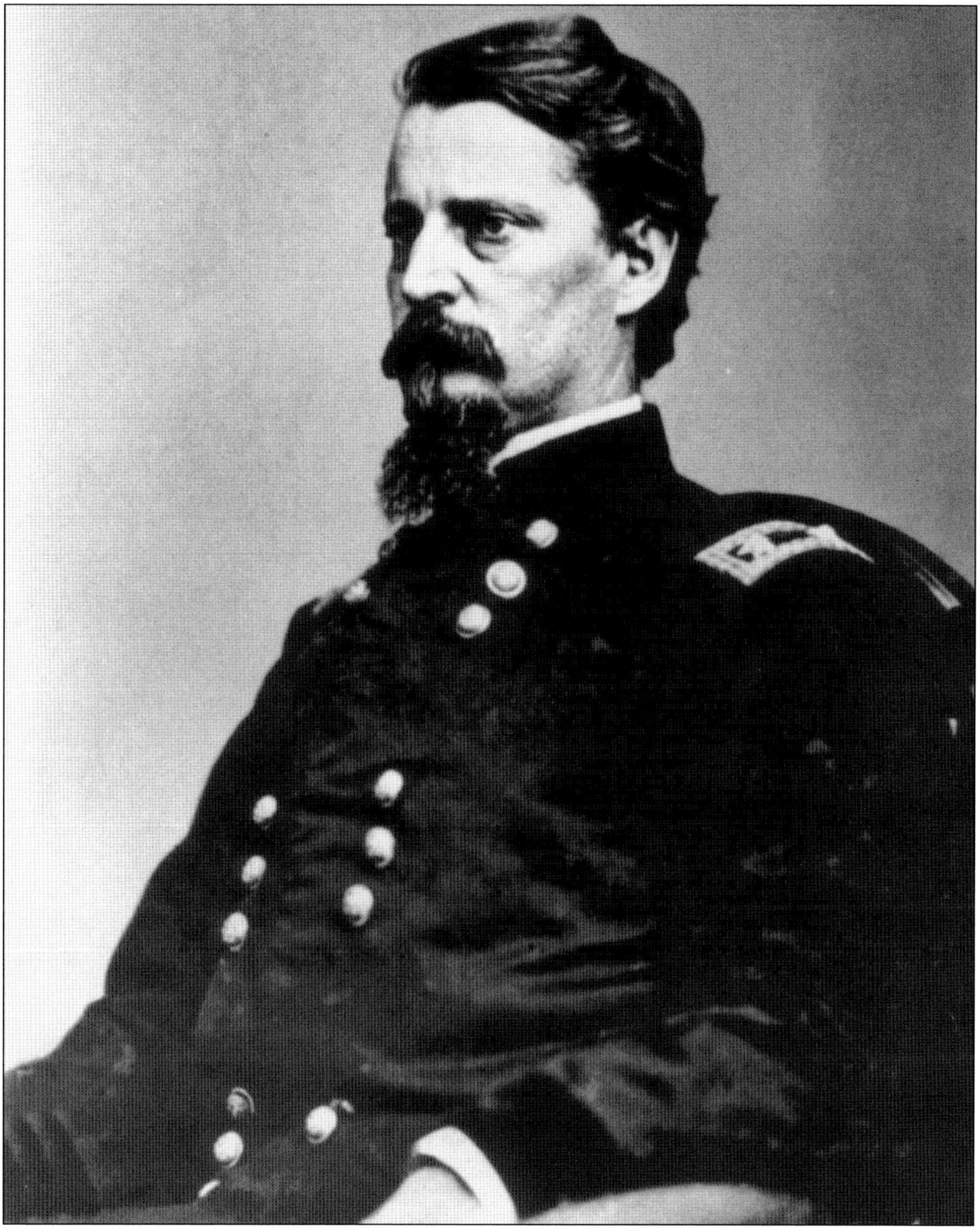

This photo was taken just as Gen. Winfield Scott Hancock's star was rising. Born in 1824, Hancock graduated from West Point and won honors in the Mexican War of 1846–1848. After duty in Fort Myers, Hancock went west and was chief quartermaster in Los Angeles when the Civil War began. His closest friends urged him to join the Confederate Army, but the Pennsylvanian declined. In the Union Army, Hancock was a "superb" commander. He chose the ground to defend in the Battle of Gettysburg, and on the third day of that encounter he was defending the middle line when Pickett made his immortal charge. In the heat of the battle, Gen. Lewis Armistead was fatally shot just as he led his men into Hancock's lines. (Hancock was Armistead's dearest friend.) In 1880, General Hancock ran for president of the United States in a close election against James A. Garfield.

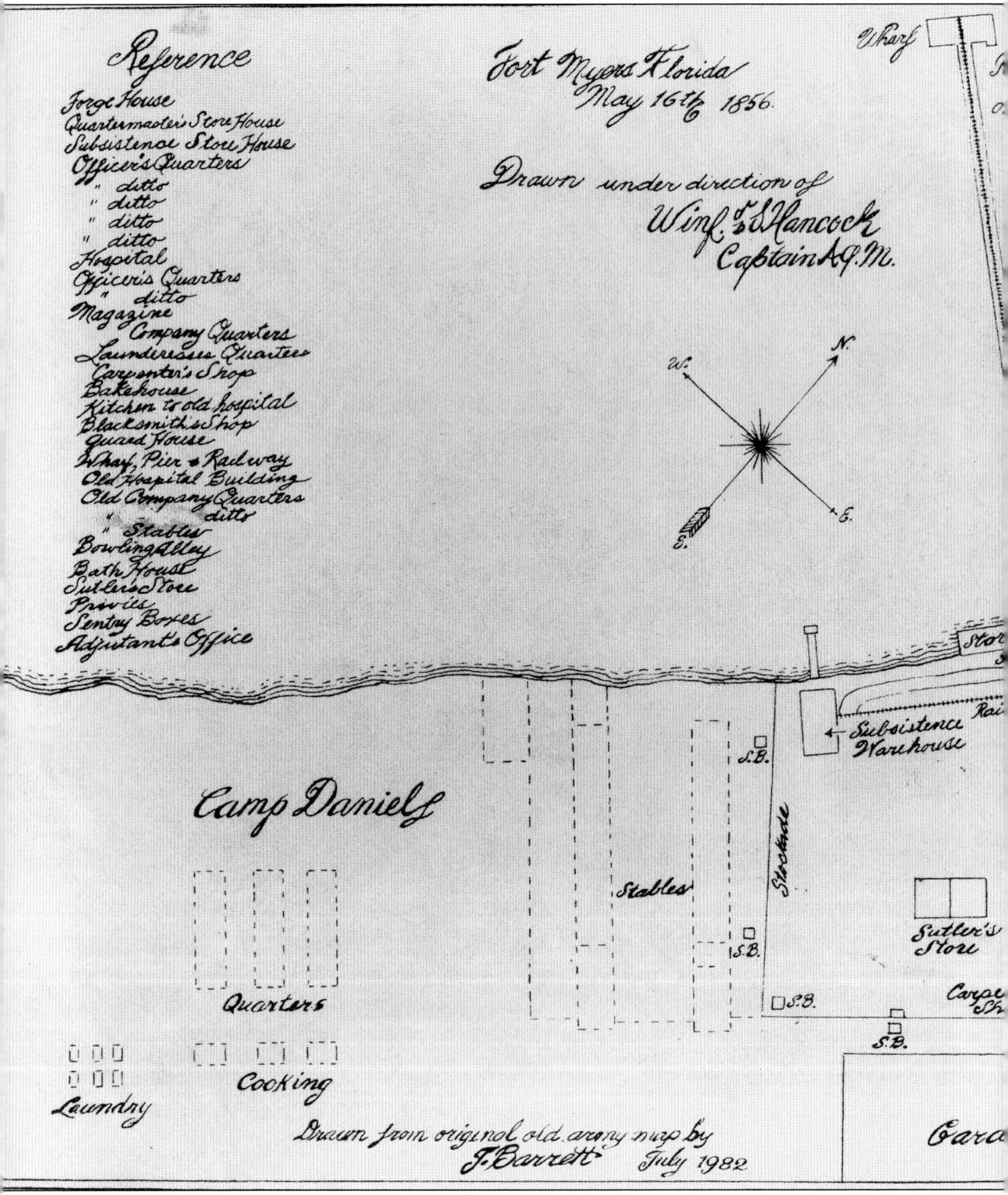

By 1855 Fort Myers had become one of the largest and most prestigious forts in Florida. That year Capt. Winfield Scott Hancock (previous image) was appointed quartermaster; together with Maj. Justis McKinstry they made a thorough survey of the 57 buildings that comprised the facility, a report that still exists in the state archives at Tallahassee. A year later Hancock drew

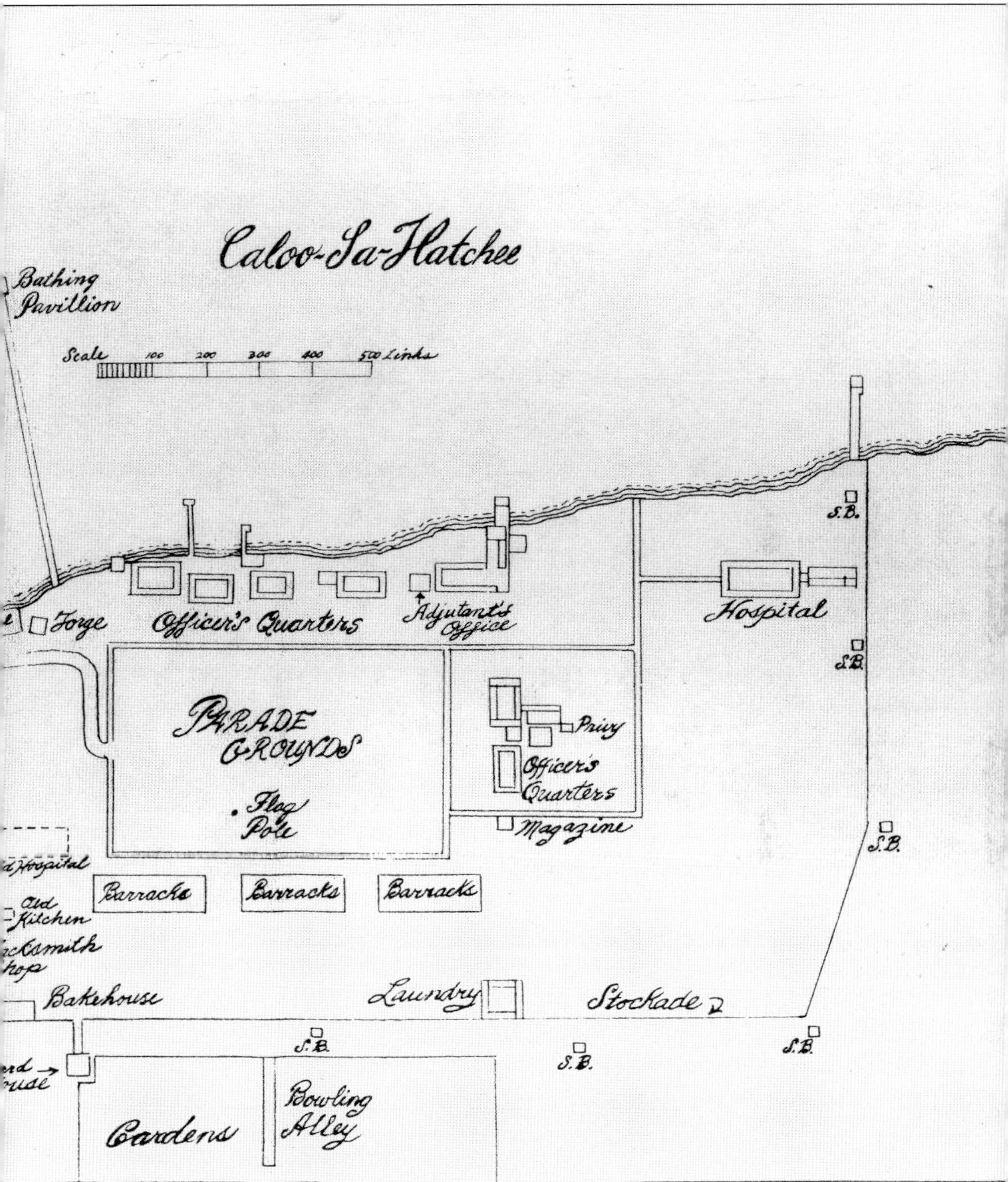

the above map, which has since been copied from the original. Captain Hancock is also remembered as the father of the first child born at Fort Myers. In 1857 Almira Hancock gave birth to Ada Elizabeth Hancock. Mrs. Hancock wrote a book about her life, and one chapter describes life at the Caloosahatchee post from a woman's point of view.

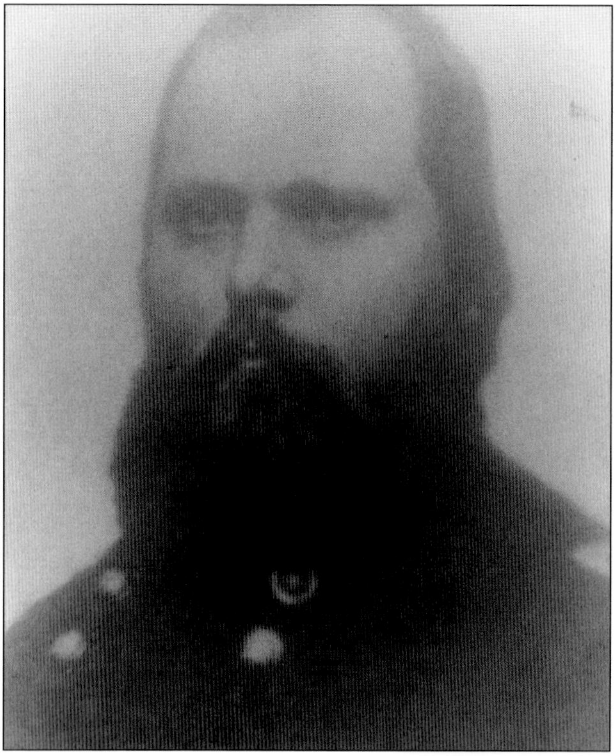

In 1855, the government was relentlessly pursuing its Indian Removal campaign. Lt. George Hartsuff (left) and a survey crew departed Fort Myers for the Big Cypress Swamp on a reconnaissance mission, with orders not to provoke the Seminoles. Hartsuff's soldiers, though, discovered the whereabouts of Chief Billy Bowlegs and destroyed his garden. The Third Seminole War began!

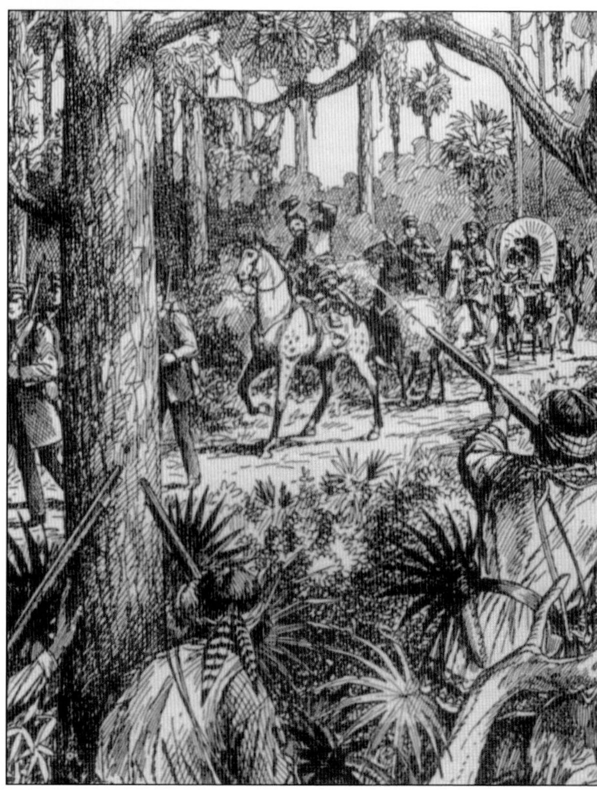

After the garden provocation, Bowlegs and his warriors went on the warpath and ambushed the Hartsuff party with grisly success. Hartsuff himself was badly wounded in his tent while awaiting breakfast. Later, he became a Civil War general. His death in 1874 (from pneumonia) was in part related to his Native-American bullet wounds.

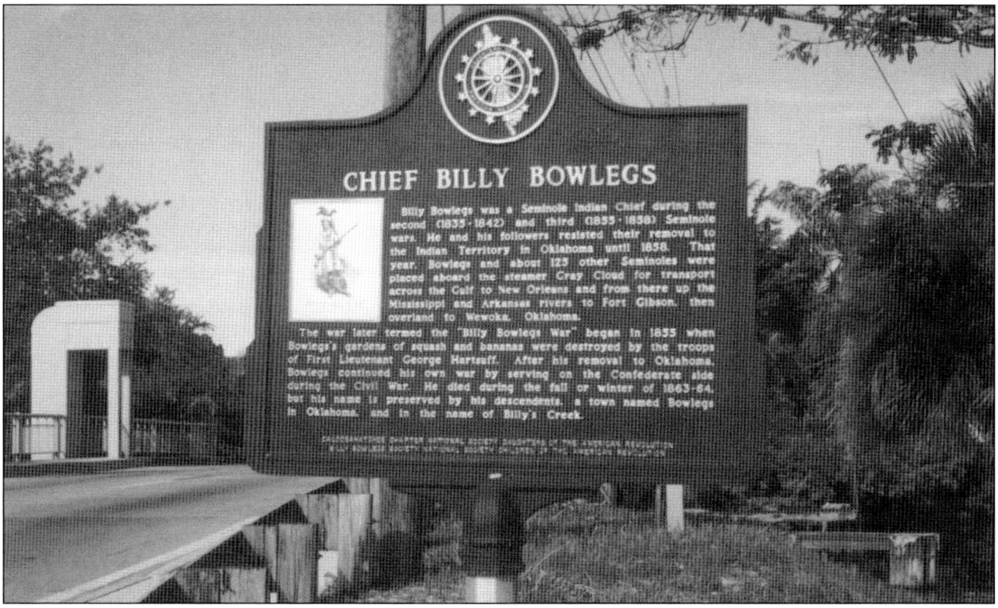

The Third Seminole War (the Billy Bowlegs War) swirled unmercifully about South Florida. Native Americans would strike, kill, burn, and loot, only to disappear and re-emerge elsewhere. After nearly three years of guerrilla warfare, surrender terms were ironed out, the Bowlegs tribe camped for weeks at the above creek near Fort Myers. Here they awaited a peaceful deportation.

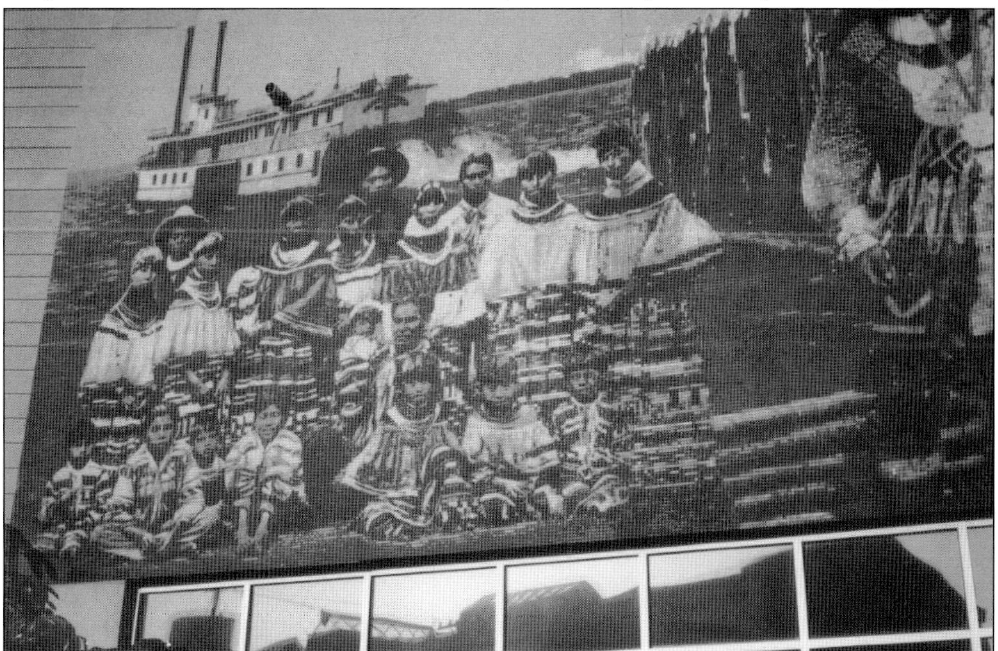

An historic mural adorns the Federal Building in Fort Myers, part of which depicts May 4, 1858, when 121 Native Americans (including Bowlegs) departed on the steamboat *Grey Cloud* for the West. A few hundred Native Americans, though, retreated to the Everglades. The Indian Removal schemes cost the government some $40 million, two-thirds of its average annual revenue.

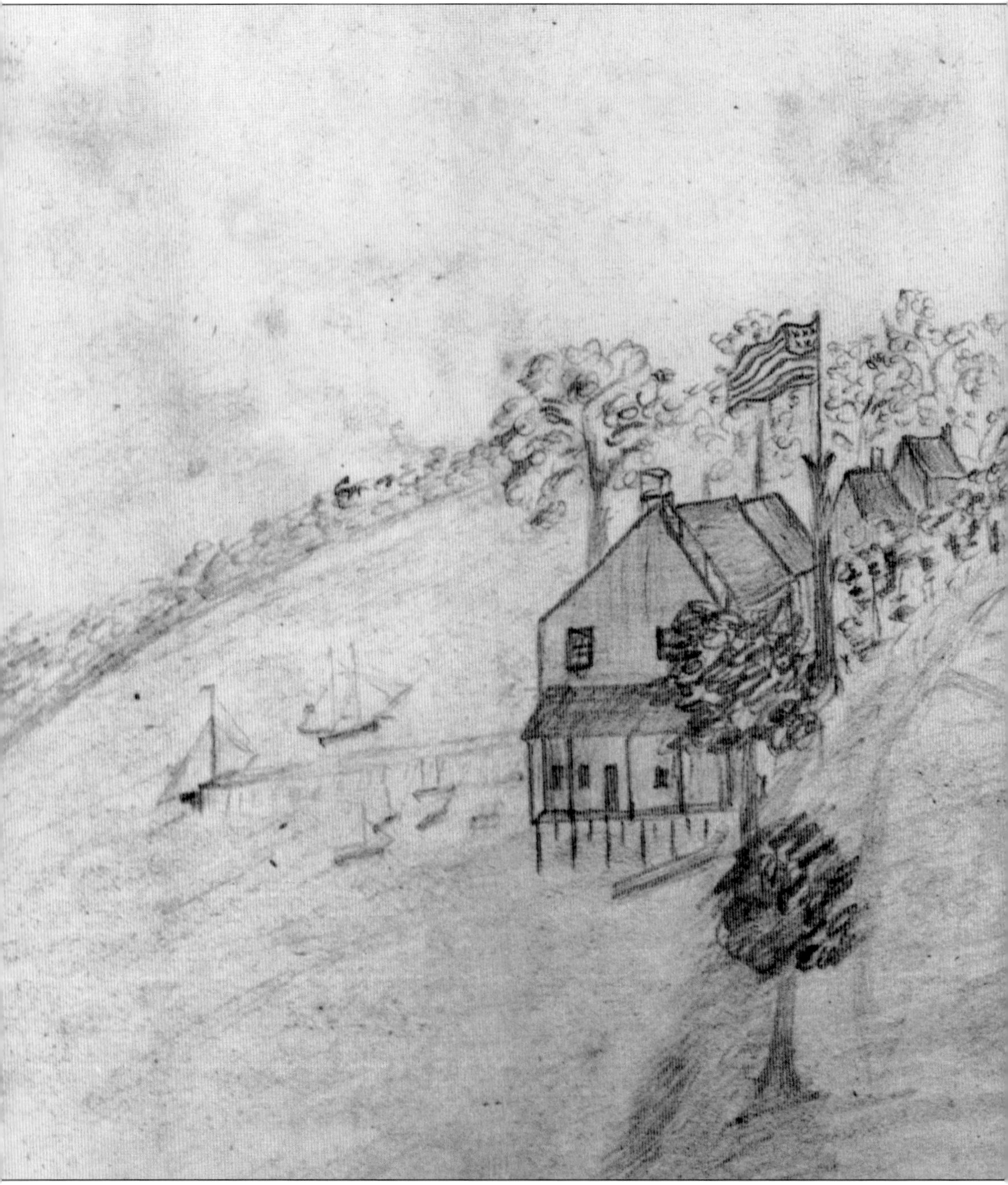

Fort Myers was re-occupied by Federal soldiers during the Civil War beginning in January 1864. Capt. Richard A. Graeffe commanded the 47th Regiment of Pennsylvania Volunteers. The sketch seen above was prepared by Captain Graeffe and accompanied a report that noted the poor condition of many buildings. The 2nd Regiment of the Florida Calvary was also billeted

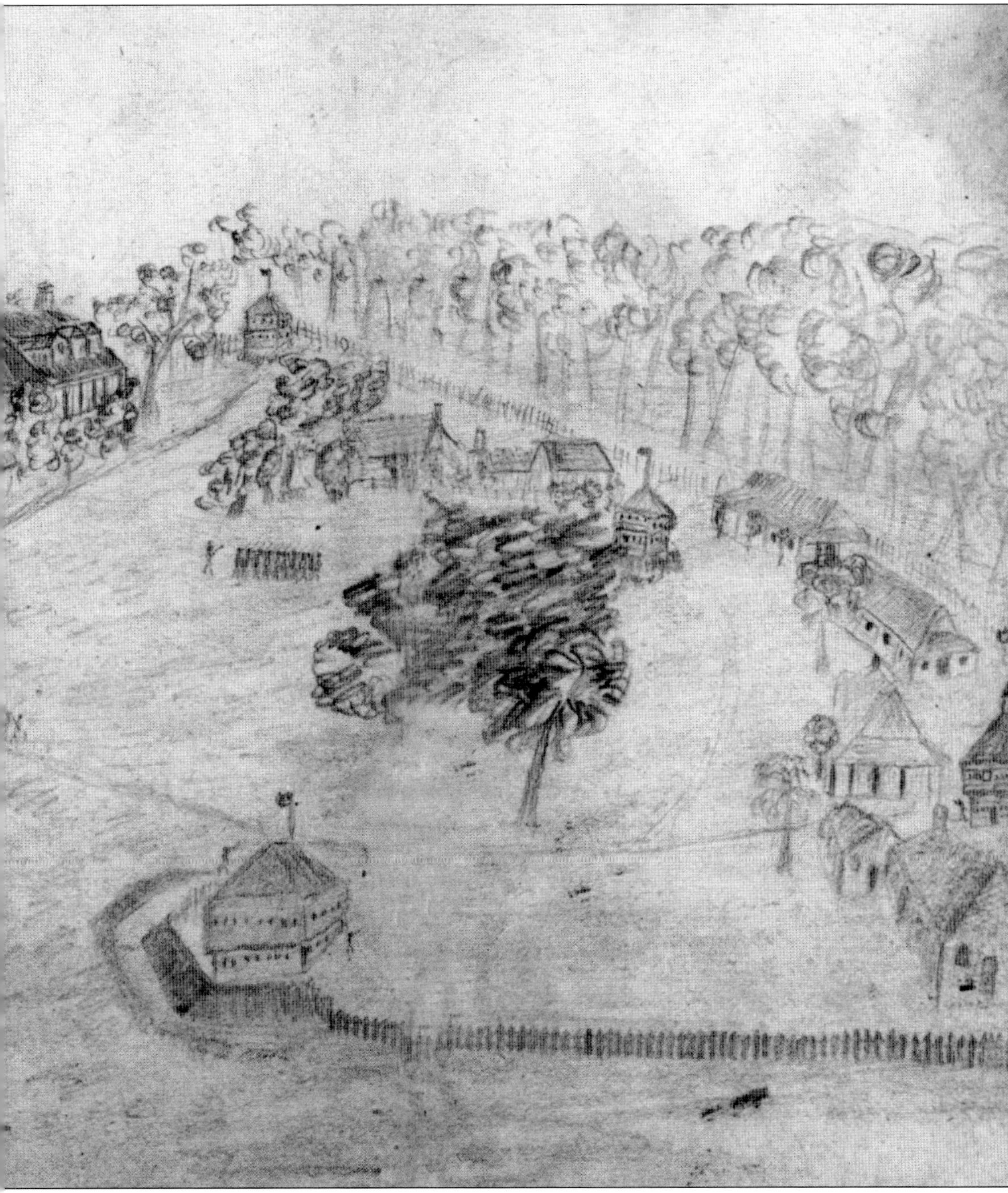

at Fort Myers, and was made up of mostly Floridians who opposed secession. Many were experienced cattlemen who carried out the fort's real mission of raiding area cattle ranches. The captured herds were then brought to Fort Myers for shipment elsewhere, thus depriving beef to the Confederate Army in Georgia.

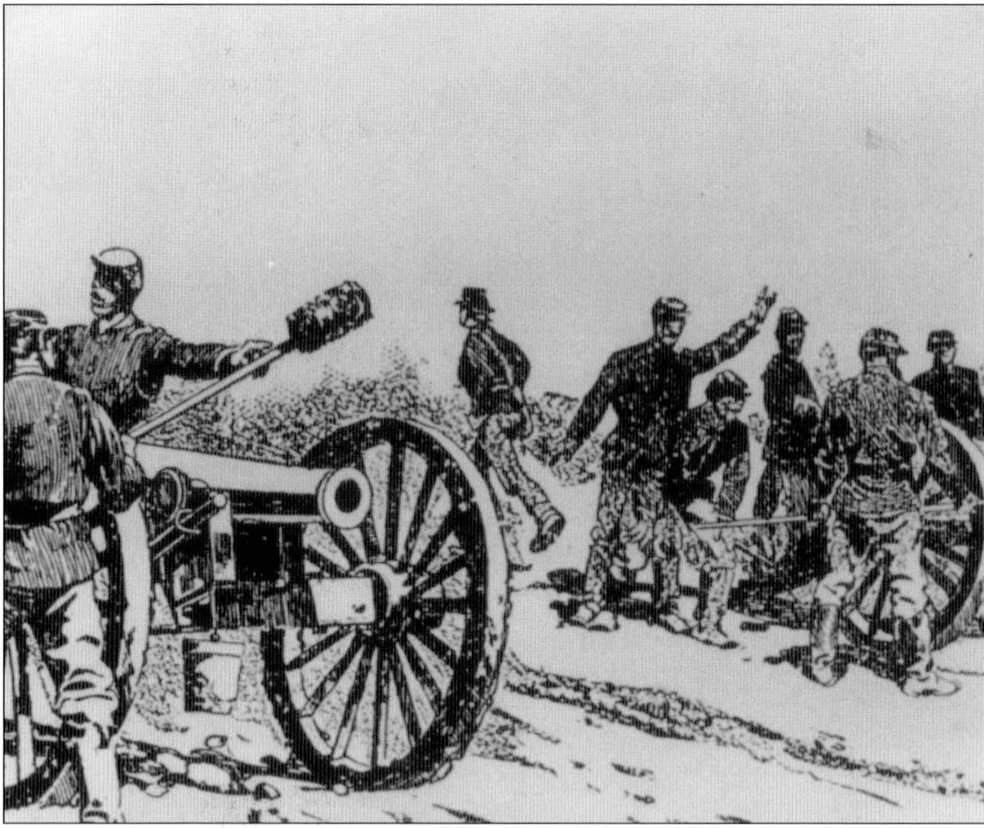

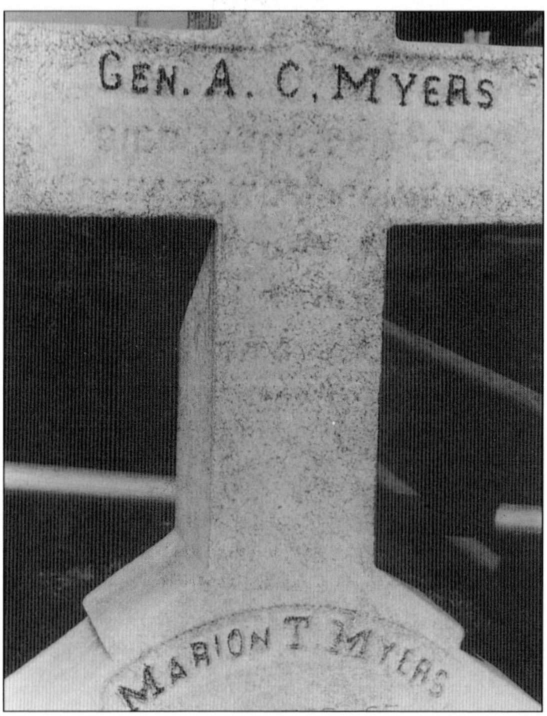

The cattle raids from Fort Myers proved very successful, too much so for rebels. In retaliation, the Confederate "Cattle Guard" attacked Fort Myers on February 20, 1865. They arrived with a single field gun while the fort soldiers returned fire with cannons. A desultory exchange continued for an afternoon with no known casualties. The Cattle Guard then withdrew, and Union forces left Fort Myers that March.

Col. Abraham Myers, a South Carolinian, became the quartermaster general of the Confederate Army, but in March of 1863 Jeff Davis fired him for being incompetent. Myers went abroad after the war and returned to live in Washington, D.C. He died in 1889 and was buried in Alexandria, Virginia (gravestone above). Note that his family promoted him!

Two

THE HAMLET

When Manuel Gonzalez was delivering mail and supplies to Fort Myers by boat in the 1850s, he could not help observing what a well-kept community the military post presented. Back in those days the southwest quadrant of Florida was almost devoid of human habitation. There were, of course, a few fishing villages from Cedar Key south, but Tampa was the only town of any size.

When the Third Seminole War (the Billy Bowlegs War) ended in 1858, Gonzalez likely thought about living in abandoned Fort Myers, but the political turmoil of the Civil War intervened. In 1864, Fort Myers was re-occupied by Federal troops until the hostilities were almost over.

Not long after the last soldier left the parade grounds, many fisherfolk and villagers descended upon Fort Myers and raided its 57 buildings. The well-built barracks, storehouses, stables, and officer's quarters furnished much-needed siding, flooring, windows, and door frames, all of which had been hewn and milled by Pensacola lumber yards.

Manuel Gonzalez re-appeared in February 1866, observed the wreckage, and decided he could salvage something livable. He then sailed back to Key West for his family and returned with wife, Evalina, their children, and his brother-in-law, along with his best friend, Joseph Vivas, and Joseph's new bride, Christiana.

The Gonzalez and Vivas families were the first to occupy the old fort grounds with the intention of staying. Though Gonzalez never intended to start a squatter's settlement—the fort still belonged to the government—his presence started to attract other early settlers. In the next two years the mysterious Nelson Tillis appeared as did James Powell and Bill Clay.

Manuel Gonzalez eventually moved out of the fort and homesteaded 160 acres under the Homestead Act of 1862, about the time government surveyors began their work in the Caloosahatchee area. Powell, in turn, moved across the river and planted the area's first orange grove while Bill Clay, a professional moonshiner, moved to Twelve Mile Creek so he could ply his trade near a fresh water source. That left Joseph Vivas. Vivas's wife, the former Christiana Stirrup, had been an orphan adopted by the Gonzalez family. Vivas, a carpenter by trade, had married the 16-year-old girl in Key West the day before they moved to Fort Myers. No doubt the military setting became special to the couple, and they eventually bought land within the fort's perimeter.

The famed Hendry clan began to arrive in Fort Myers in 1873. Its patriarch, Georgia-born Capt. Francis Asbury Hendry, ran a cattle ranch some 70 miles north of the Caloosahatchee. After the Civil War, Captain Hendry and the families of his brother William, his cousin Charley, and brother-in-law, Jehu Blount, moved their cattle to grazing fields some 30 miles east of Fort Myers. Life on the range was lonely for the womenfolk, and after Mrs. Charles Hendry lost her daughter to illness she insisted on moving to Fort Myers proper. Charles was the first family member to arrive at the fort, and in the following summer, Captain Hendry appeared and rebuilt one of the officer's quarters. Other family members followed, and the population of Fort Myers increased some tenfold.

The Hendry clan moved to Fort Myers for another important reason—to be near the cattle port of Punta Rassa, at the mouth of the Caloosahatchee. The old army barracks there were now owned by the International Ocean Telegraph Company, which allowed its docks and facilities to be used by area cattlemen, for a profitable market had opened to Cuba. The Hendrys (and others) were now driving their herds from the grasslands of mid-Florida, where the small "scrub" cattle of early Spanish days flourished in the wild. All the cow hunters had to do was round them up and they were in possession of an instant cash crop.

Thus, the hamlet of Fort Myers began to unfold, and the once-grand fort on the Caloosahatchee, dilapidated by circumstances, was now occupied by civilians.

But one small question remained: who really owned the land they were living on?

Manuel Gonzalez, an early Fort Myers settler, was born to take risks. When 14 years old, he left his native Spain in a small boat with other teenagers. Their destination was Cuba, but they missed, and shipwrecked on the Florida coast. Eventually Gonzalez lived in Key West, and after his navigation skills improved he became a mail boat captain. In the 1850s he was on the Tampa-Fort Myers-Key West run, a portentous activity.

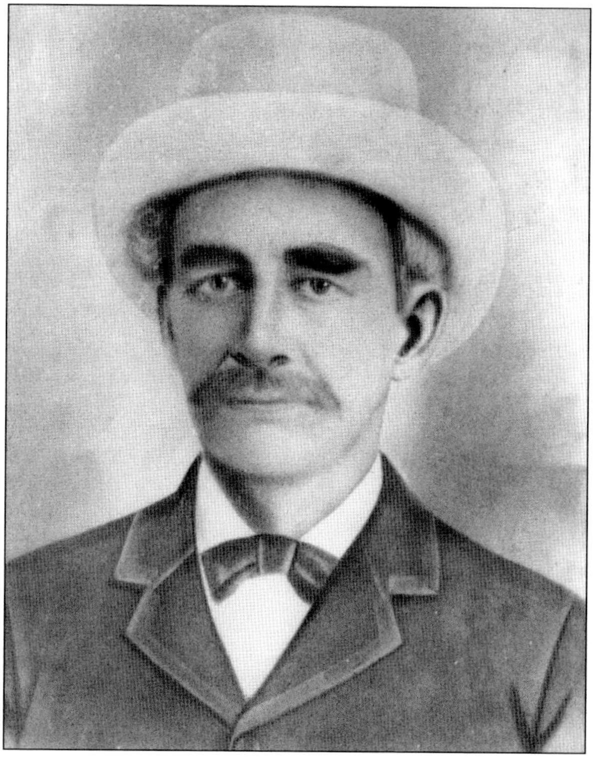

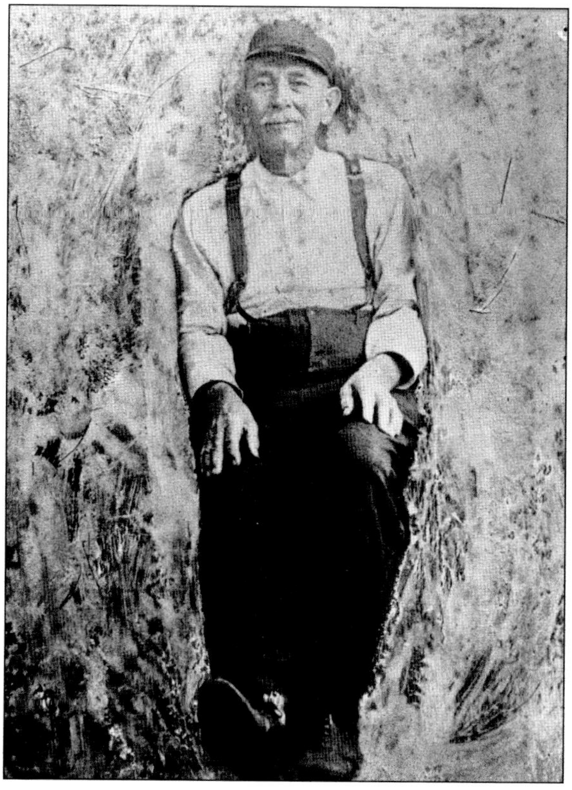

In 1866 Manuel Gonzalez decided to leave Key West and settle on the abandoned grounds of Fort Myers. He brought along his best friend, Joseph Vivas, and his brother-in-law, John Weatherford. When they arrived they were shocked to see the marauded fort buildings, but the party stayed and some years later Weatherford crouched into a tree and had himself photographed.

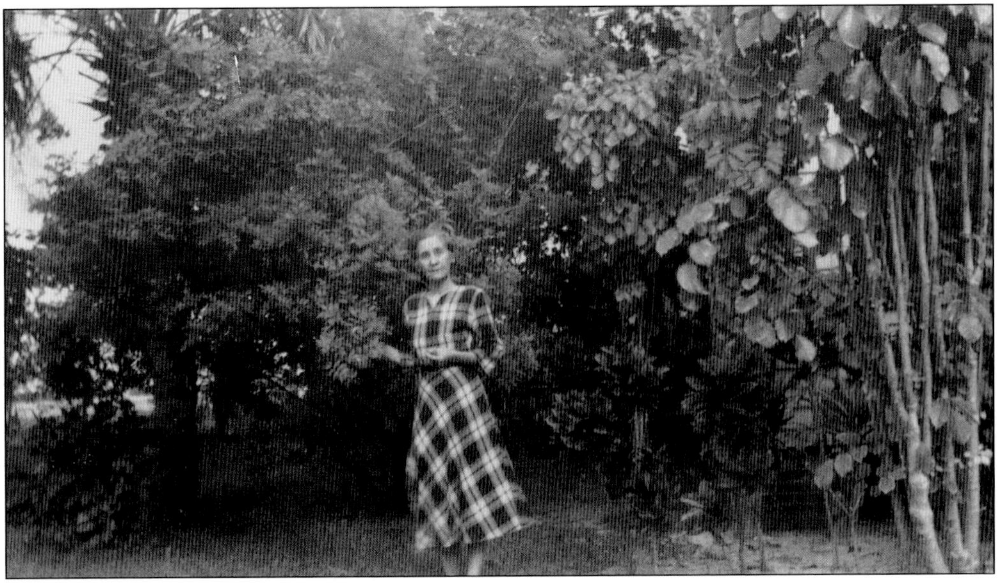

Christiana Vivas was 80 years old when this photograph was taken. Her foster father was the aforementioned Manuel Gonzales; his best friend, Joseph Vivas, married Christiana. The newlyweds spent their honeymoon in an old fort named for a soldier in love.

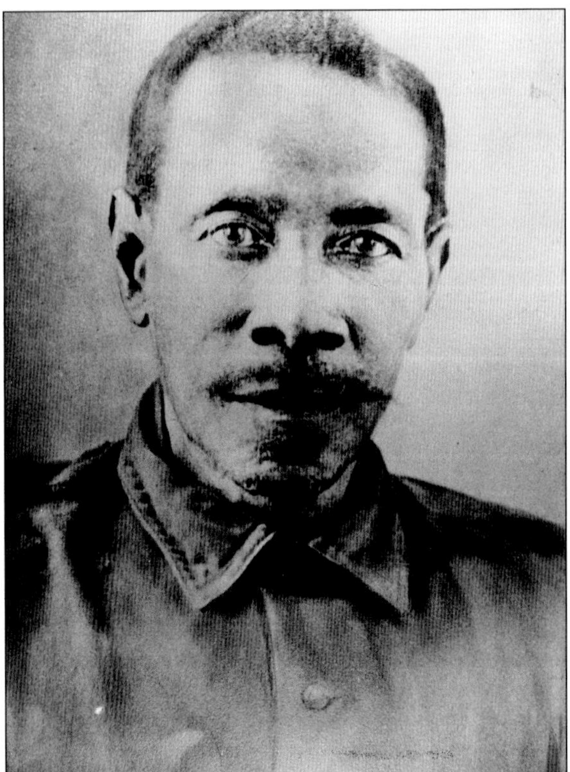

Mystery surrounds the arrival of Nelson Tillis in Fort Myers, his departure, and the man himself. He was among its earliest settlers, but it is uncertain when the man arrived or where he was from. Tillis lived here some 40 years with a white wife who gave him 11 children. He left town alone in 1910 when work became scarce and died in the Bahamas. Many of his descendants still live in Fort Myers today.

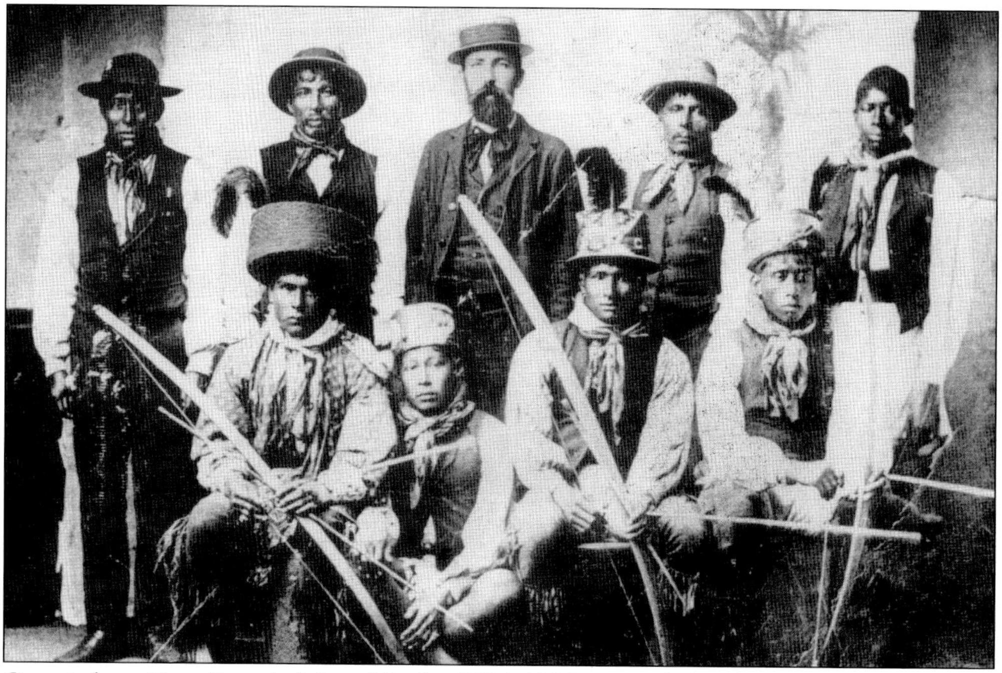

Georgia-born Capt. Francis Asbury Hendry (1833–1917) is regarded as the "Father of Fort Myers." He served in the Confederate Army and became one of the state's biggest cattlemen. He arrived in Fort Myers in 1873, served in the state senate, and underwrote or supported virtually every civic improvement. Here, he poses with special friends—the Seminoles. (Courtesy of Florida State Photo Archive.)

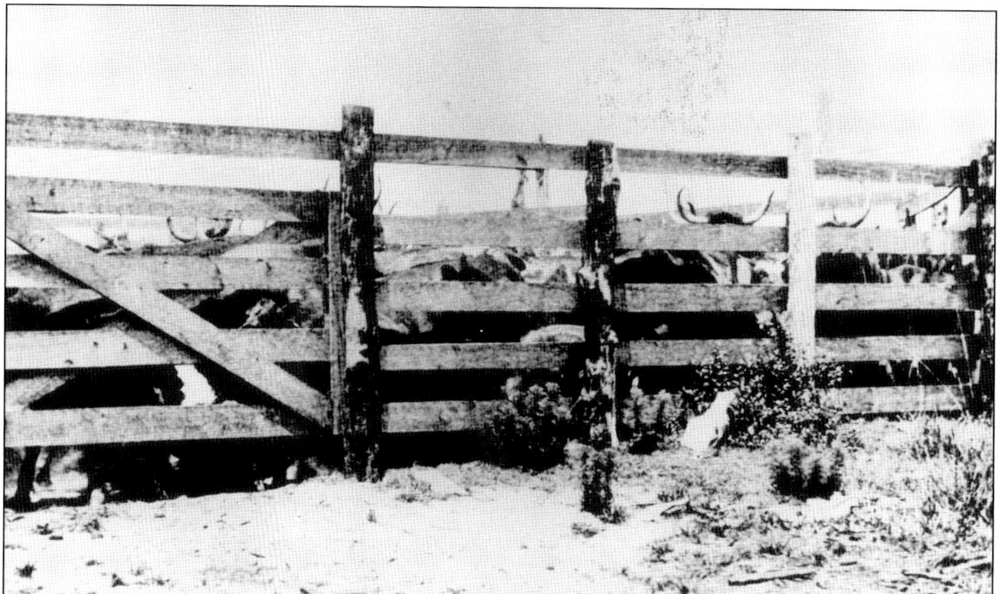

Many readers are familiar with the Sanibel Causeway and its toll house at Punta Rassa; but in the days of cattlemen Captain Hendry and Jake Summerlin, the area was dotted with cattle pens. Whereas many thought the Florida specimen was scrawny and tough, they were prized in Cuba. Some 18,000 head departed here in 1872.

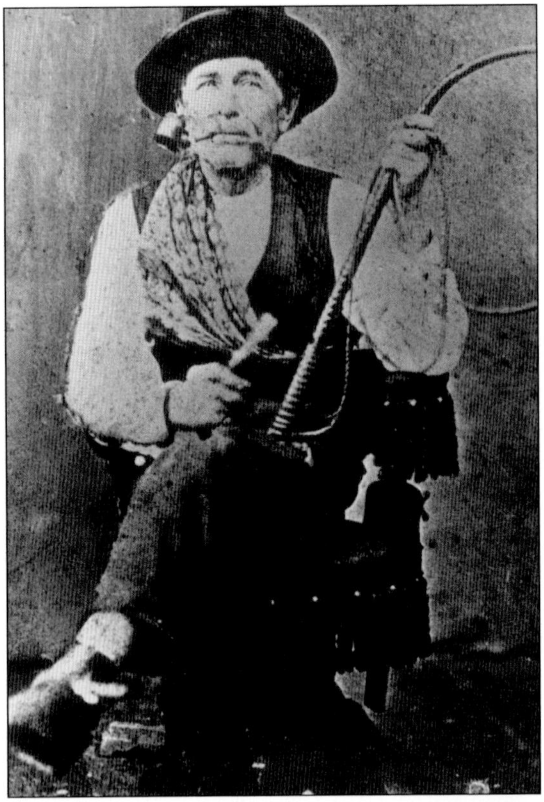

Jacob "Jake" Summerlin, "King of the Cowmen," made a fortune shipping cattle to Cuba from Punta Rassa, near the mouth of the Caloosahatchee. In bygone days, cattle were brought down in easy stages from mid-Florida. Cattlemen loved the rough-and-tumble life at Punta Rassa, where Summerlin built corrals, loading docks, and living quarters for his drovers. (Courtesy of Florida State Photo Archive.)

The old army barracks at Punta Rassa became a telegraph office after the Civil War. George Shultz was the first telegrapher and before long he was providing room and board to cattlemen. The cattle chutes themselves are at lower left. Later, the barracks would attract and house wealthy sport fishermen.

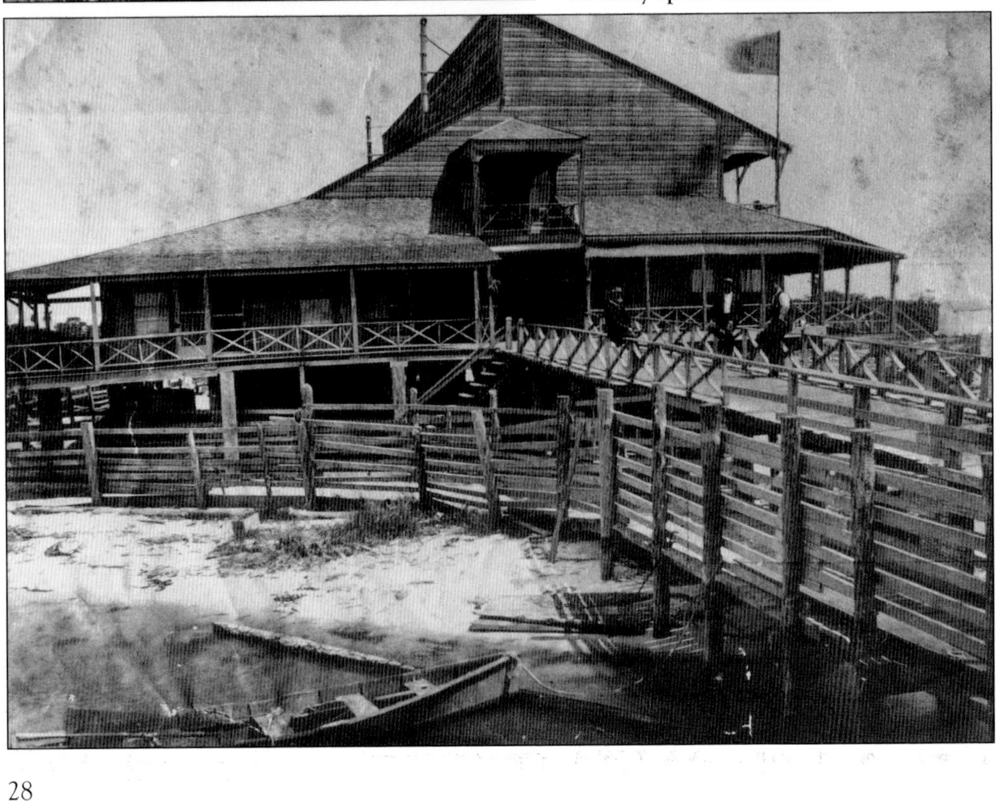

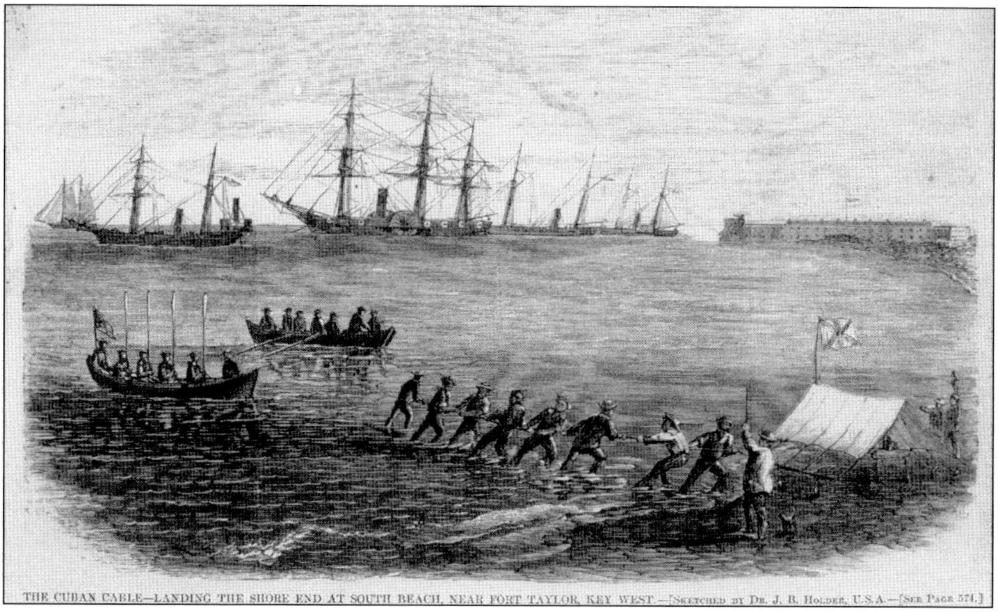

Telegraph service between the United States and Cuba was inaugurated by the International Ocean Telegraph Company, and its overland line from northern Florida opened to Punta Rassa on May 29, 1867. An underwater cable was then laid to Key West, then Havana. How it was pulled ashore at Key West appeared in *Harper's* magazine that September. (Courtesy of Florida State Photo Archive.)

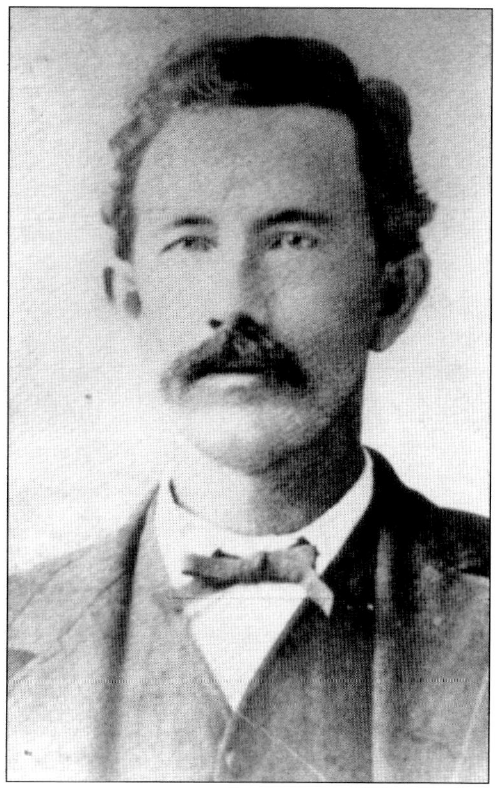

C.W. "Waddy" Thompson was a telegrapher assigned to the Fort Myers relay station. His claim to fame? He was the first person to marry in Fort Myers—to Laura Hendry, daughter of Captain Hendry. Waddy's clan remained loyal to Fort Myers, just as his great-grandchildren have. Douglas Thompson, Waddy's great-great-grandson, enhanced this book's cover photo.

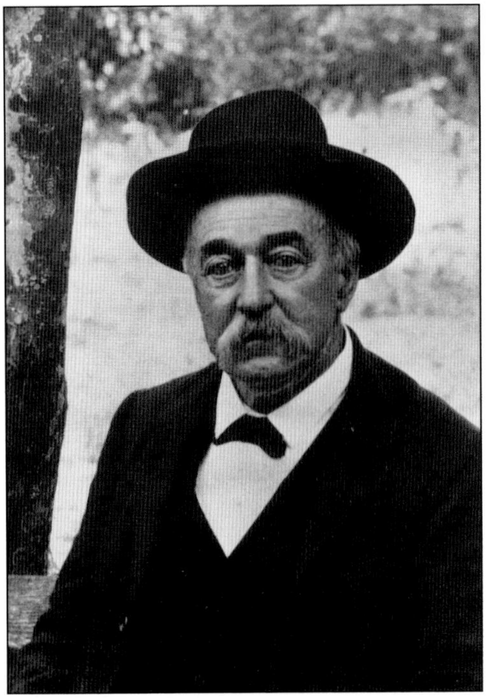

Maj. James Evans, a Virginian, founded the "town" of Fort Myers. Evans had been part of a government crew that surveyed the Caloosahatchee area in 1859. He liked the fort, staked a claim, and in the following year planted coconuts, tropical shrubbery, even coffee beans. But the Civil War intervened. Evans served in Lee's army, vanished afterwards when radical Republicans wanted to hang rebel officers, and then re-appeared.

The Evans land claim in Fort Myers embraced some 139.6 acres, but when he re-appeared in 1873, he discovered 10 families firmly entrenched on his land. Accepting the inevitable, he paid for the land ($175) and recorded his plat at Key West in 1876. Evans was a kindly soul, and allowed the families to remain and sold them land at uneven prices.

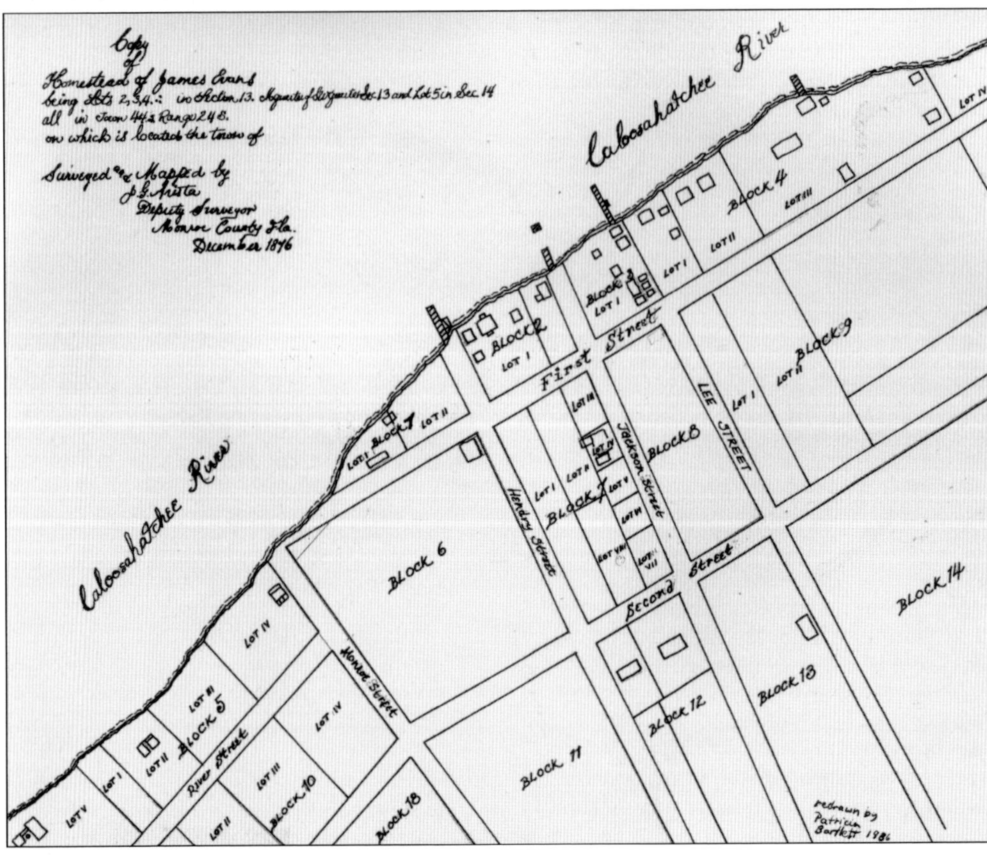

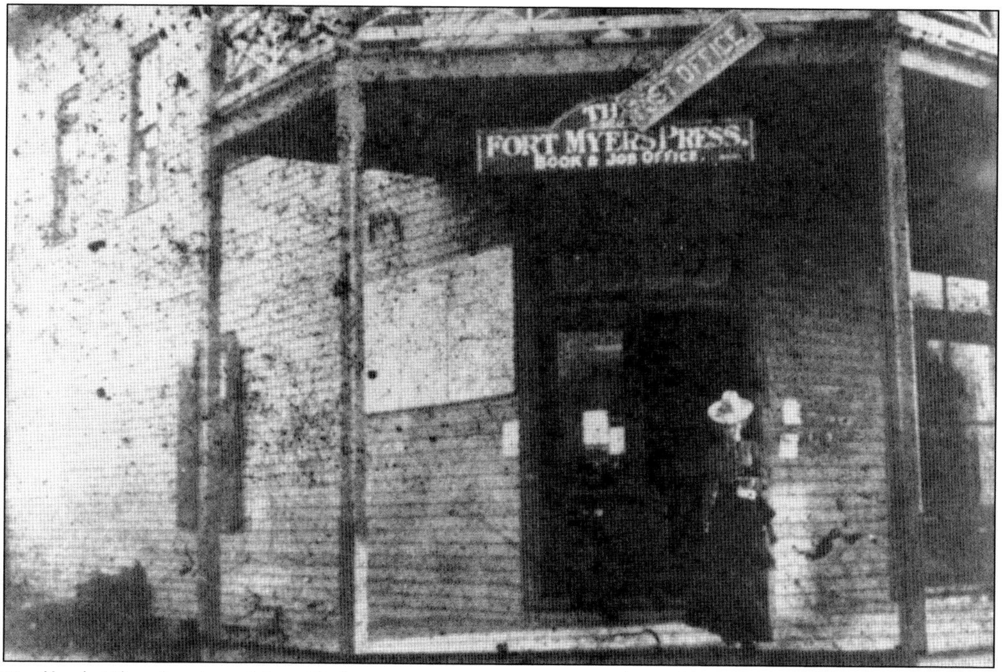

Stafford Cleveland, a New York newspaper man, was advised to go south for his health. Intending to set up shop in Fort Ogden, he instead ended up in Fort Myers—printing press and all—because the boat's captain thought a newspaper was just what his town needed. The first issue of the *Fort Myers Press* appeared on November 22, 1884. Cleveland died the following year, but the newspaper survived.

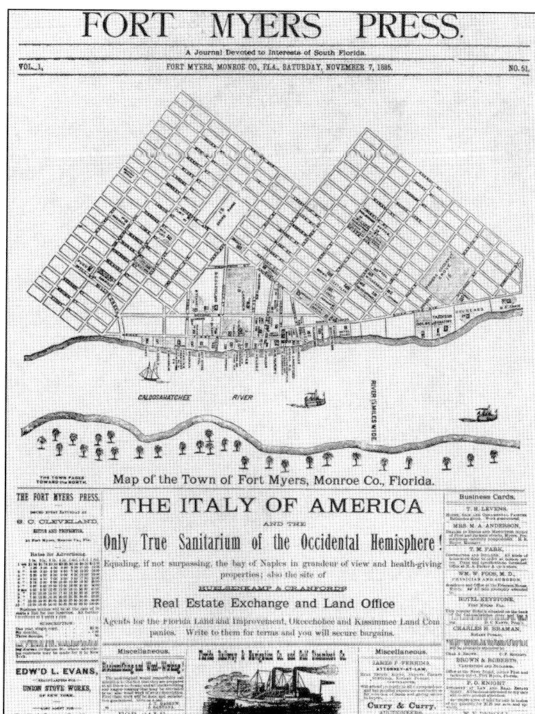

FORT MYERS PRESS.

A Journal Devoted to Interests of South Florida.

VOL. 1, FORT MYERS, MONROE CO., FLA., SATURDAY, NOVEMBER 7, 1885. NO. 51.

CALOOSAHATCHEE RIVER

RIVER 1½ MILES WIDE

Map of the Town of Fort Myers, Monroe Co., Florida.

THE FORT MYERS PRESS.

S. C. CLEVELAND,

THE ITALY OF AMERICA

AND THE

Only True Sanitarium of the Occidental Hemisphere!

Equaling, if not surpassing, the bay of Naples in grandeur of view and health-giving properties; also the site of

HUELSENKAMP & CRANFORD'S

Real Estate Exchange and Land Office

Agents for the Florida Land and Improvement, Okeechobee and Kissimmee Land Companies. Write to them for terms and you will secure bargains.

Business Cards.

T. H. LEVENS,

MRS. M. A. ANDERSON,

T. M. PARK,

WM. W. FOOS, M. D.,

HOTEL KEYSTONE,

CHARLES H. BRAMAN,

BROWN & ROBERTS,

F. O. KNIGHT

W. E. DRISCOLL,

Miscellaneous.

FOR SALE.

A DECIDED BARGAIN.

Miscellaneous.

JAMES F. PERKINS,

ATTORNEY-AT-LAW,

Curry & Curry,

AUCTIONEERS,

And Commission Merchants,

EDW'D L. EVANS,

UNION STOVE WORKS,

OF NEW YORK.

Bradley's Famous Fertilizers,

Cleveland was a Republican, but he quickly swam with the Democratic majority of Fort Myers. Back then, the town was still part of Monroe County. The front page of Cleveland's paper featured a map, just the way Major Evans had platted the town. In this November 7, 1885 issue, plenty of vacant lots are available.

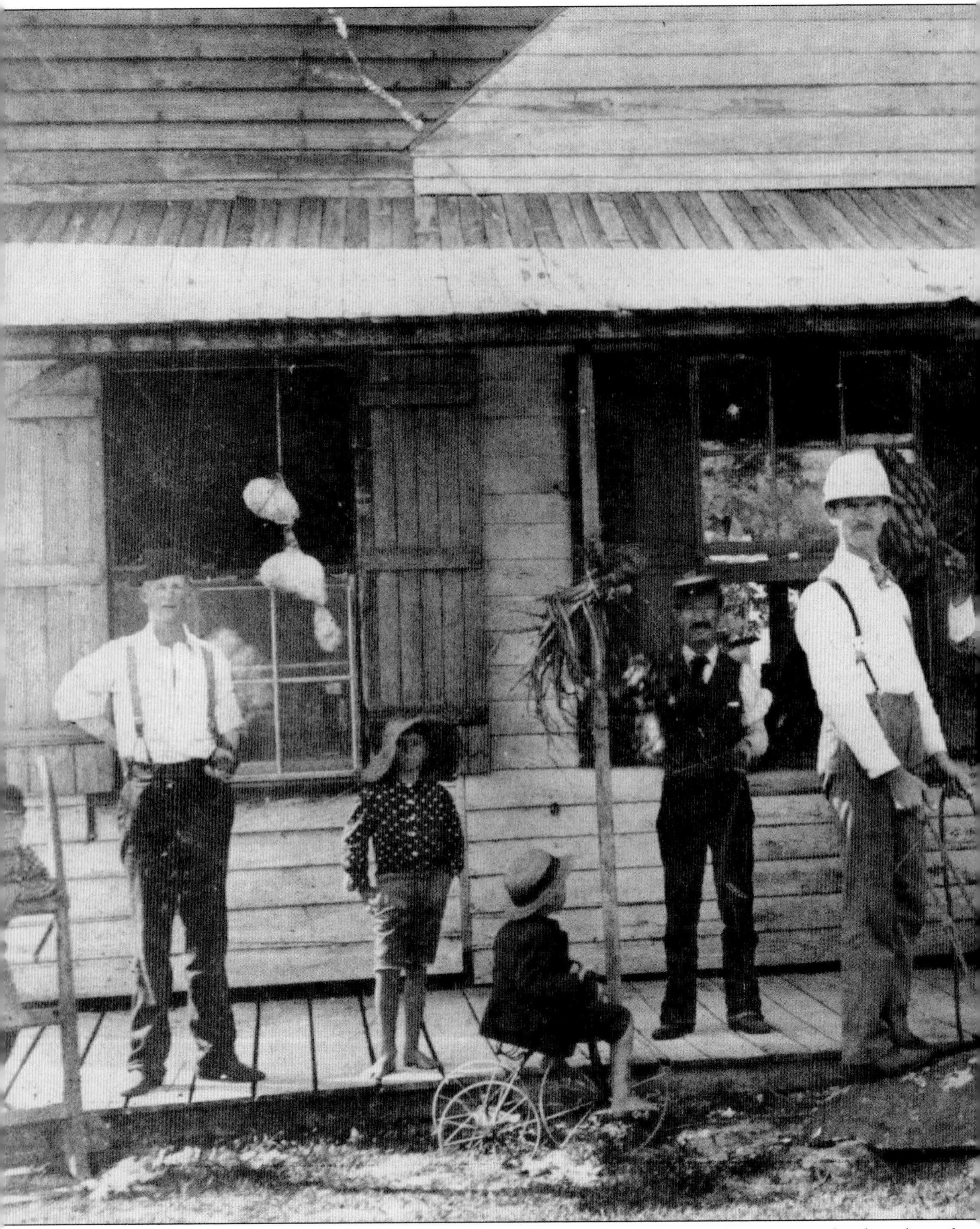

In 1873, the famed Hendry clan moved off their cattle range and came to the hamlet of Fort Myers. Jehu J. Blount, brother-in-law of Captain Hendry, opened the first general store. Virtually unknown to the modern generation, the general store of yesteryear sold just about everything needed for everyday living, from hats and shovels to flour to nails. Blount's

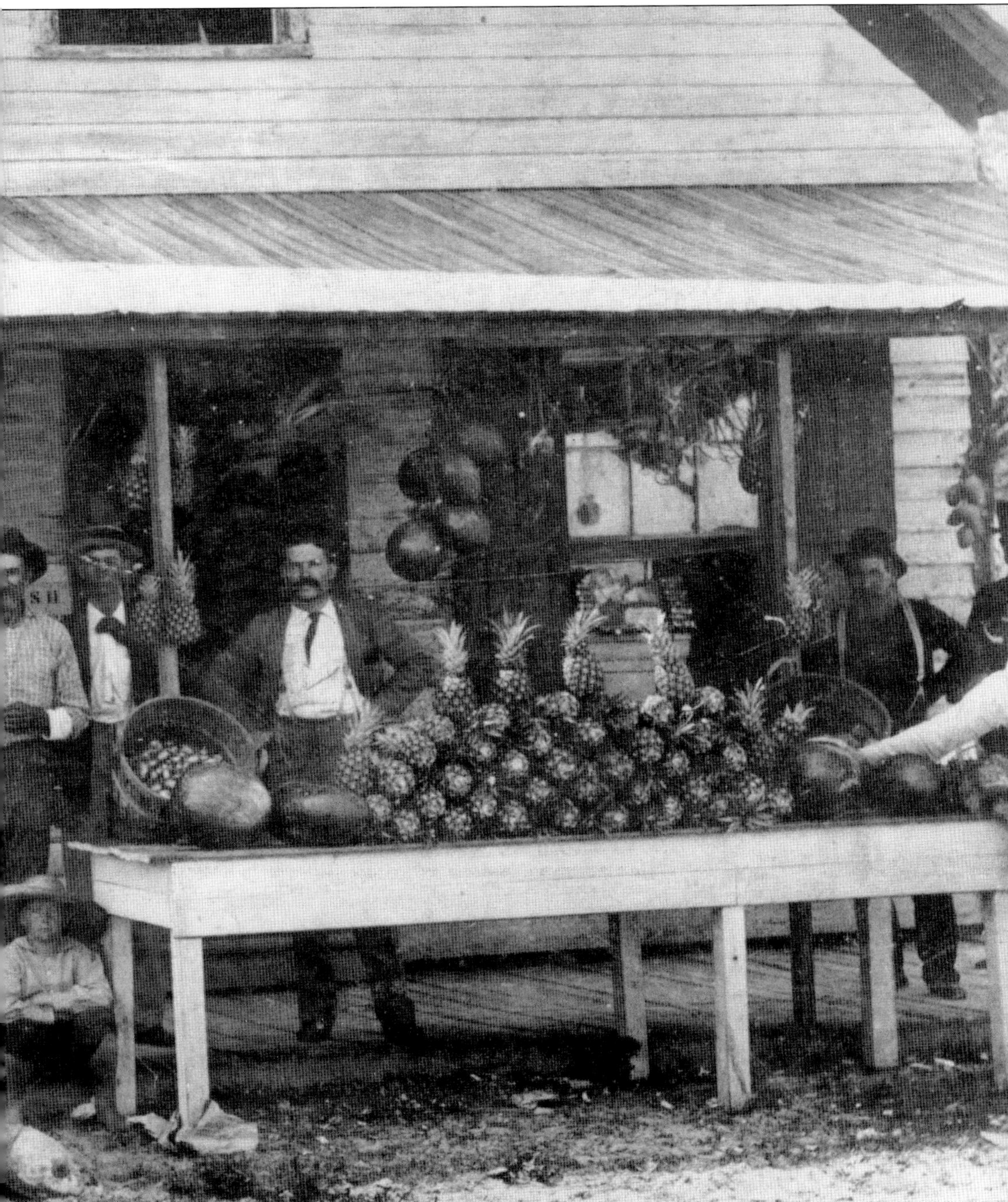

emporium cornered First and Hendry Streets. In this splendid 1886 view, pineapples—an area staple, used in the town seal—are prominently displayed. An interesting collection of headgear is also visible, as is a tricycle with no tires. Our award for the best pose goes to the chap straddling that giant sea turtle.

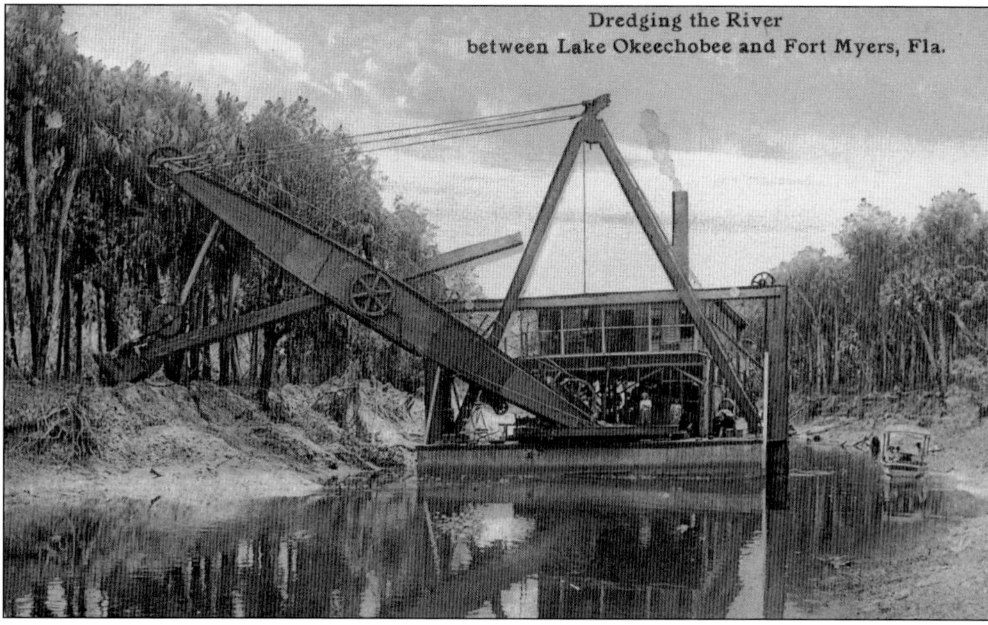

Every day boaters delight in the waters of the Caloosahatchee, but how the river looked a hundred and more years ago was very different than today. The channel was far narrower and shallow, plus an enormous amount of vegetation overhung the waterway. In time, though, dredges appeared, and the twists and turns were straightened above Fort Myers.

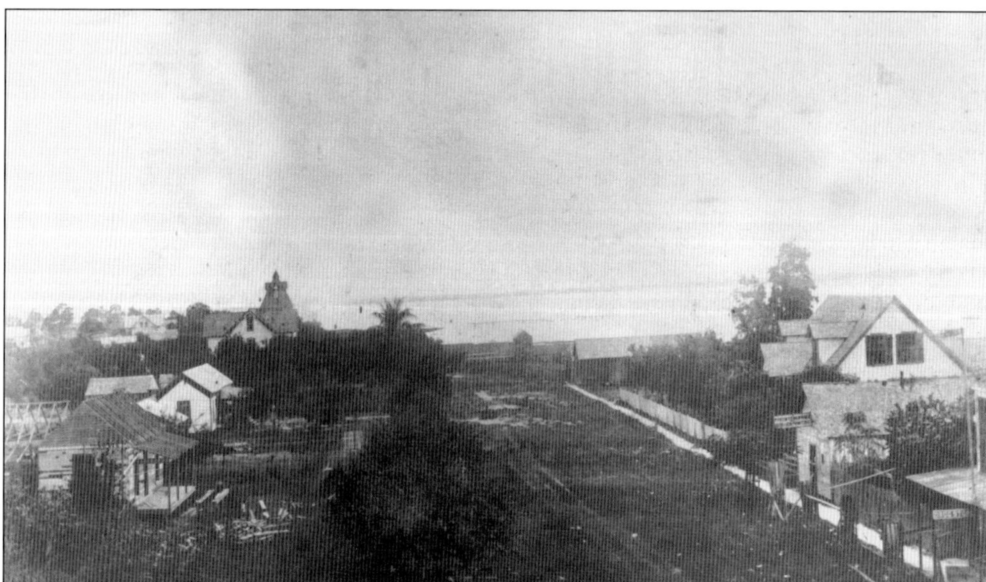

This image, taken in the late 1880s, shows First Street "fading" into the Caloosahatchee. By turning back to page 30 (bottom), the reader can pinpoint this oddity on Major Evans's plat. One can only imagine the patience that was needed to navigate the rutted thoroughfare, especially in the wet summer months.

Three

THE TOWN

Fort Myers did not develop with magic rapidity during the 1870s. Homesteaders, of course, trickled in, attracted by the community's tropical climate and fertile soil, but Fort Myers was still an isolated outpost on the peninsula. It lacked a transportation network, and few markets existed for locally grown fruits and vegetables. Back then the economy relied on one industry—the cattle business—and Fort Myers itself became an important trading post.

During the 1880s, however, the image of a rough and tough cowtown began to soften. Steamboat service arrived and commercial activities increased. The principal exports of the decade included cattle, sugar, molasses, fish scales, shells, bird plumes, deer skins, and the hides of alligators, otters, bears, panthers, and beavers.

In 1881, the famed Hamilton Disston began his huge dredging and reclamation projects. By dredging and deepening the Caloosahatchee above Fort Myers, and connecting two small lakes, a navigable link was finally achieved with Lake Okeechobee.

Four years later two major events occurred in Fort Myers. First, a famous "electrician" by the name of Thomas Alva Edison paid a chance visit. Edison liked what he saw and purchased a handsome parcel on the Caloosahatchee. In 1886 his winter retreat ("Seminole Lodge") opened, and the following year it boasted electric lights, the town's first.

Another milestone took place in August 1885, when Fort Myers officially became a "town." Poorly constructed frame buildings dotted the business landscape and housed general stores, saloons, livery stables, blacksmith shops, and small businesses. Absent were paved streets and sidewalks; cattle and pigs freely roamed about. There was also no public water system, and cisterns and shallow wells provided the only drinking water. Seminole Indians often wandered into town from the Everglades to sell or trade their wares, and many partook of "firewater."

Developments down at Punta Rassa also affected Fort Myers. George Shultz, the man who ran the telegraph relay station in the old army barracks, started to rent rooms to fishermen, who tried their skill in local waters catching kingfish, sea trout, Spanish mackerel, and the glorious Silver King—tarpon! Before long the cheap rooms and good meals became very popular. (The barracks stood near today's Sanibel Causeway toll house.) In March of 1885 one of Shultz's guests actually caught a tarpon with a rod and reel—a first—and the story was transmitted around the world in newspapers and sporting journals. Almost immediately Shultz was besieged with a newer clientele: wealthy sport fishermen, captains of industry, renowned politicians, and playboys. Before long the old army barracks became known as the Tarpon House.

After the first schoolhouse burned in Fort Myers, Monroe County commissioners refused to build another. That the commissioners failed to furnish the town with certain bridges and roads also contributed to ill feelings. Thus, a movement was begun for a new county. Thanks to civic-minded folks like Capt. Francis Asbury Hendry, Lee County was carved out of Monroe County in May 1887. Fort Myers was voted the county seat and soon a courthouse was erected.

In the next decade, the fertile growing lands of the Caloosahatchee region became widely known. In December 1894 the devastating "Big Freeze" struck, and the temperature dropped to 10 degrees in mid-state. Citrus groves were instantly destroyed or severely damaged, but not in Lee County! When grove owners heard the news, a buying frenzy took place. Prices for orange and grapefruit acreage skyrocketed, and the region's reputation for superb growing conditions became firmly established.

Among the new citrus investors was Ambrose McGregor, who had made a fortune with Standard Oil. McGregor and his wife, Tootie, discovered tarpon fishing at nearby Punta Rassa, and eventually came up the Caloosahatchee to Fort Myers. They, like Edison, liked what they saw, and in the next few years, the McGregors purchased some 32 properties. They also loaned money to an up-and-coming businessman named Harvie Heitman, who built the first brick building in the town. Other men of wealth found Fort Myers inviting too, such as New York furniture merchant Hugh O'Neill, who erected the town's first "quality" hotel. His clientele? Wealthy sportsmen.

Five years after Fort Myers was incorporated, the federal census of 1890 revealed a town population of 575 people. A decade later, 943 souls could be counted. The same census of Lee County showed a population of 1,414. By 1900, the number crept up to some 3,000 men, women, and children.

In the pages ahead we see how the town of Fort Myers evolved. For certain, its reputation as a frontier cowtown was changing.

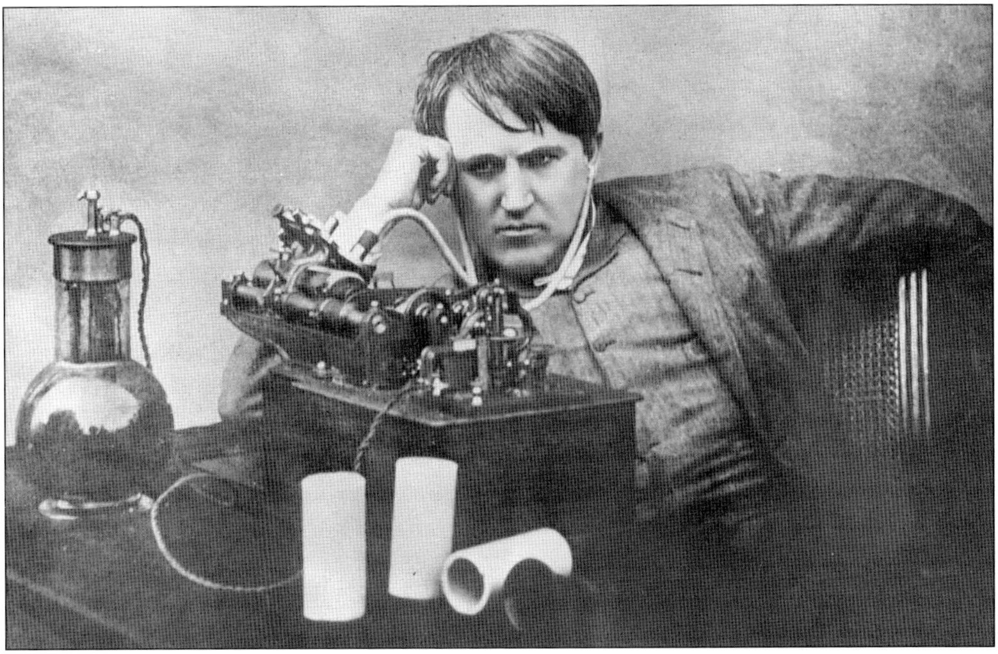

This photo of a brooding 39-year-old Tom Edison was taken after five sleepless nights of trying to improve one of his popular inventions. It turns out Edison never perfected the phonograph. He left that to others, who not only improved it but made huge fortunes as well.

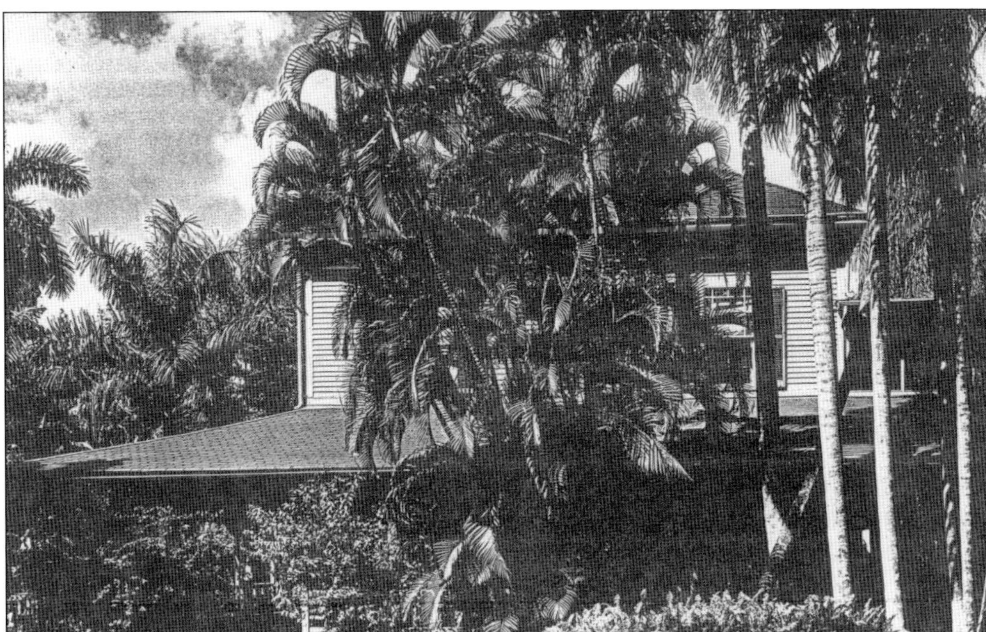

When Edison first visited the hamlet of Fort Myers on March 6, 1885, he was impressed with the friendly people, the town's isolation, and the dry warm weather. He purchased land on the Caloosahatchee for a winter home and called it Seminole Lodge (seen above). The famed inventor returned the following winter on his honeymoon with Mina Edison, his second wife.

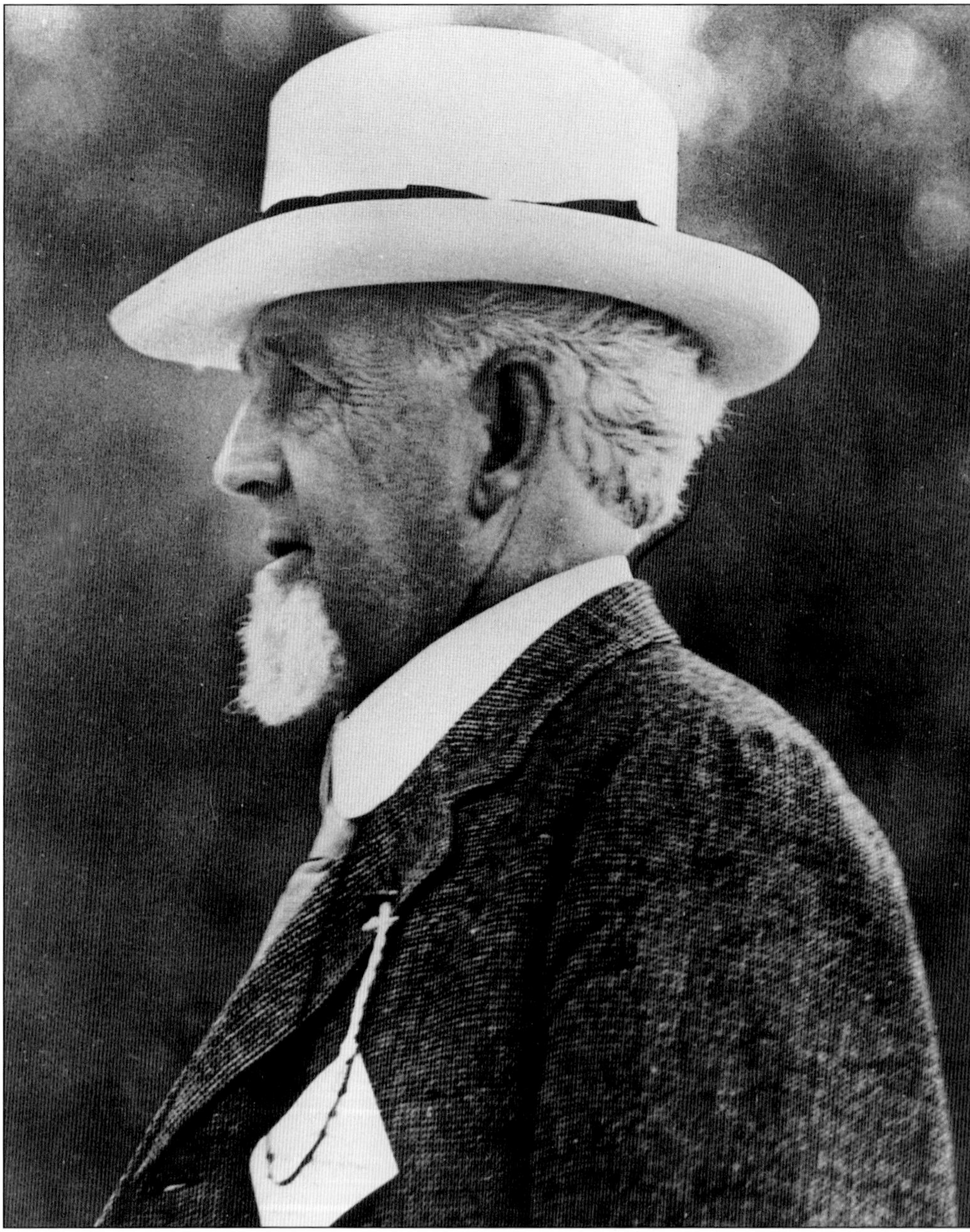

Readers will recall Capt. Francis Asbury Hendry, the "Father of Fort Myers." During the 1850s, Hendry raised cattle near Fort Meade, some 70 miles north of the Caloosahatchee. In 1854, he was a dispatch bearer during the Indian wars and later became a captain in the Confederate "Cattle Guard," the battalion that attacked Fort Myers. After the war, he drove his cattle to the grazing fields some 30 miles east of Fort Myers. When the Hendry clan moved to Fort Myers in 1873, the hamlet's population increased tenfold. It was during this time that Hendry shipped enormous herds of cattle to Cuba using Jake Summerlin's facilities at Punta Rassa; by 1880 he owned some 50,000 head and was considered the cattle "king" of South Florida. Captain Hendry also took a leading role in having Fort Myers incorporated in 1885, and, as we will see, he solved the "problem" of Monroe County.

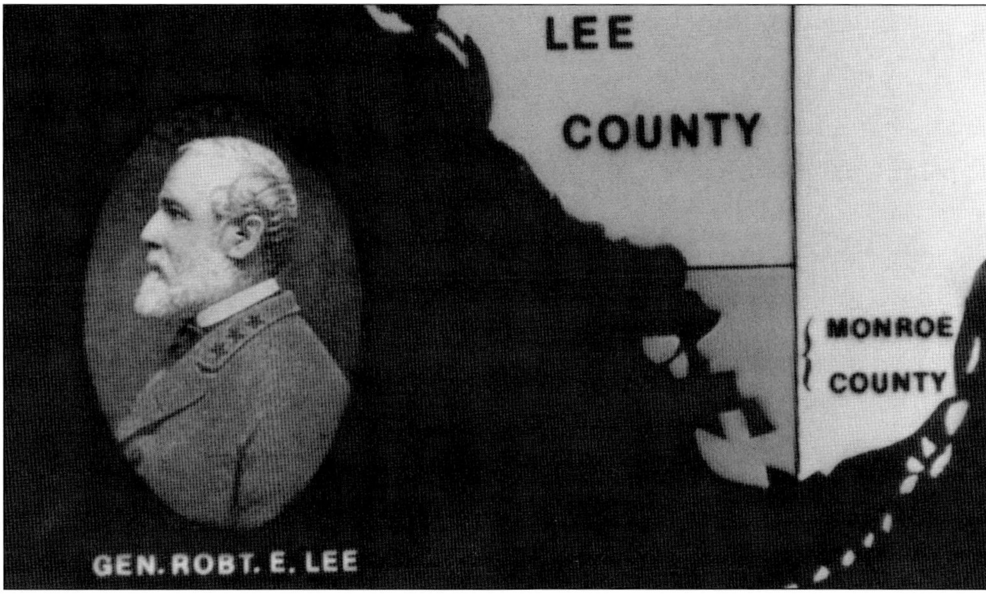

Monroe County, Florida, was the largest county in the United States in 1887, but the county seat was in Key West, which meant a week's trip by sailboat from Fort Myers. When county officials refused to rebuild the burned down Fort Myers Academy, Capt. Francis Asbury Hendry and others got the legislature to create Lee County, named in honor of the famous general.

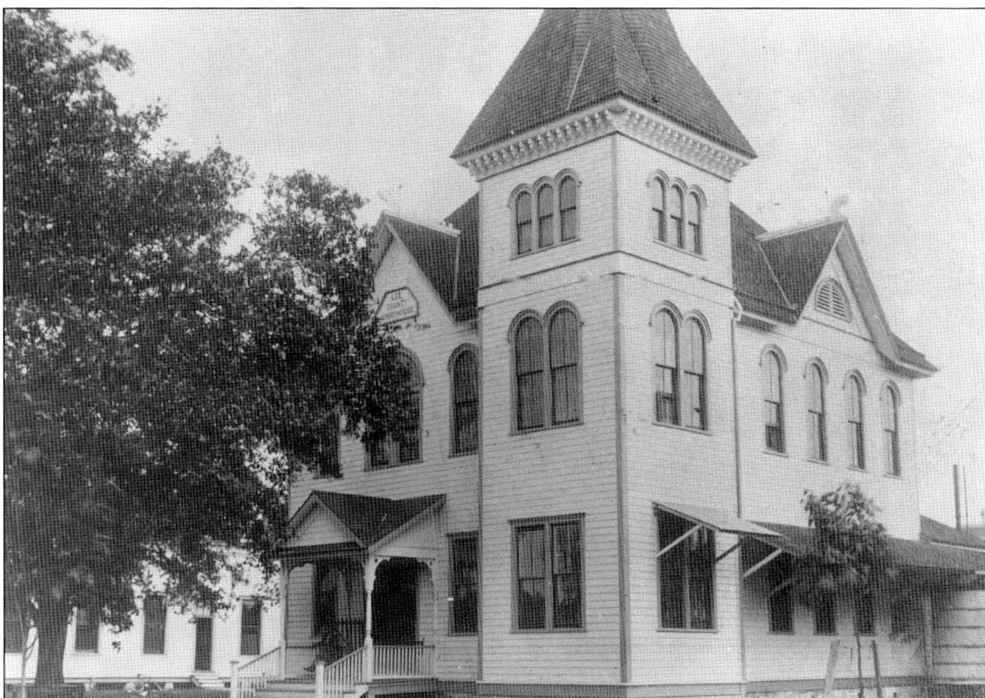

After Lee County was created in 1887, a county seat was needed; Fort Myers handily won the vote over Alva and Fort Denaud. A courthouse was now needed, and the modest one seen here opened in 1894 for $3,600—almost the cost of the land.

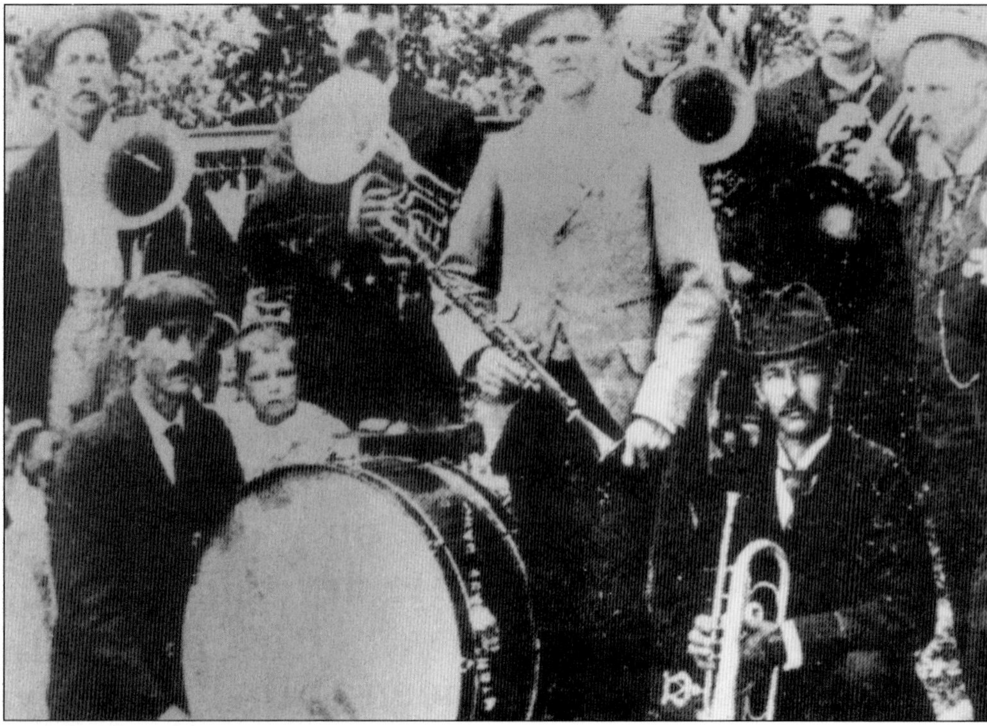

Fort Myers folk organized a town band in 1885. Dues allowed for the purchase of music and instruments, and its warmly dressed members made their first public appearance the following March at the home of Thomas Edison and his new wife. Later, a "Professor" Francis Perry became its leader and local entertainment began on a regular basis.

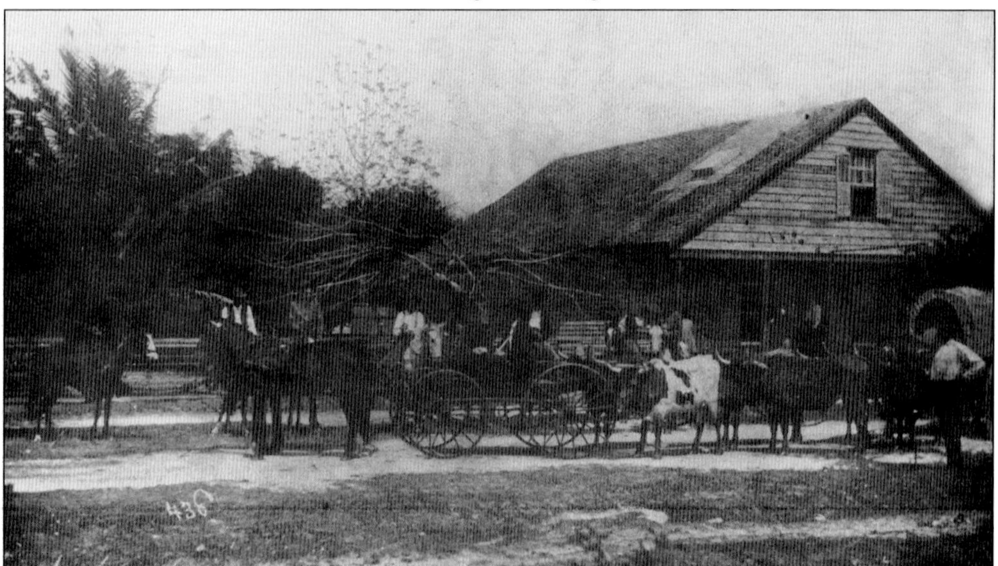

The power of oxen often shuttled wagons between Fort Myers and the Everglades. Road conditions were, of course, pathetic, and roads often proved impassable in the rainy summer season. The Everglades itself offered up bird plumes and the hides of coons, bears, otters, and especially alligators. Countless manifests would then depart Fort Myers by steamboat.

Ambrose McGregor was a shining product of the Gilded Age, that period of great industrial expansion between the Civil War and the next century. McGregor aligned himself with John D. Rockefeller and amassed a fortune in Standard Oil stock. He came to Punta Rassa in the winter of 1891 for tarpon fishing, and along the way he and his wife, Tootie, fell in love with Fort Myers.

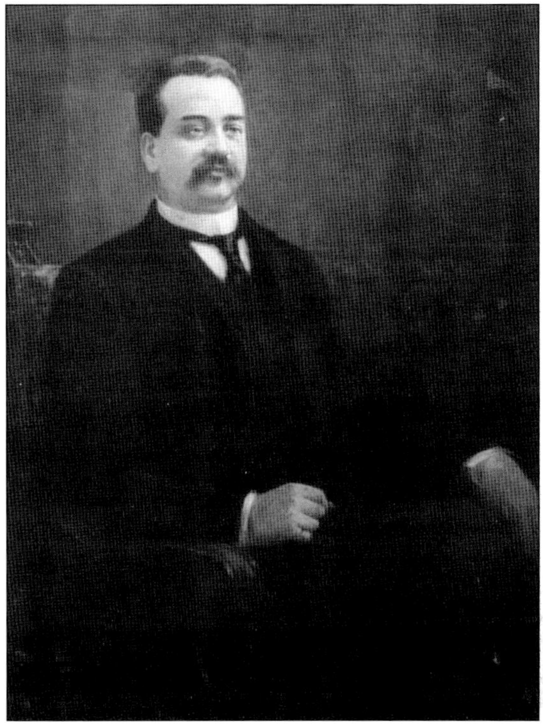

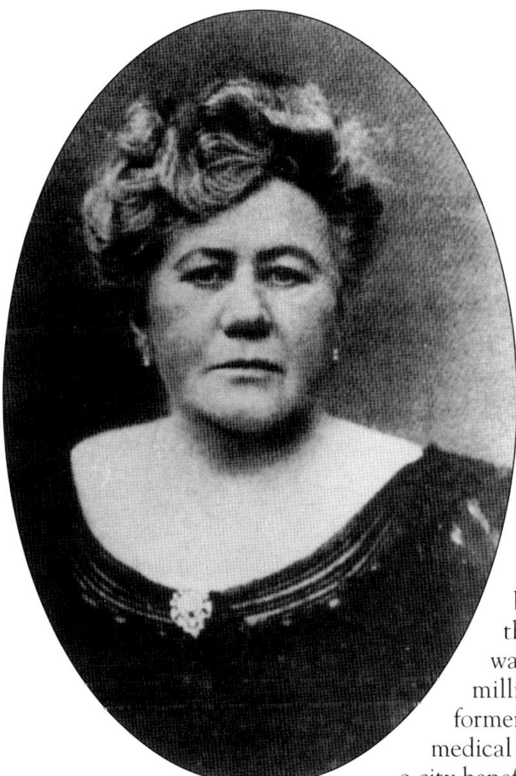

Tootie Barber of Cleveland, Ohio, was in love with a medical student in the 1870s, but instead married Ambrose McGregor, thinking his future would be brighter. It was. Ambrose died in 1900, and in 1905 the millionairess married Dr. Marshall Terry—her former sweetheart—who had become a national medical figure. Tootie spread her wealth and became a city benefactress.

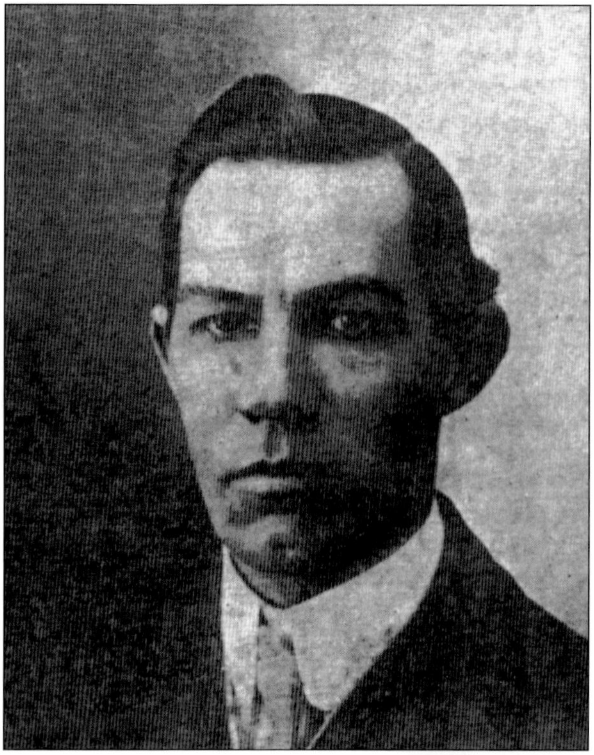

Harvie Heitman arrived in Fort Myers in 1888, at age 16, and within six years he was in business for himself. In 1897, he built the first brick building in Lee County with financial help from Ambrose McGregor. In 1905, Tootie McGregor financed his brick hotel, which he named "The Bradford" in memory of Tootie's deceased son. His road to riches had begun.

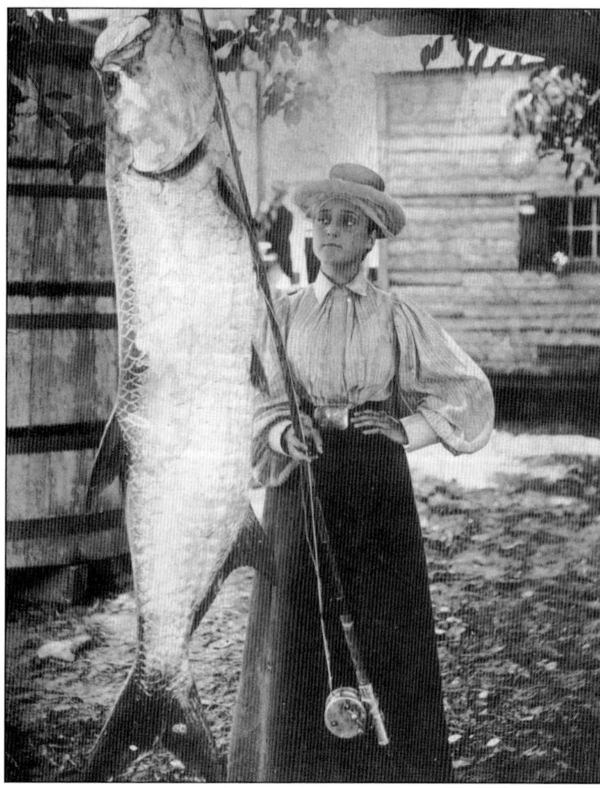

Readers will recall George Shultz, the first telegrapher at Punta Rassa. George boarded itinerant cowpokes and rich fishermen at the old army barracks. His daughter Florida is seen here after hooking a 185-pound tarpon. In 1897 she hooked another catch—Fort Myers businessman Harvie Heitman. On October 6 they married.

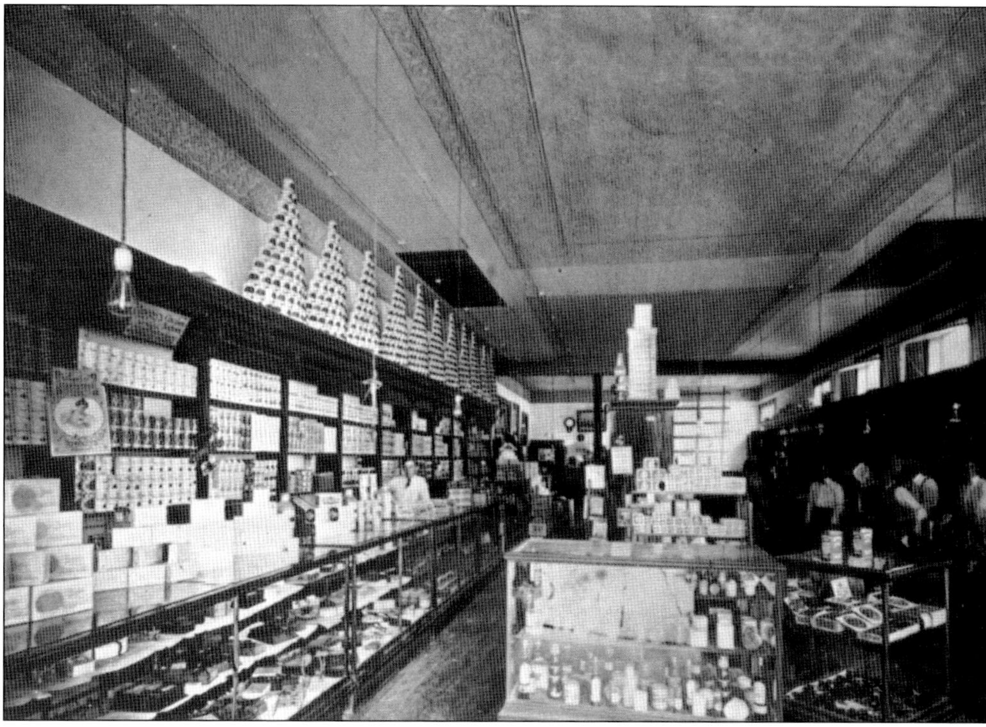

The above picture shows the interior of Harvie Heitman's grocery store. Its offerings were so varied that it even provisioned Caloosahatchee steamboats with fresh-baked and preserved goods. Harvie's brother Gilmer also became a business dynamo. Gilmer started the first telephone exchange and later bought the Franklin Arms Hotel. (Courtesy of Florida State Photo Archive.)

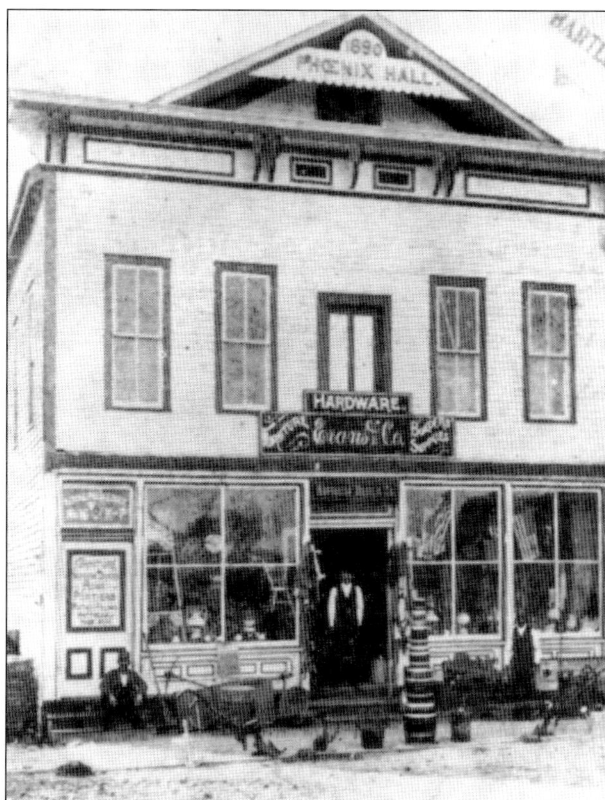

Edward Evans managed a hardware store together with Harvie Heitman. Its second floor was called Phoenix Hall, and it was used for town meetings and entertainment like itinerant vaudeville shows. The fire department, when organized, hung its bell atop the roof.

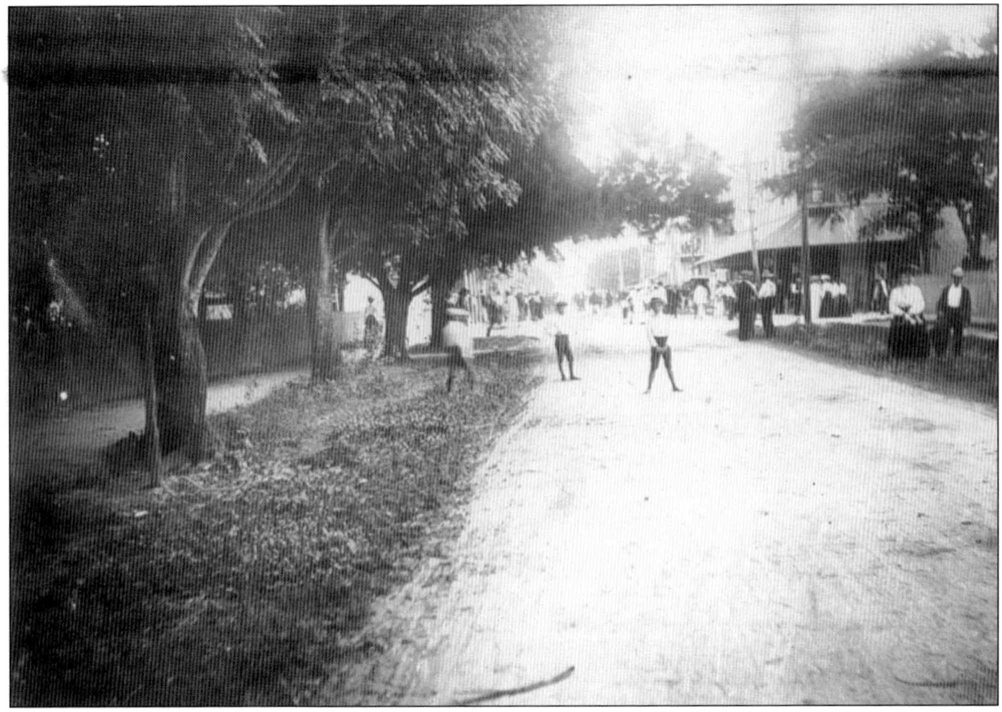

Around 1900 a local Fort Myers photographer composed this image of First Street. Kids could not resist posing, nor the adults at far right. The aforementioned brick Heitman Building lay in the distance. The picket fence at left was part of the Frierson boardinghouse, which was built with concrete walls—a deterrent to termites.

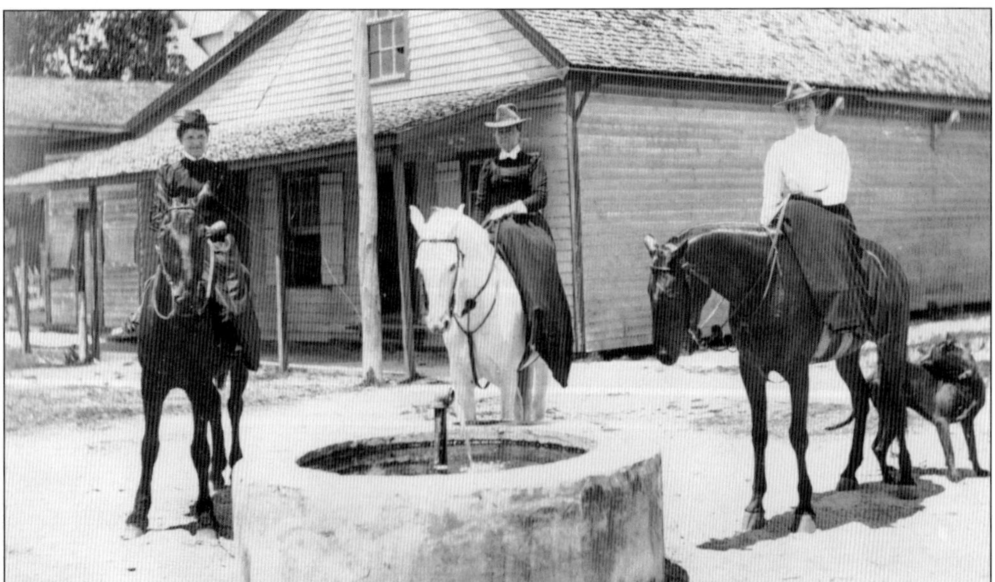

This photo of three ladies on horseback was taken in the center of town at the intersection of Hendry and First Streets. The water trough for horses was fed by an artesian well, placed there in 1905, and removed in 1910. We know the photo was taken on a Sunday because the grocery store in the background is closed. The lady at center is Florida Shultz Heitman.

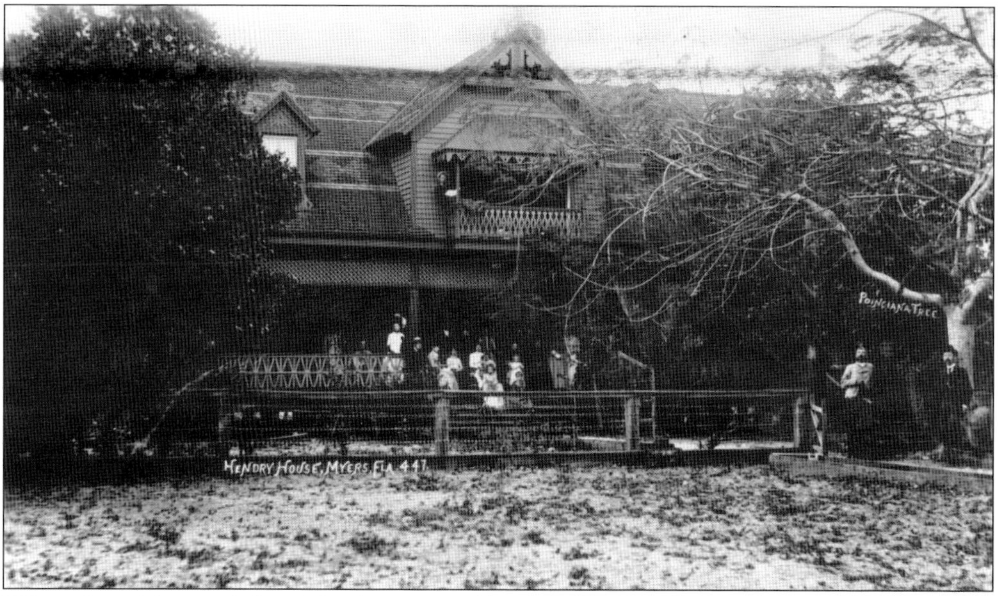

When Capt. Francis Asbury Hendry eventually moved back to his ranch 30 miles east of Fort Myers, he sold his house to son Louis in 1888. Louis, in turn, added 14 rooms and opened the above hotel. The structure was located right at the riverfront, which proved ideal for guests coming and going on steamboats.

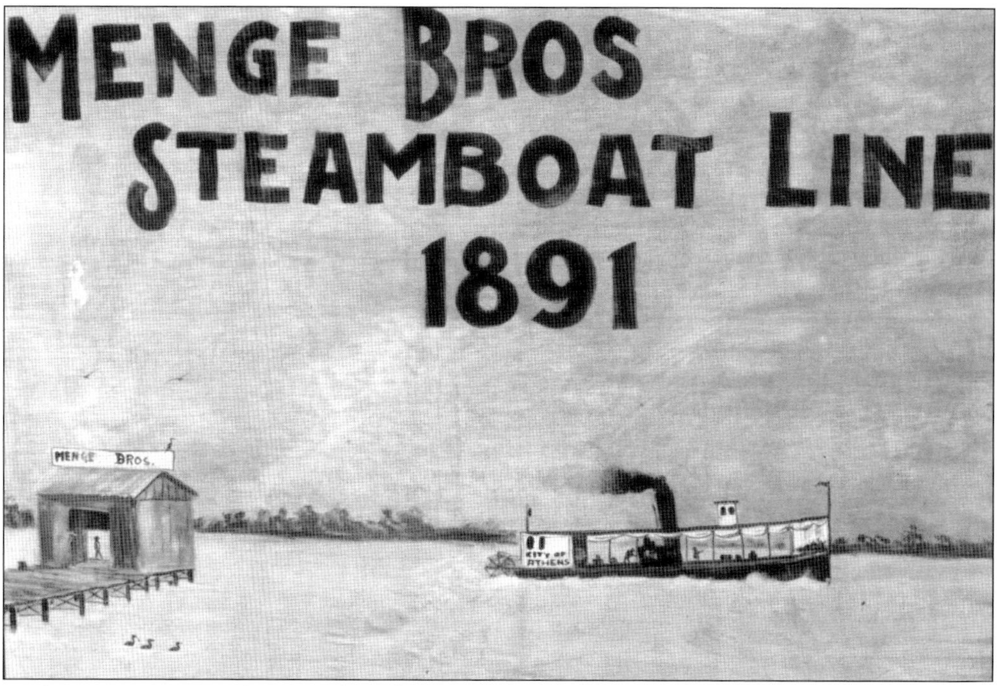

Fred Menge got into the steamboat business in 1888 when his employer, Hamilton Disston, stopped dredging the Caloosahatchee. Fred married a daughter of Capt. Francis Hendry and remained in the fledgling town. He started operations with two small supply boats (purchased from Disston) and gradually increased the fleet. One of his skippers was Manuel Gonzalez, the town's first settler.

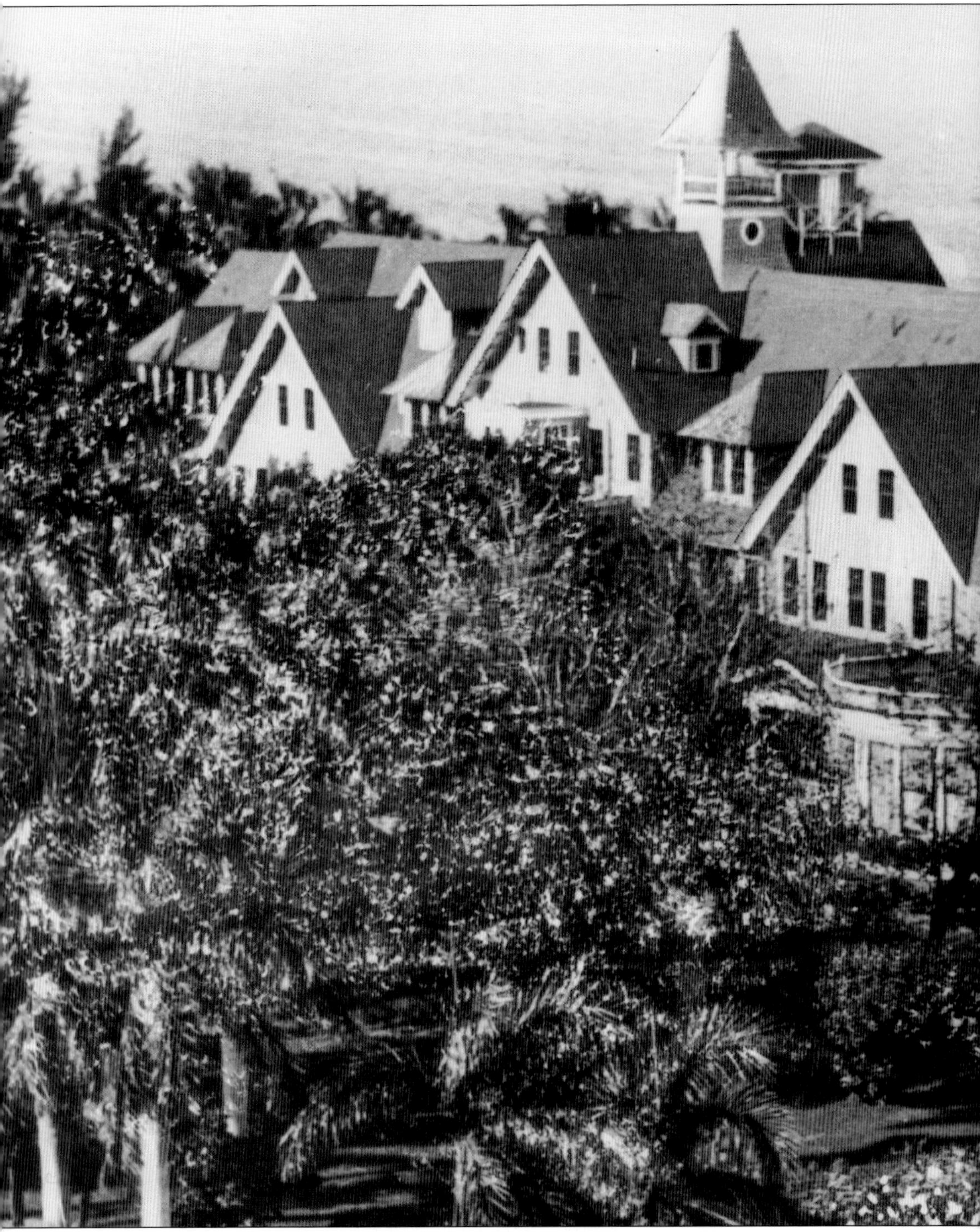

Hugh O'Neill was a New York City department store magnate who supplied furniture for hotels. In 1892 he came to Florida on business and fished at Punta Rassa for tarpon. O'Neill, like Tom Edison, came up the river and fell in love with Fort Myers. He bought Louis Hendry's hotel (page 45 top), tore it down in 1897, and built the fabulous 50-room Fort Myers Hotel. Not only

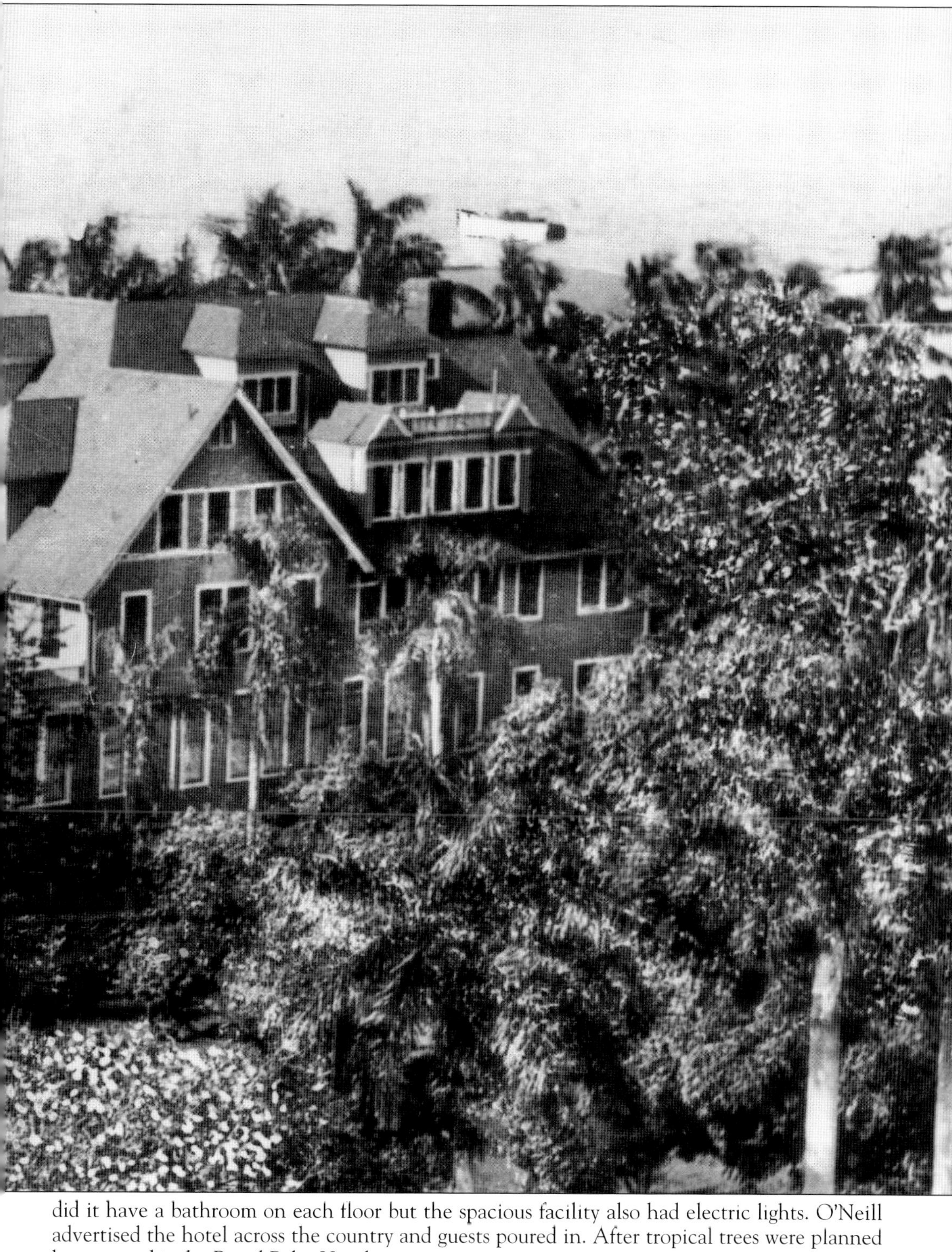

did it have a bathroom on each floor but the spacious facility also had electric lights. O'Neill advertised the hotel across the country and guests poured in. After tropical trees were planned he renamed it the Royal Palm Hotel.

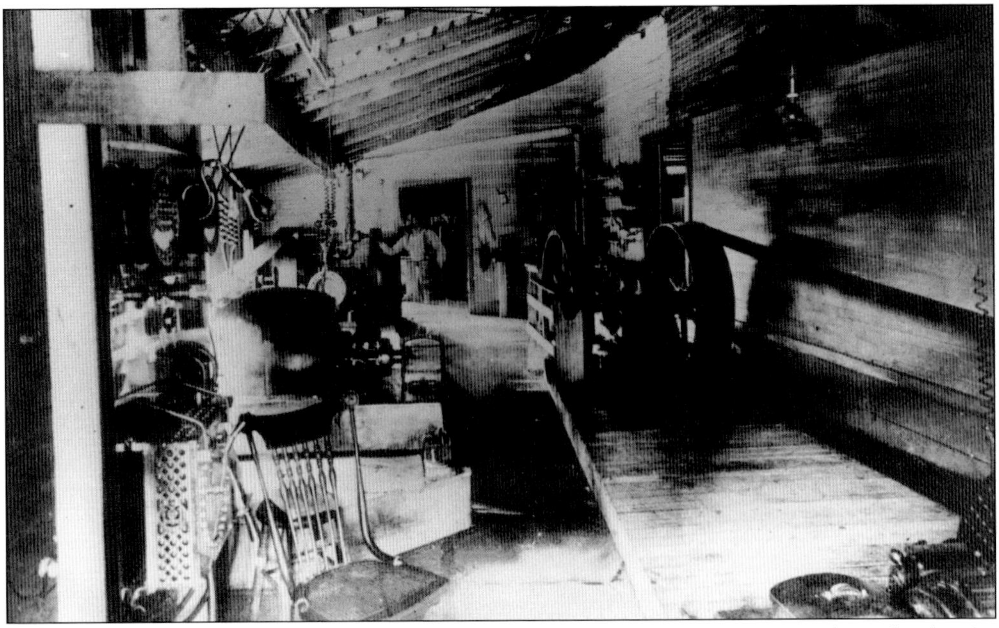

In 1887, Thomas Edison installed electric lights in his new winter home, Seminole Lodge, but he did not return to Fort Myers until 1901. In the meantime, Albertus Gardner had been thinking about installing his own generator in the family canning business. With a contract from both the town (for ten street lights) and the Royal Palm Hotel, he started the above private utility.

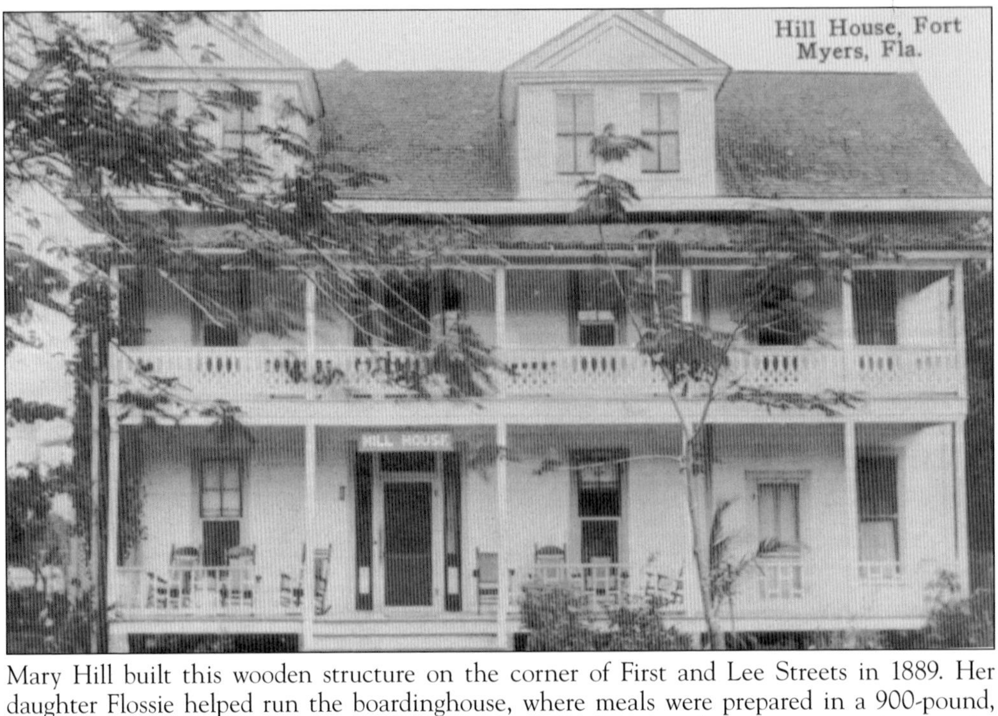

Mary Hill built this wooden structure on the corner of First and Lee Streets in 1889. Her daughter Flossie helped run the boardinghouse, where meals were prepared in a 900-pound, cast-iron, woodburning stove. Flossie had ambitions, however, and she later opened a popular womens clothing store on Jackson Street.

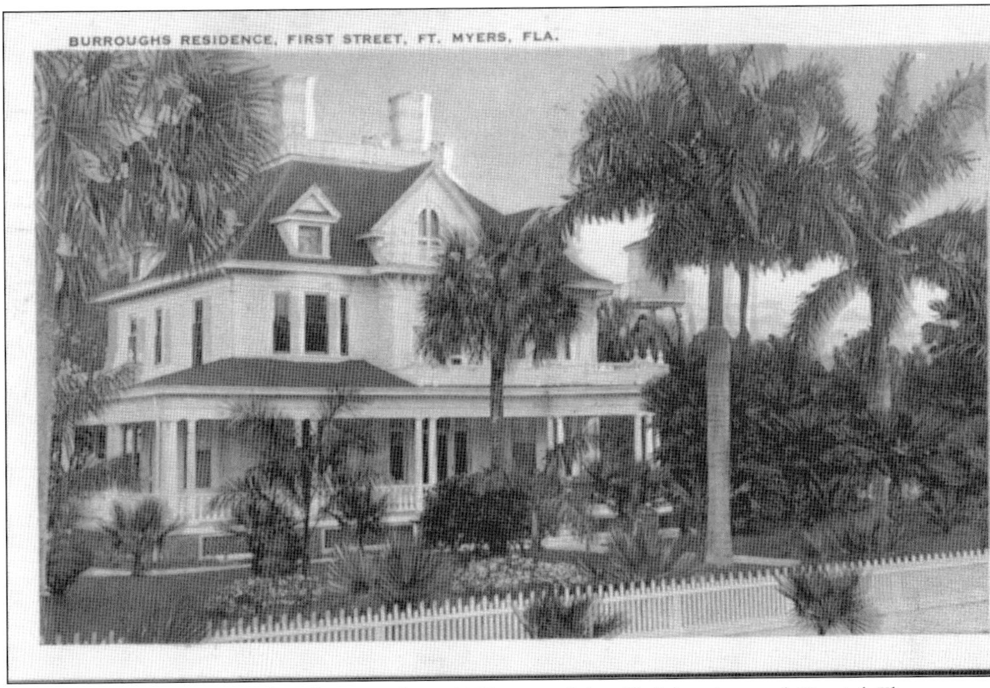

Two visitors at the Royal Palm Hotel in 1889 were John T. Murphy and Daniel Floweree of Montana. Both were wealthy cattlemen who had come to Punta Rassa to fish and watch cattle being shipped to Cuba. They were unimpressed with the scrawny Florida critters, but both were impressed with Fort Myers. Murphy built the above estate in 1901, which in 1918 became the Burroughs home.

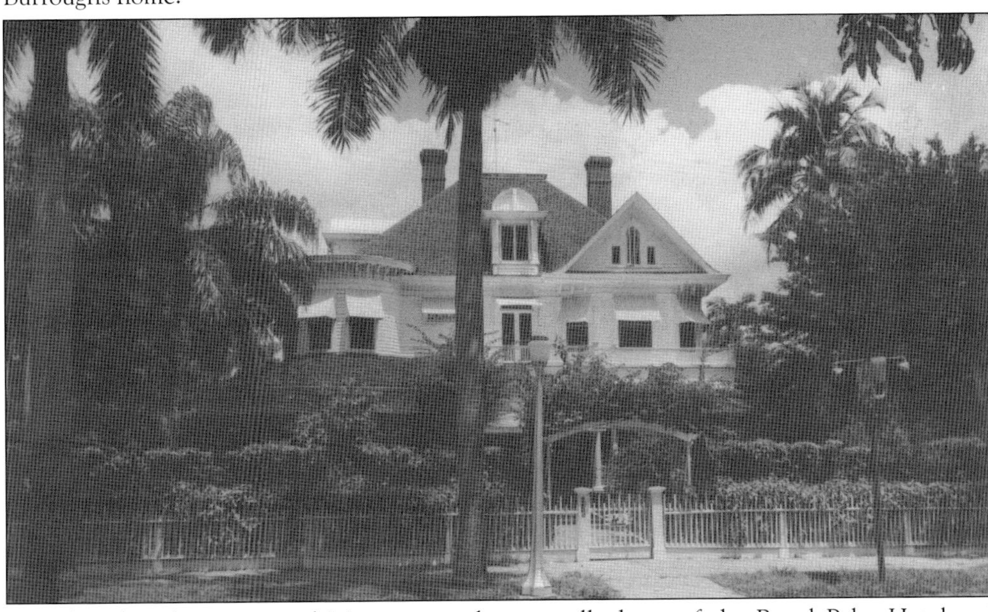

One day the aforementioned Montana cattlemen walked out of the Royal Palm Hotel and decided to buy river frontage near First and Fowler Streets. Murphy won a coin toss and got the corner lot. Floweree's mansion (seen here) cost $20,000—$5,000 more than Murphy's, which also opened in 1901.

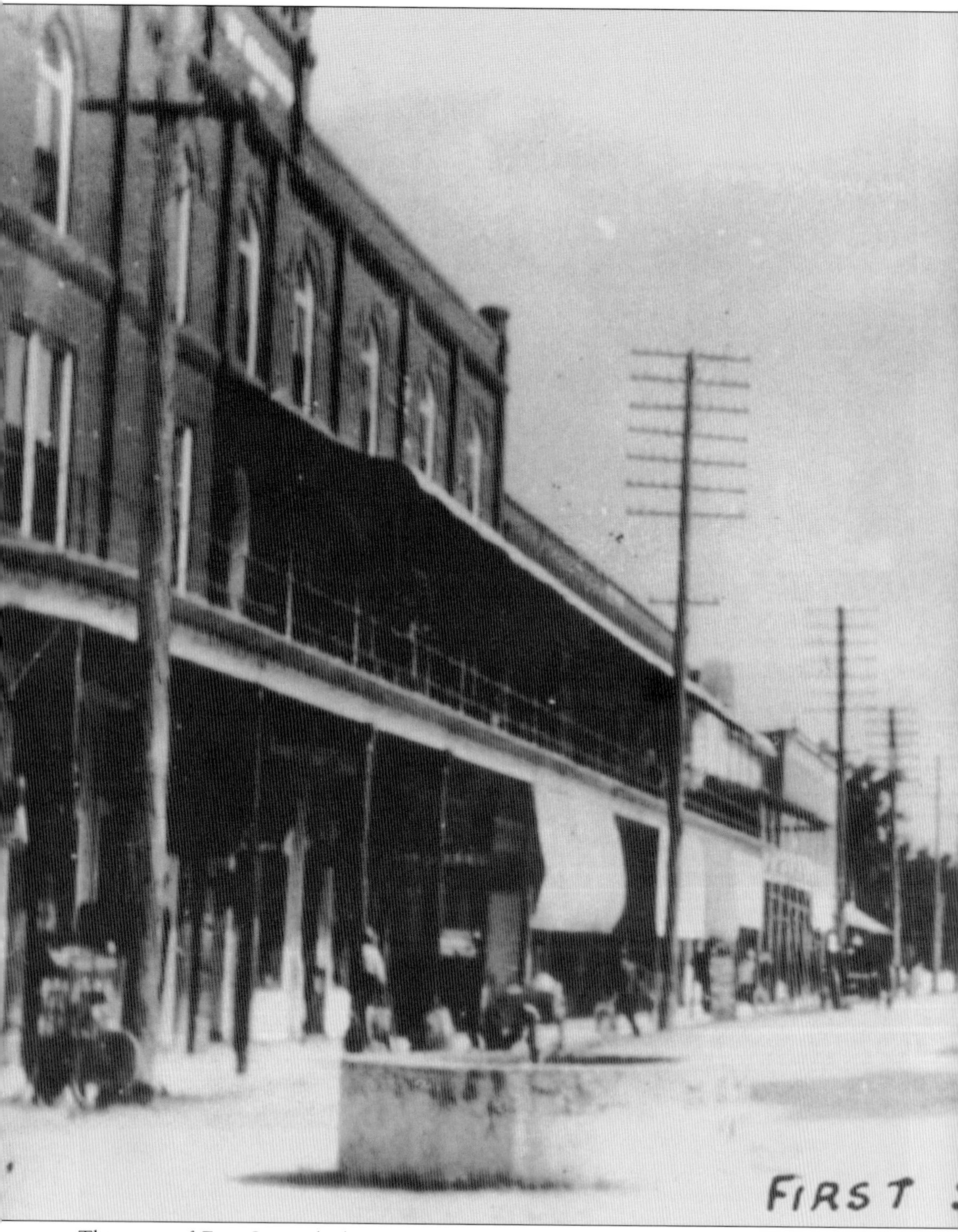

This view of First Street, looking east from Hendry, was taken in 1909. Visible in the left foreground is the watering trough for horses, while behind it is Harvie Heitman's Bradford Hotel. Across the street (first building on right) is Evans Hardware; its top floor was called

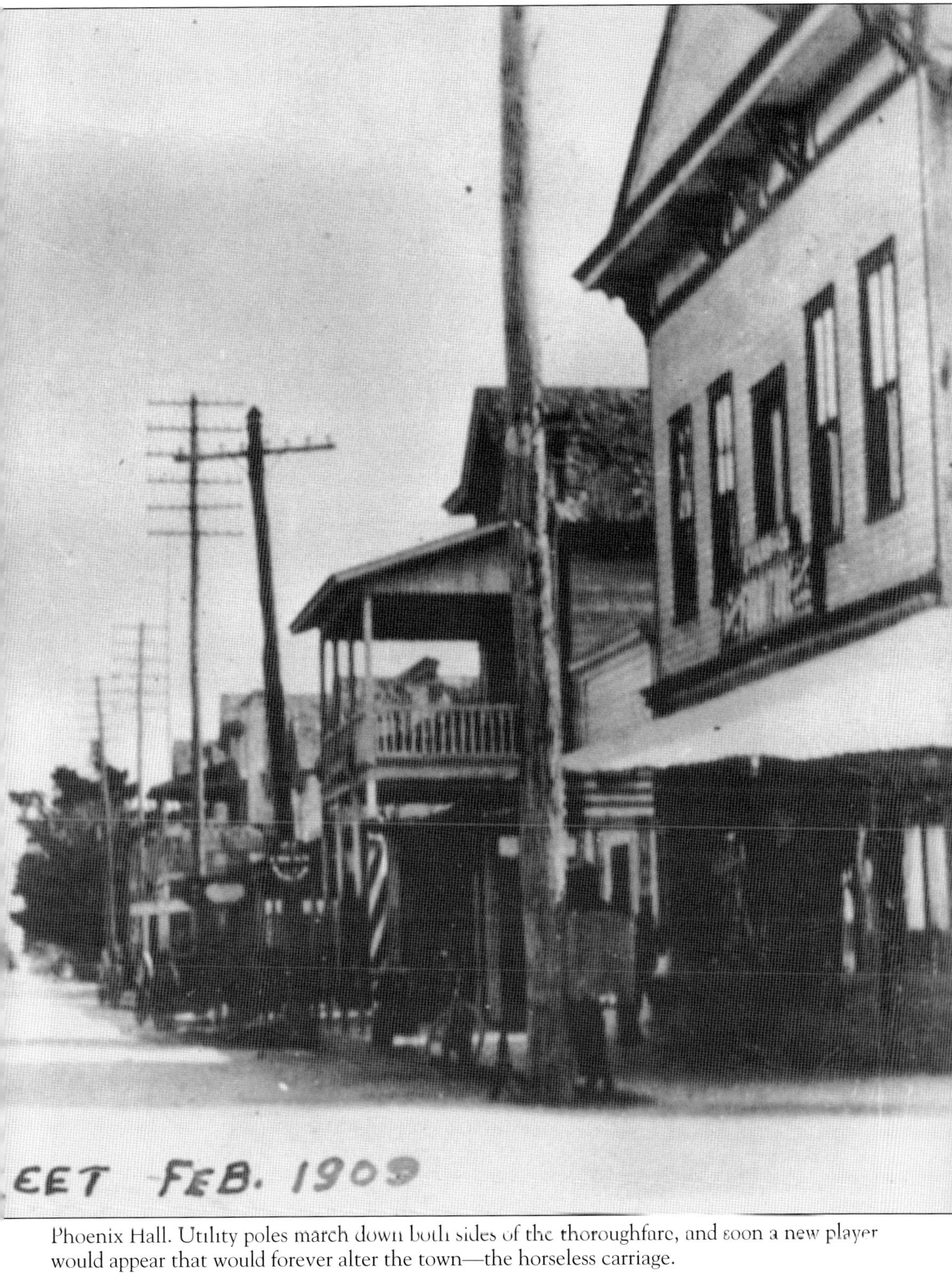

Phoenix Hall. Utility poles march down both sides of the thoroughfare, and soon a new player would appear that would forever alter the town—the horseless carriage.

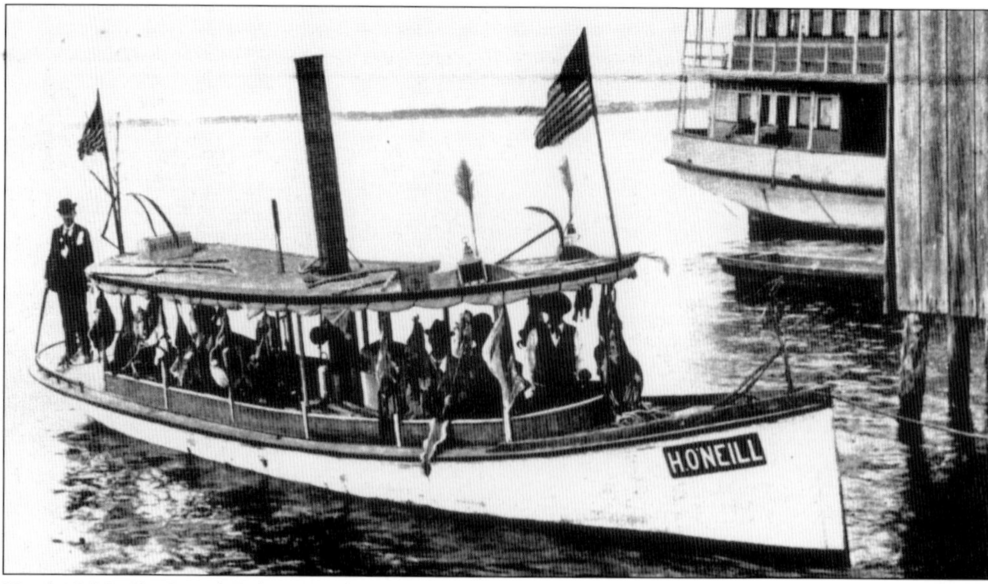

Hugh O'Neill's Royal Palm Hotel attracted many wealthy sportsmen. Back then, Florida had a super abundance of wildlife due to its warm climate, heavy rainfall, and lush growth. The O'Neill vessel would leave the hotel in the early morning and travel to nearby forested hammocks on the Caloosahatchee, returning with the boat festooned with wild turkeys.

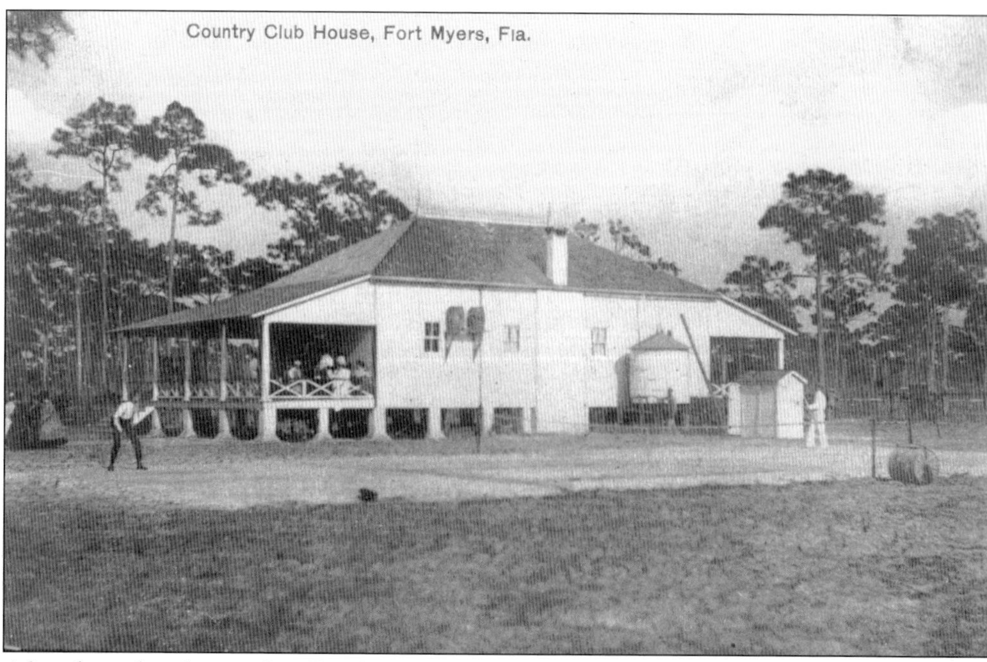

After the railroad arrived in Fort Myers in 1904, visitors wanted a golf course and clubhouse. Tootie McGregor Terry donated a 40-acre site east of the town and club memberships were sold for $100 apiece. In 1907, a clubhouse appeared and work continued on the links. However, the club's distant location and the lack of good roads spelled doom, and the dream failed.

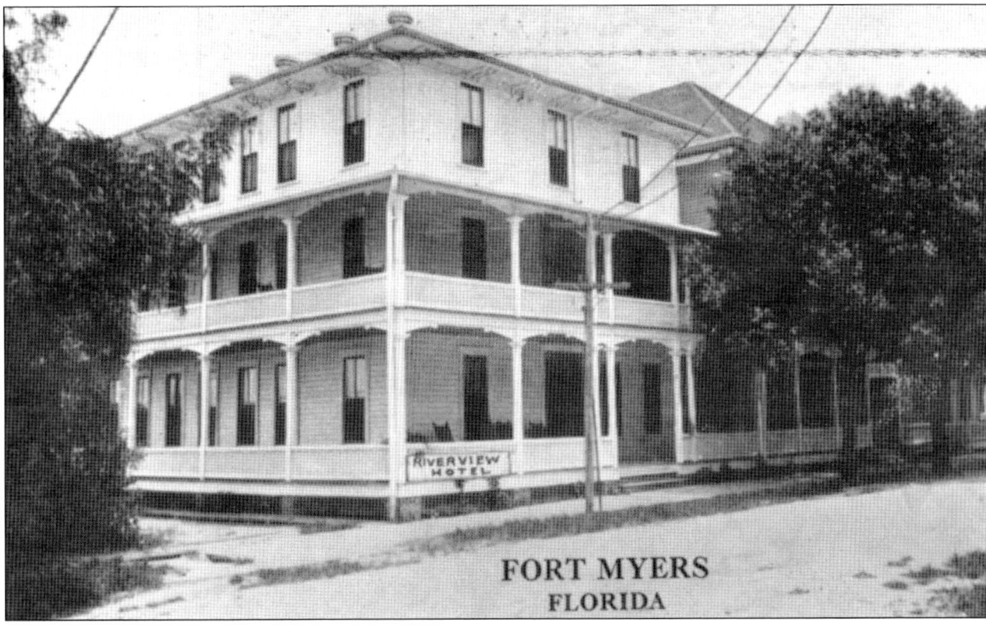

The Riverview Hotel building, first located on the edge of Fort Myers, began life in 1883 as the Keystone Hotel. Thomas Edison spent part of his honeymoon there, calling it a "flea trap." Later it became the Fort Myers Inn, then the Caloosa House. In 1895, the structure was moved to the center of town, enlarged, and renamed the Riverview. New management got rid of the fleas.

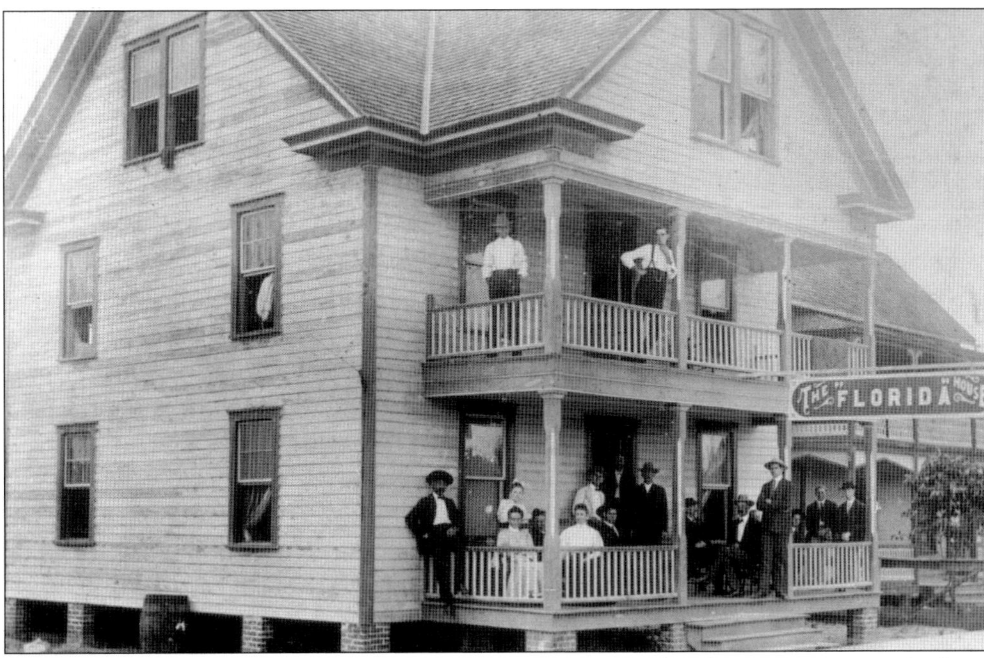

The 20-room Florida House was two blocks from the original Atlantic Coast Line Railroad station at Main and Monroe Streets. Hotel porters greeted trains and helped guests with their luggage. Here, a few registrants pose for the cameraman in 1910. Most windows of the hotel are open, allowing for river breezes, but window screens are notably absent.

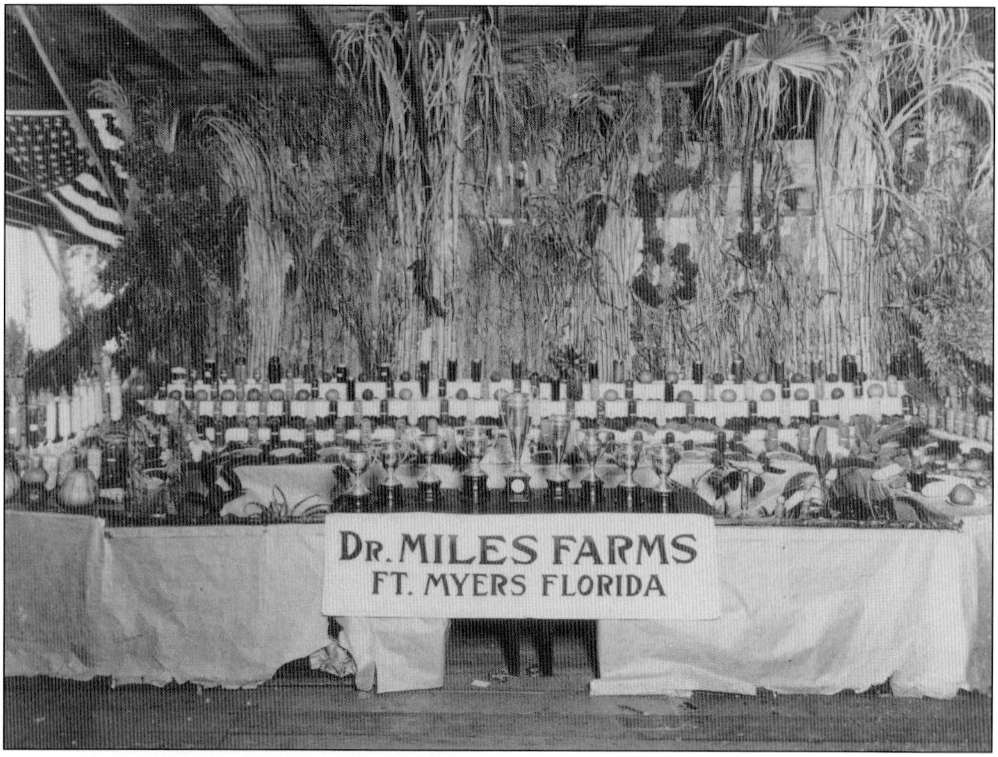

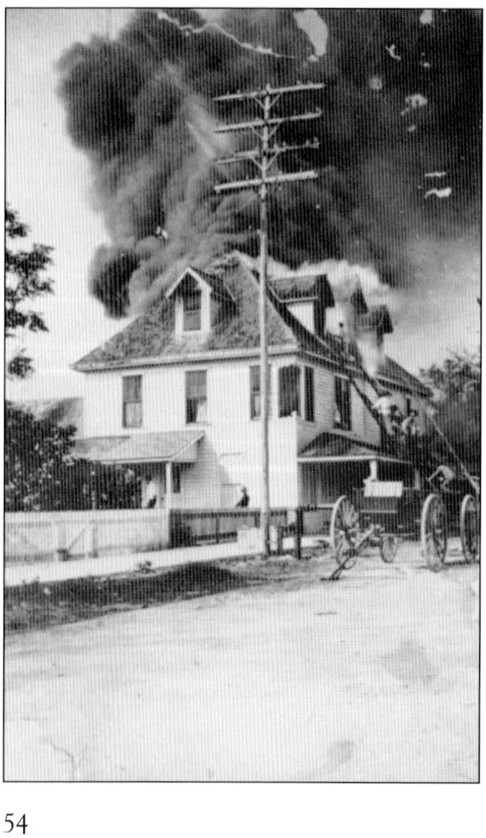

When Dr. Franklin Miles came to Fort Myers in 1905, he relinquished management of Miles Laboratories in Indiana to kinfolk. Miles himself became intensely interested in Florida agriculture and bought some 16,000 acres of area land. Not only did he raise vegetables and sugar cane, but he taught local farmers how to obtain better crop yields. His lab back home later rolled out Alka-Seltzer.

On May 2, 1901, the first fire in a dozen years burned down the house of Mrs. Carrie Bass. At the time, a Dr. Winkler was operating a steam laundry on the premises, and the fire started in a laundry stovepipe. Fortunately the fire began slowly, which allowed neighbors to carry out furniture before the home was destroyed.

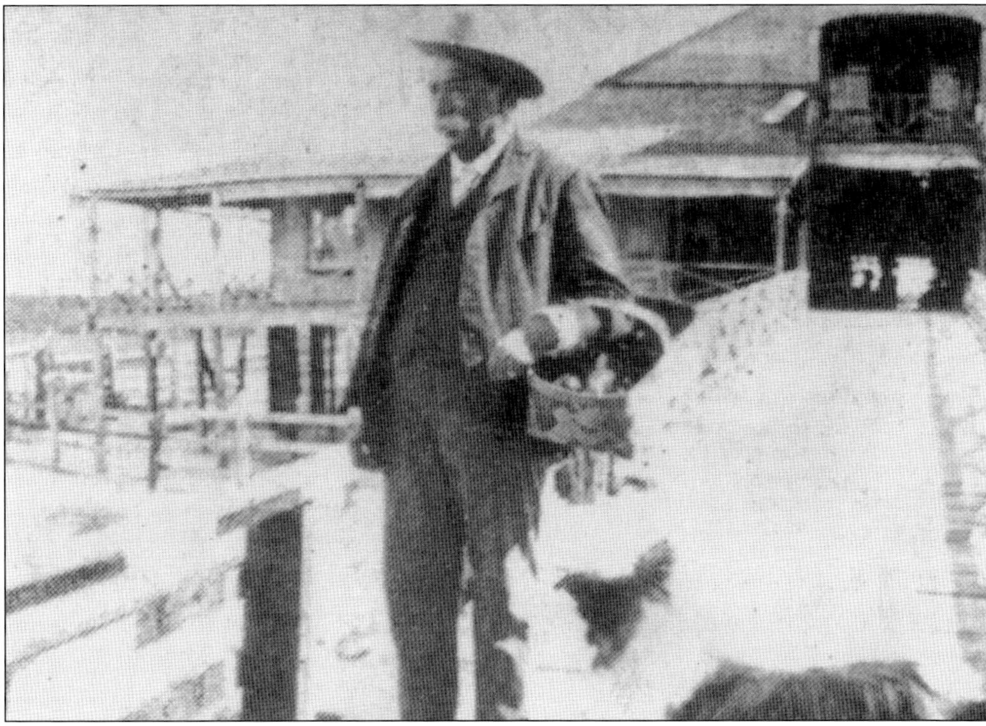

George Shultz came to Punta Rassa in 1867 as a 24-year-old telegrapher from Newark, New Jersey. His employer, the International Ocean Telegraph Company, had been given the old Civil War army barracks, which Shultz eventually turned into the "Tarpon House" for cattle drovers and wealthy sports fishermen. The popular attraction stood near today's Sanibel Causeway tollhouse.

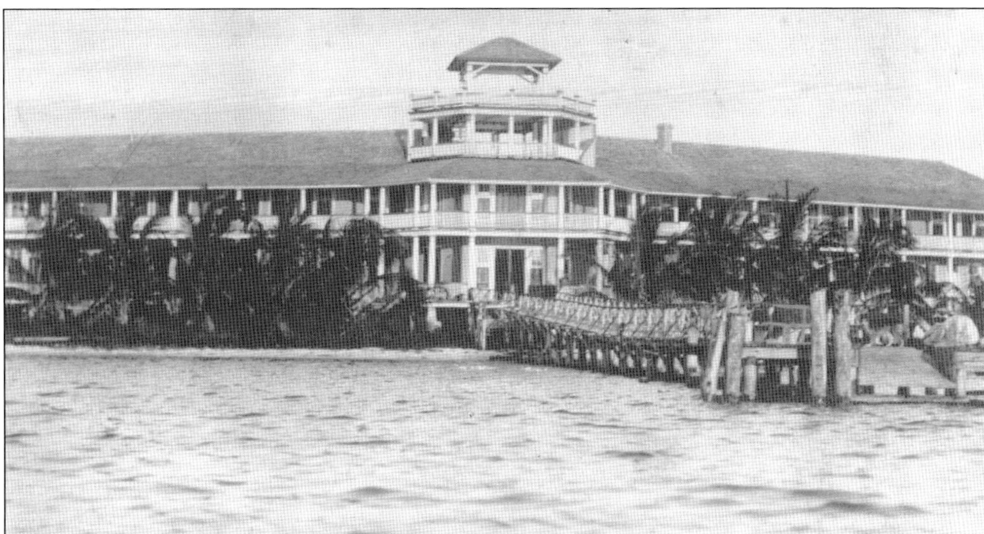

After the old army barracks burned at Punta Rassa in 1907, George Shultz raised money to erect the above structure. The Shultz Hotel was built like a bird with spread-out wings, every room having a water view. Even family suites were available. Unfortunately the stately structure burned to the ground in 1913. Shultz, a local legend, died in 1921.

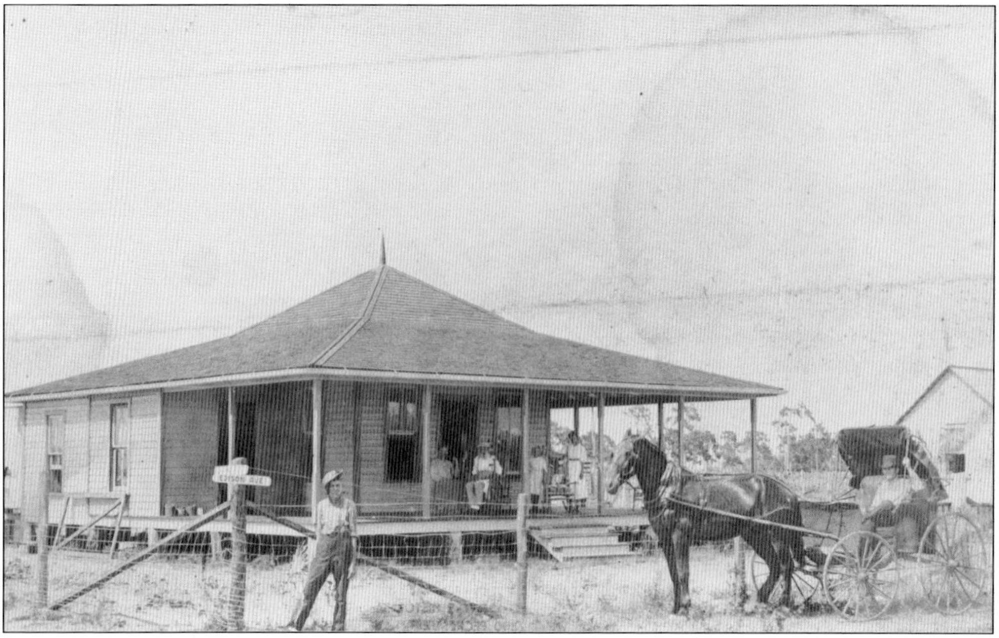

With internationally famous Thomas Edison spending his winters in Fort Myers, it was inevitable that his name would be used for various purposes. Soon after buying property on the Caloosahatchee, a street east of his home was named Edison Avenue. Houses like the one above were typically constructed from then on.

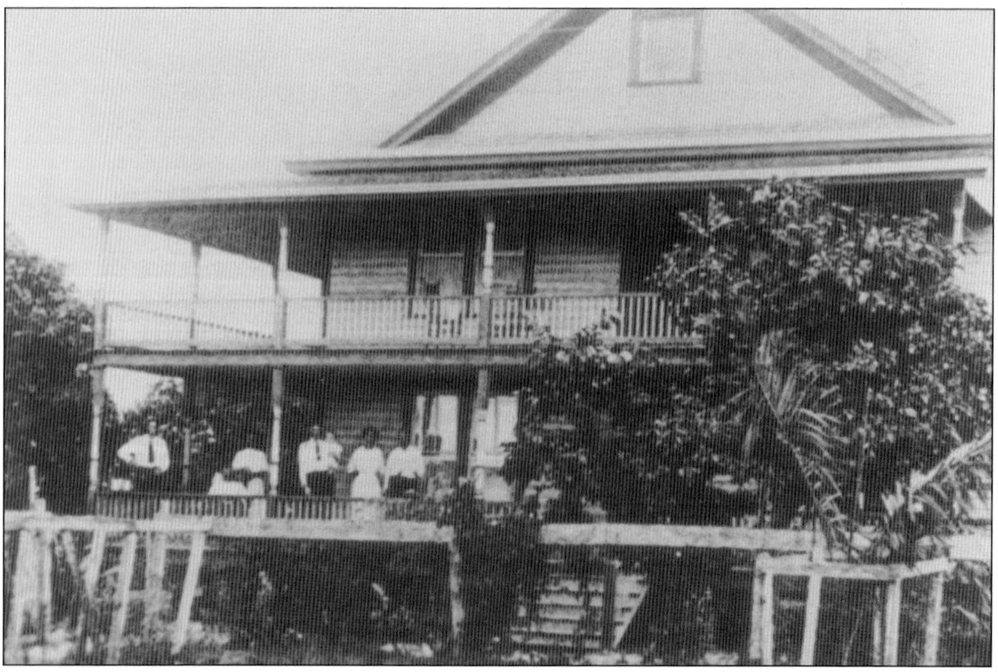

Several boarding homes were built in Fort Myers to accommodate the "domestics" who worked the winter season. Rooms and meals were furnished at affordable rates, and many workers flocked to the congenial accommodations found at Aunt Dooley's Boarding House (shown here).

Four

COMINGS AND GOINGS

Like most Florida towns, Fort Myers grew slowly because it lacked a transportation network. But once the steamboat and Iron Horse arrived, and good roads appeared, the economy of the Caloosahatchee region began to flourish. As Florida historian Kathryn Abbey once said, "Transportation and settlement always go hand in hand; the former makes possible the latter, while the latter creates demand for the former."

All manner of sailing vessels once worked the Caloosahatchee, and schedules were always subject to the vagaries of weather. In June of 1883, the first steamboat appeared—the *Manatee*—which connected Fort Myers to Manatee, another town on the west coast. The Menge brothers of Fort Myers eventually organized a local and popular steamboat firm, as did the Kinzie brothers. Both offered regular passenger and freight service and did a brisk excursion business as well during the winter season.

Finally, in 1904, the Atlantic Coast Line Railroad linked Fort Myers with the national railroad network. Tourists started pouring in, and citrus growers quickly switched to rail transportation. The Iron Horse also spurred other new industries; one of the more important of these was bringing catfish and bass from Lake Okeechobee to Fort Myers, where they were packed in barrels and sent to Northern markets.

The first "motor car" appeared in town in 1904, having left Bradenton 15 hours before. For decades poor roads cursed Fort Myers and Lee County, though many sand "paths" were eventually covered with crushed shell. The shell itself, pumped up from the river bed or taken from Native-American mounds, was washed and screened. Later, brick pavers and macadam were utilized, especially in the early 1920s, when over 20 miles of roads were paved. The famed Tamiami Trail, begun in 1915, was delayed by World War I. Intermittent construction followed until the Tampa-to-Miami highway opened in 1928.

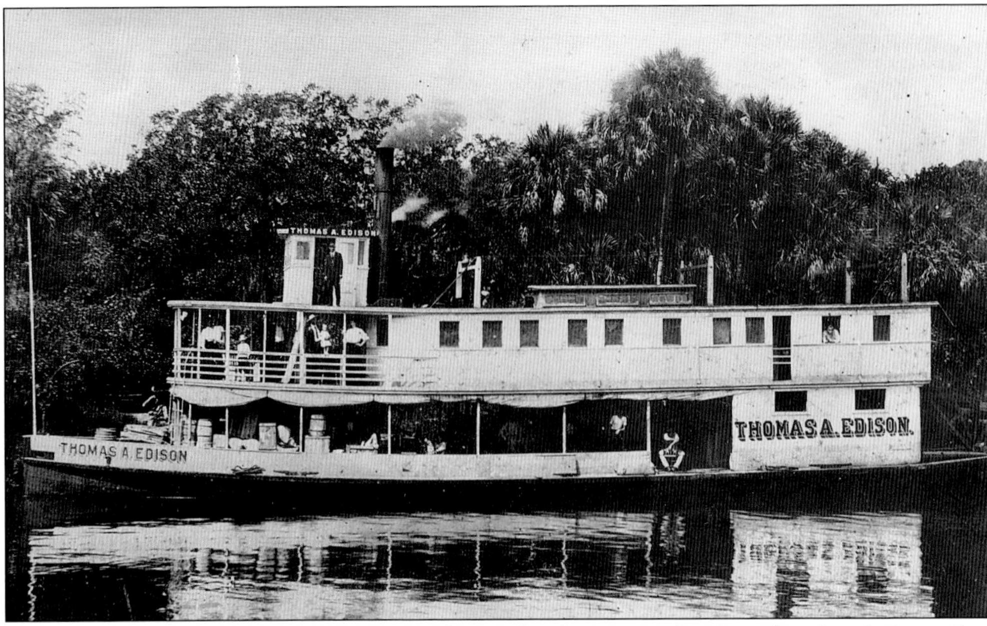

The steamer *Thomas A. Edison* was proudly run by the Menge brothers (Fred and Conrad) of Fort Myers. It had been built in Apalachicola by Sam Johnson for river travel and drew less than 2.5 feet of water. Technically the *Edison* was a stern wheeler, had two decks, and was capable of carrying 1,200 boxes of citrus.

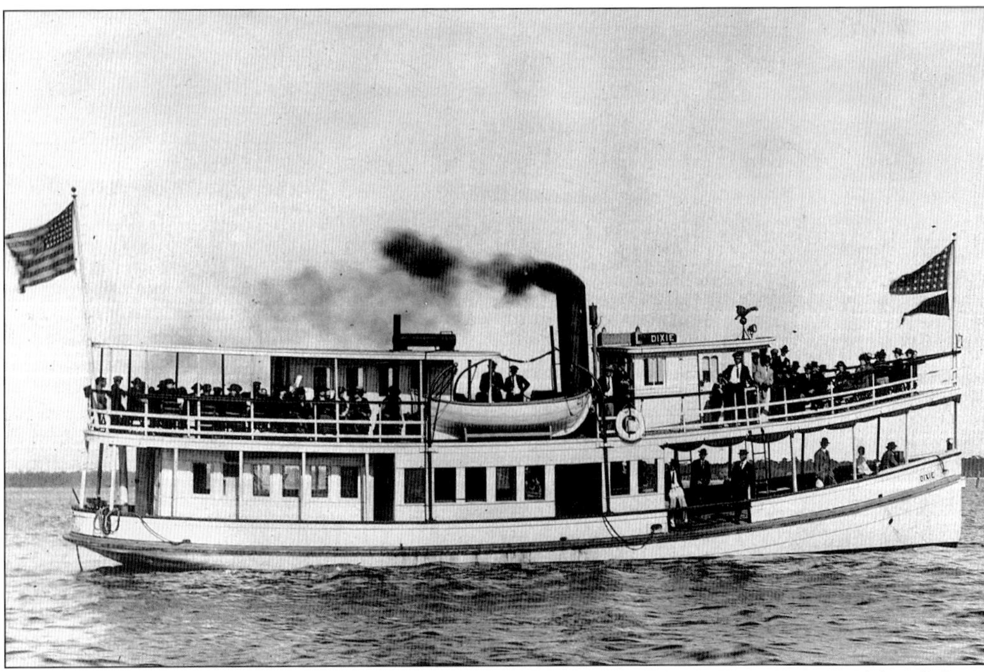

Every winter season thousands of people would board the *Dixie* in Fort Myers and head down the Caloosahatchee to the barrier islands. The Kinzie brothers (Andrew, George, and Eric) owned the popular vessel. Above its wheelhouse is an eagle carving, a gift of New York senator Charles Stadler, a prominent winter visitor.

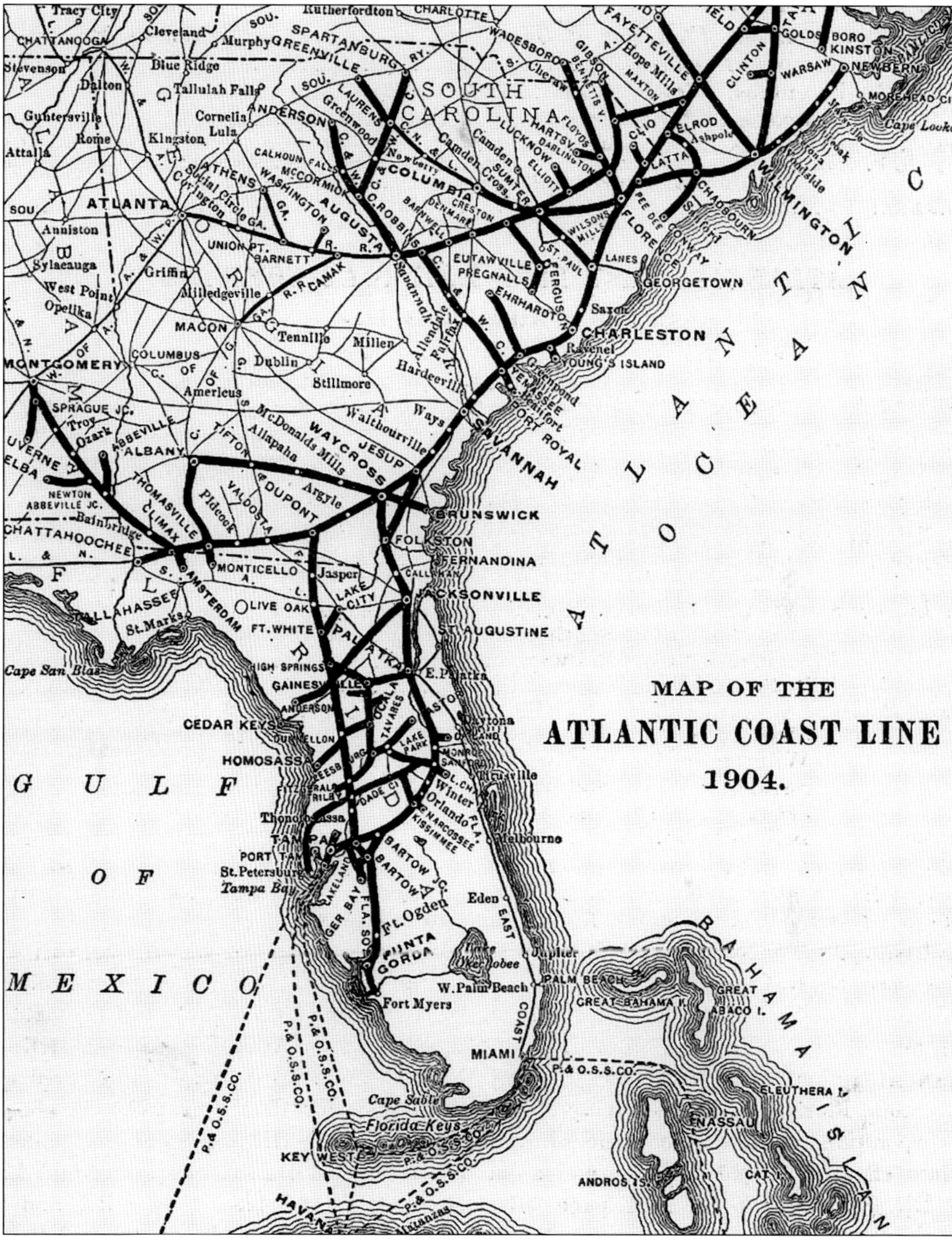

Fort Myers rejoiced when the Atlantic Coast Line Railroad arrived in 1904. Most of the firm's lines in Florida were formerly part of the Plant System of rails. For years, Fort Myers had begged Henry B. Plant for the Iron Horse, but the Connecticut Yankee brought rails no closer than Punta Gorda—this in 1886. Thus the tycoon was never locally revered. Plant died in 1899 and three years later the Plant System of rails (2,235 miles long) was sold to the Atlantic Coast Line. Walter G. Langford, a prominent Fort Myers businessman and banker, then began writing Coast Line officials about the lack of railroad service. Company officials eventually visited the City of Palms, liked what they saw, and in 1903 a 28-mile extension from Punta Gorda was begun.

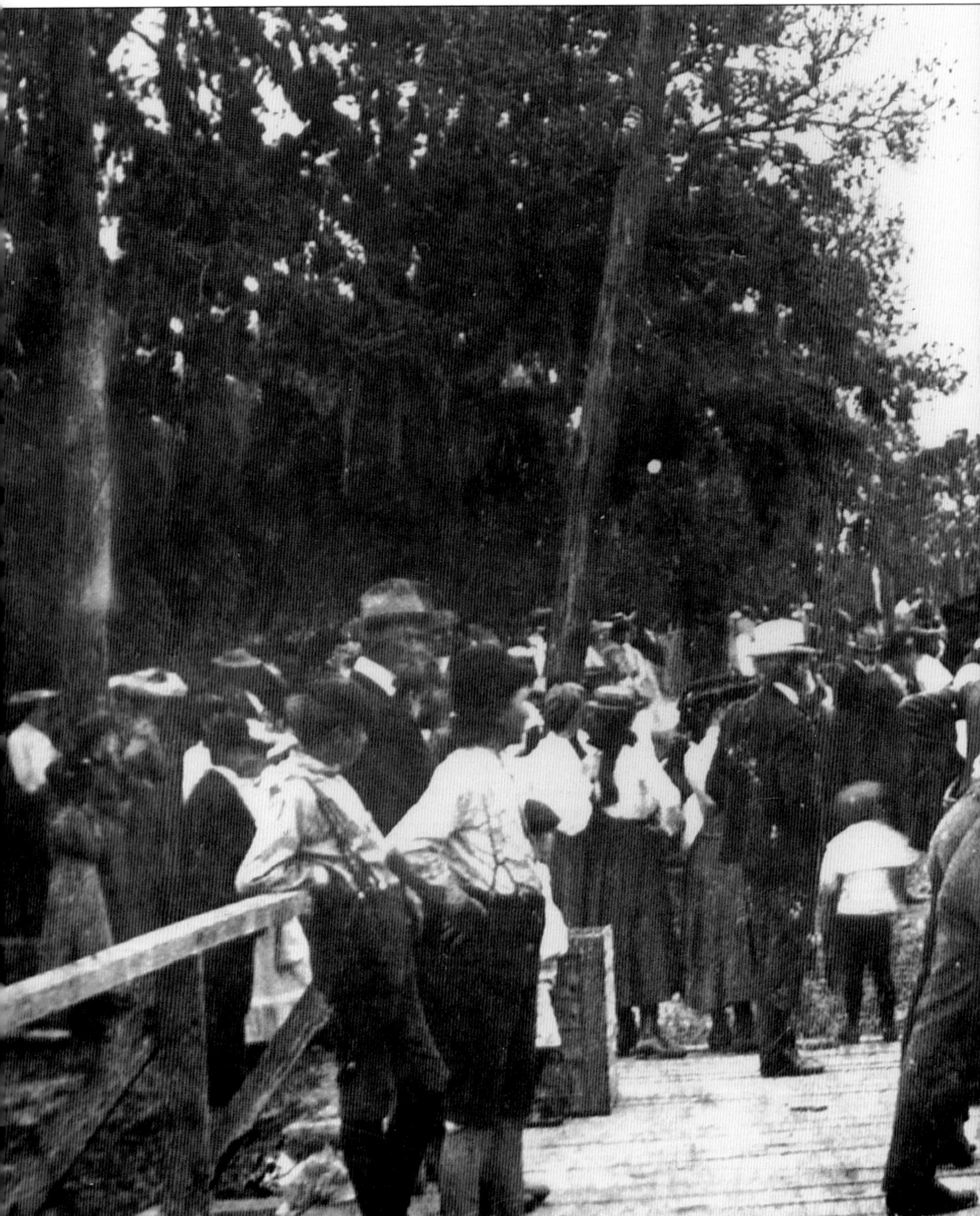

Mrs. James (Julia) Hendry, a former Miss Tampa, drove home the last railroad spike on February 20, 1904. She can be seen at far right holding a sledge hammer. Once the deed was done, church bells rang, a cannon boomed, and boat whistles blew. Jubilant citizens then draped the Coast Line steam engine with Old Glory. Sandwiches were passed out to railroad workers along

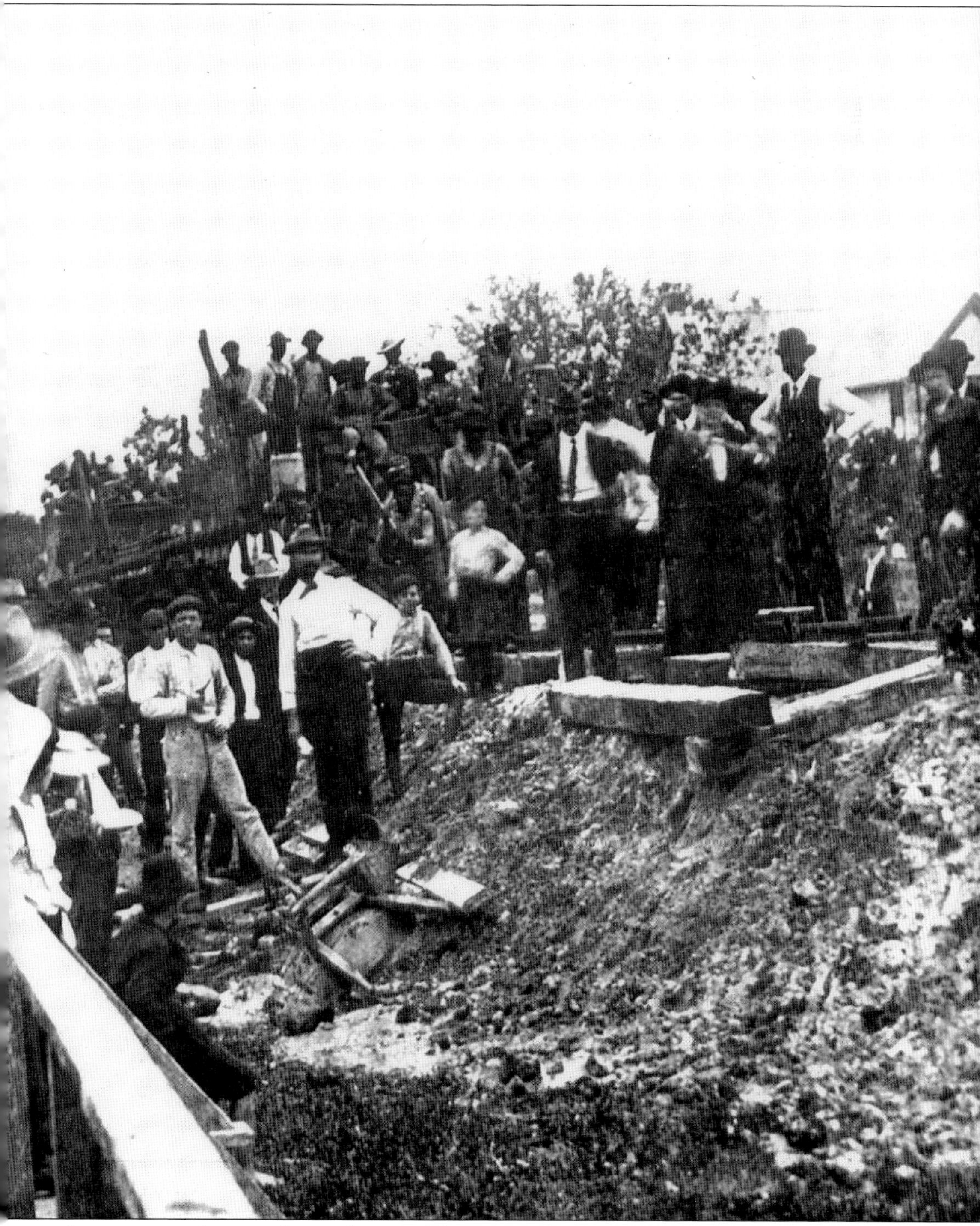

with sausages, cookies, candies, and cigars. After getting the Iron Horse, Fort Myers experienced an economic renaissance. Tourists and newcomers poured in as never before, plus new industry arose. The image of a frontier cowtown began to vanish.

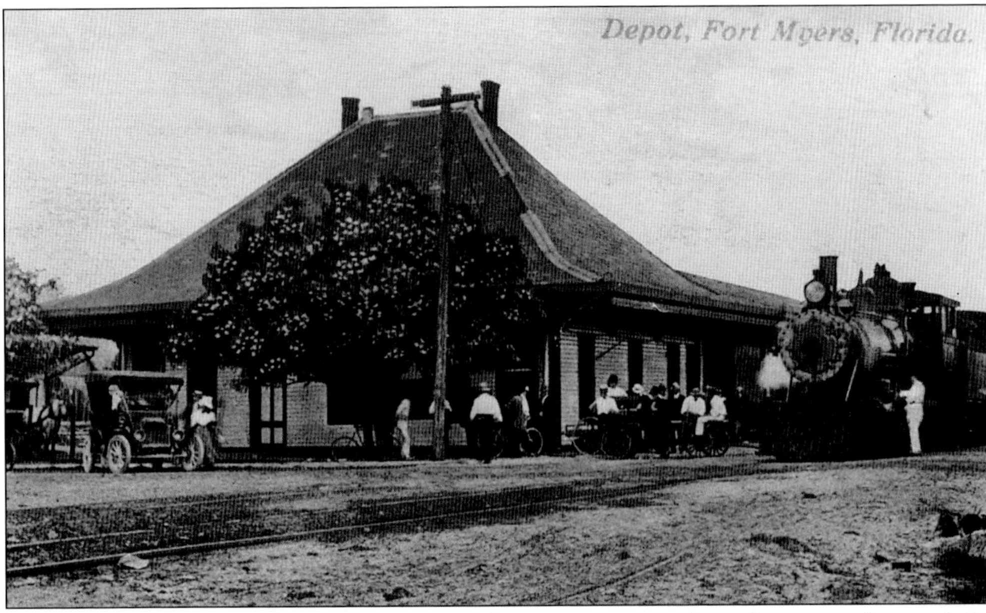

The Coast Line insisted that Fort Myers provide a no-cost route through town and grounds for a station, freight house, and wharf. To meet the demands, local businessmen formed a board of trade, the forerunner of today's chamber of commerce. A wood depot soon went up at Monroe Street, on property purchased from Mrs. Evalina Gonzalez for $6,000. Passenger train service began May 10, 1904, with two daily trains.

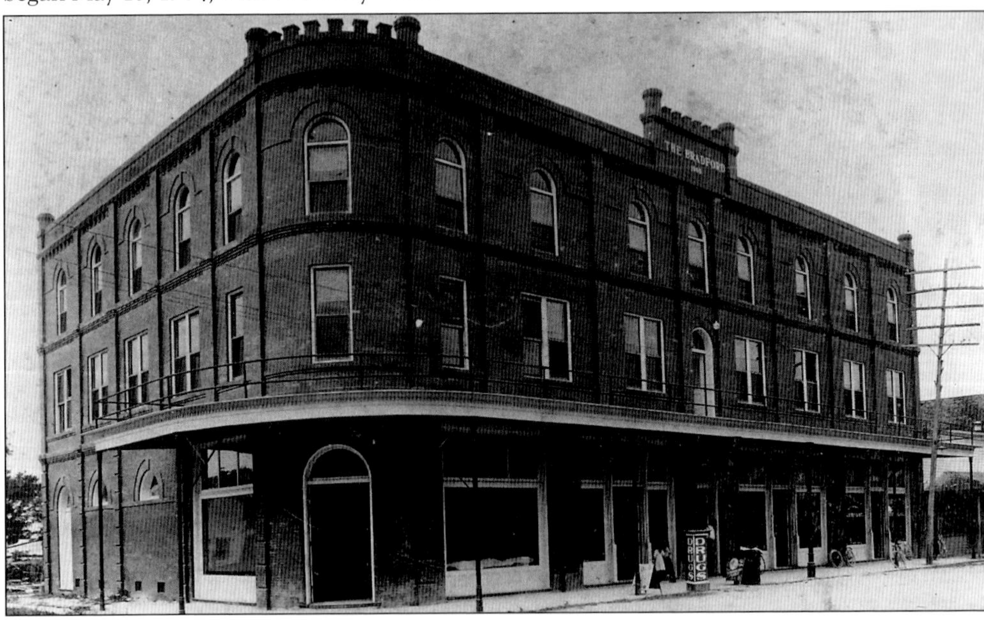

Harvie Heitman built the Bradford Hotel on First Street shortly after the Iron Horse arrived. Millionaire Tootie McGregor provided financing and the hotel was named for her deceased son. Work began in August 1904 and the brick hostelry opened the following November. It boasted 41 rooms and a spacious second-floor dining room. Sportsmen liked the Bradford, and frequently they let their hunting dogs sleep in the corridors. Additions were later built, including a fancy entrance in 1926.

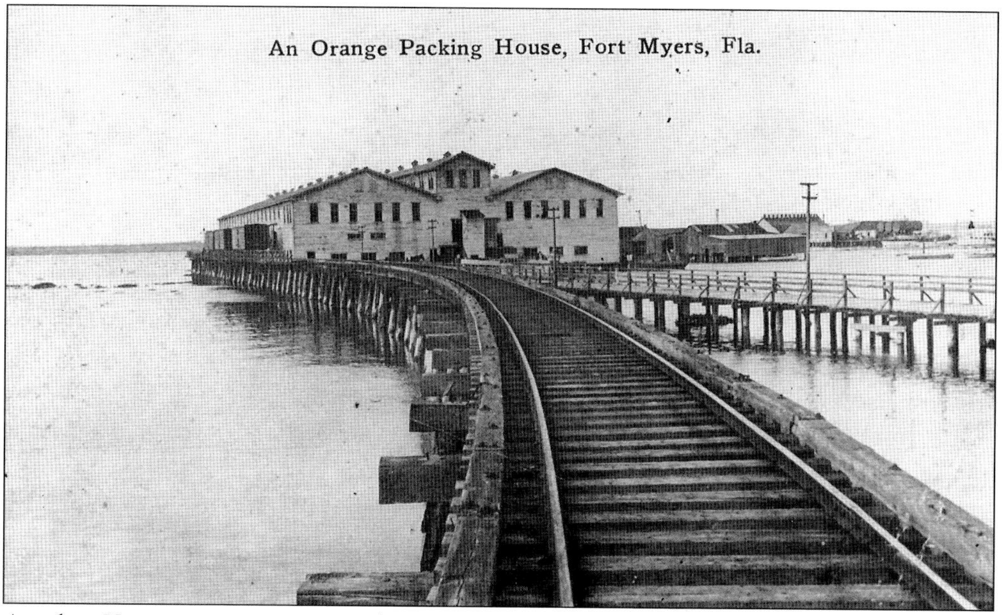

Another Heitman enterprise was the Lee County Packing Plant, which sat on piers in the Caloosahatchee. It accommodated area citrus and vegetable growers, who discovered that the Iron Horse could reach Northern markets far faster than steamboats. Products arrived by boat at the back door, then left by rail in ventilated freight cars. The plant, built in 1910, was the world's largest.

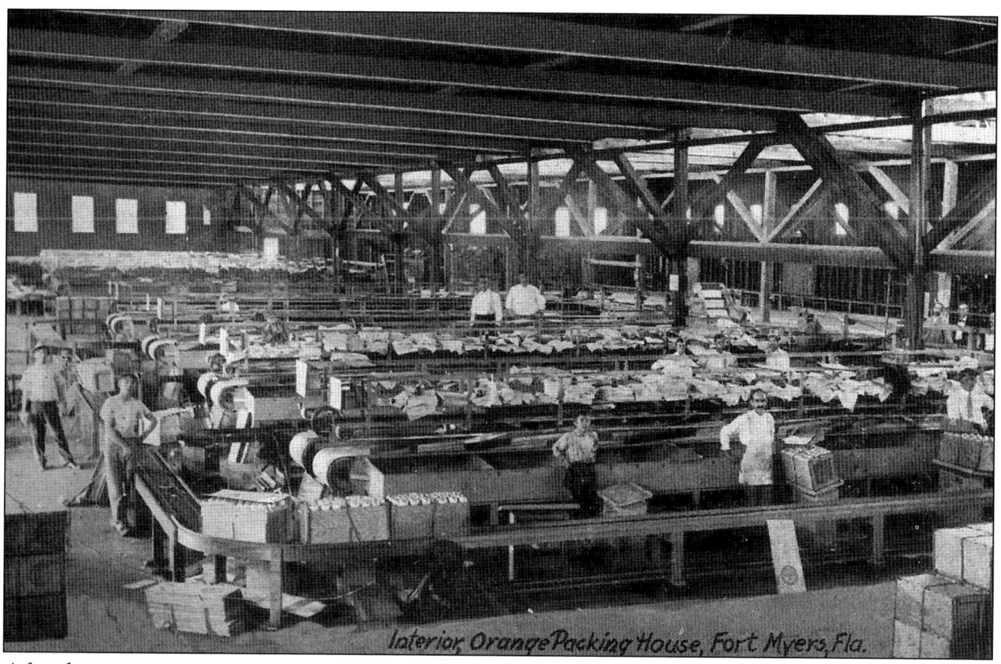

After harvesting, citrus was sent to packing houses where it was washed, graded, boxed, then shipped by rail. Quickly the traffic grew. In 1924 some 340,473 crates of oranges were dispatched, as well as 540,838 crates of grapefruit, 12,670 crates of guava, 62,980 coconuts, 11,500 pounds of grapes, and 28,807 bunches of bananas.

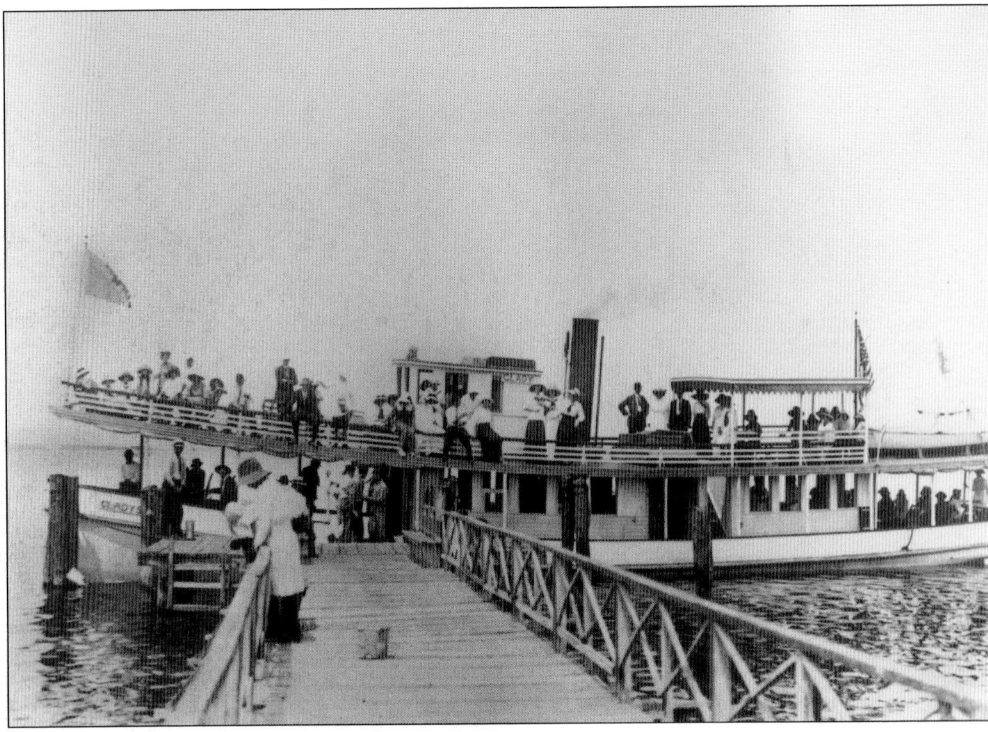

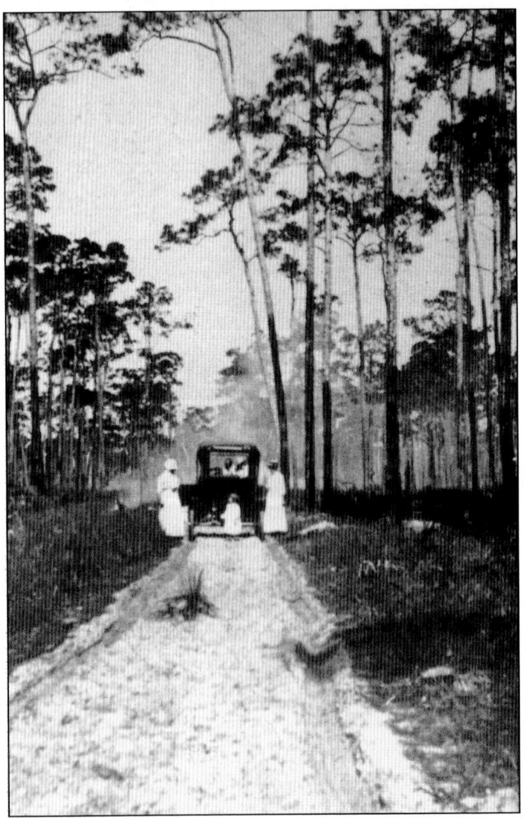

The *Gladys* usually delivered mail and freight, but the Kinzie brothers vessel also did a brisk excursion business. Day trippers departed Fort Myers and were taken down the Caloosahatchee to Sanibel, Captiva, and Pine Islands, or for a leisurely cruise around beautiful San Carlos Bay. Many patrons brought a picnic hamper, and "dressing up" for the occasion was not uncommon.

Whereas today motorists can zip with ease between Fort Myers and Estero, such was not the case in the early 1920s. Here, a Ford flatbed has sunk into the primitive sand trail that once connected those points. In 1928, the famed Tamiami Trail opened over the same course. Today it is known as US Route 41.

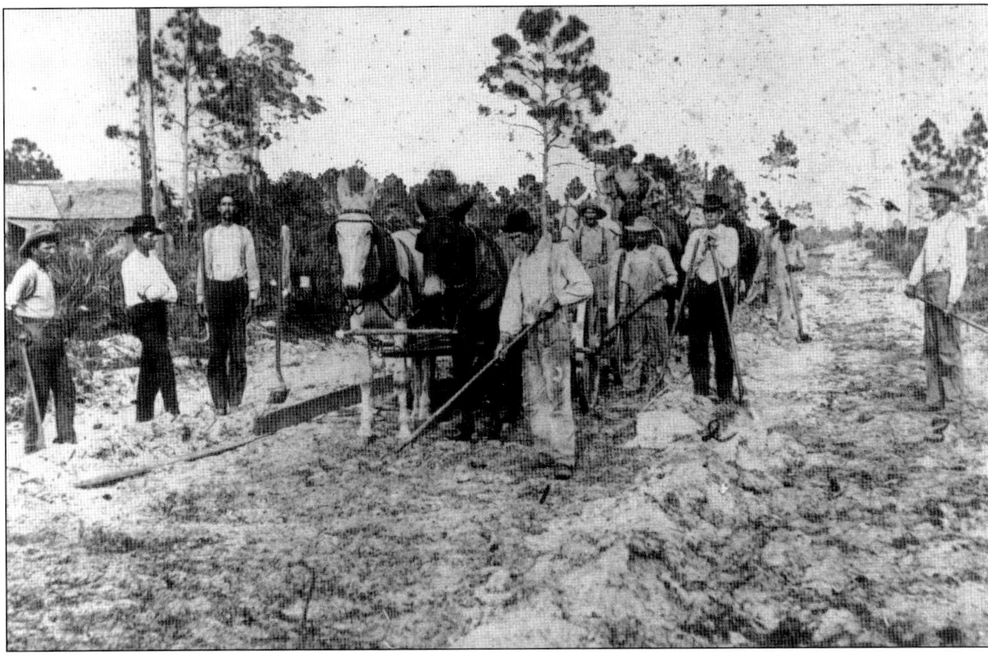

Once the motorcar supplanted the horse and carriage, citizens of Fort Myers demanded better roads. Asphalt, for instance, was applied to shell streets beginning in 1914. Later, other materials appeared, such as macadam and brick. Mechanized equipment is absent in this early construction scene. Long-sleeved shirts and hats protected workers from mosquitoes, bugs, and the hot Florida sun.

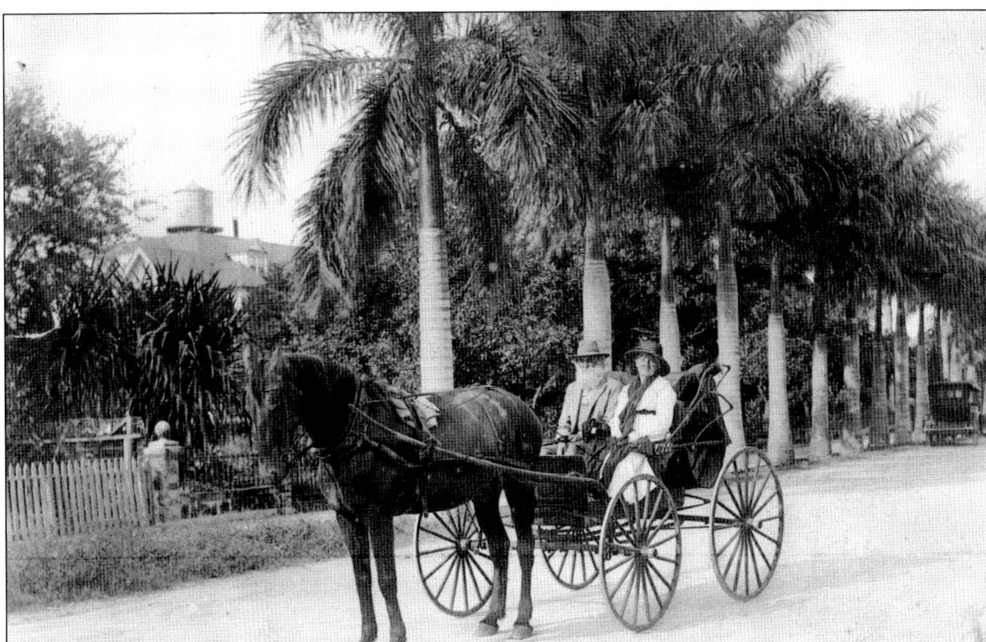

Sam Luckey and his bride cared not for the horseless carriage. Here, the couple poses for the cameraman on First Street in Fort Myers c. 1925, but this handsome thoroughfare really belonged to motorcars, one of which is parked in the background at the Royal Palm Hotel.

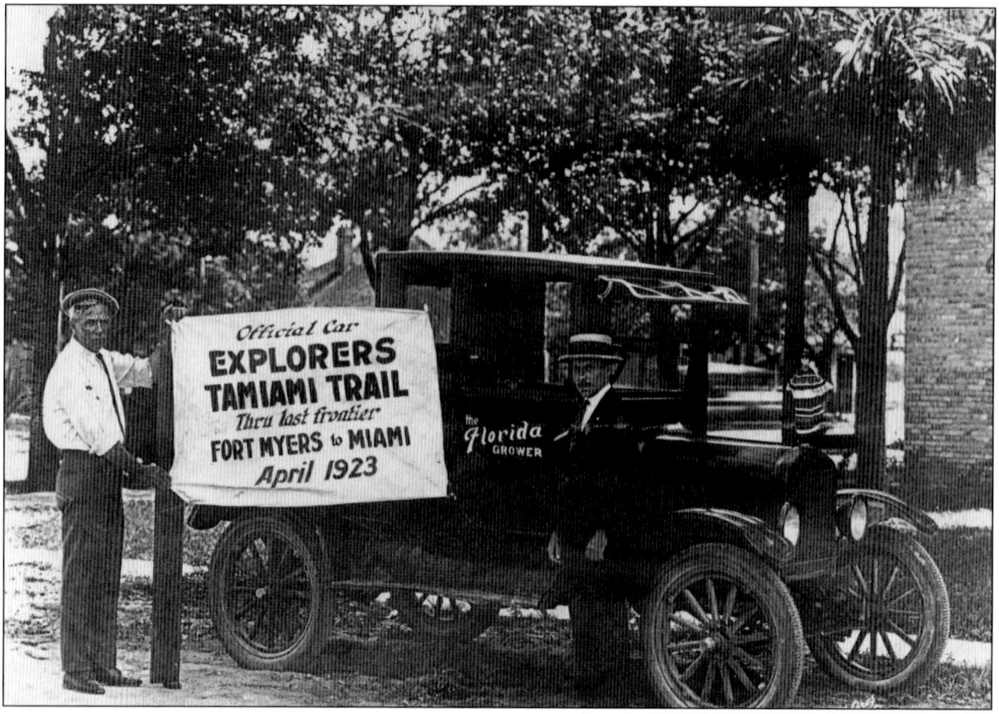

Many folks believed that the Tamiami Trail would never conquer the forbidding Everglades, but not the "Explorers" from Fort Myers! To prove it, this trail-blazing motorcade (26 men and 10 cars) left town April 4, 1923, over the approximate route. Incredible problems and setbacks were encountered, but they reached Miami on April 25. Their hair-raising episodes made the national press.

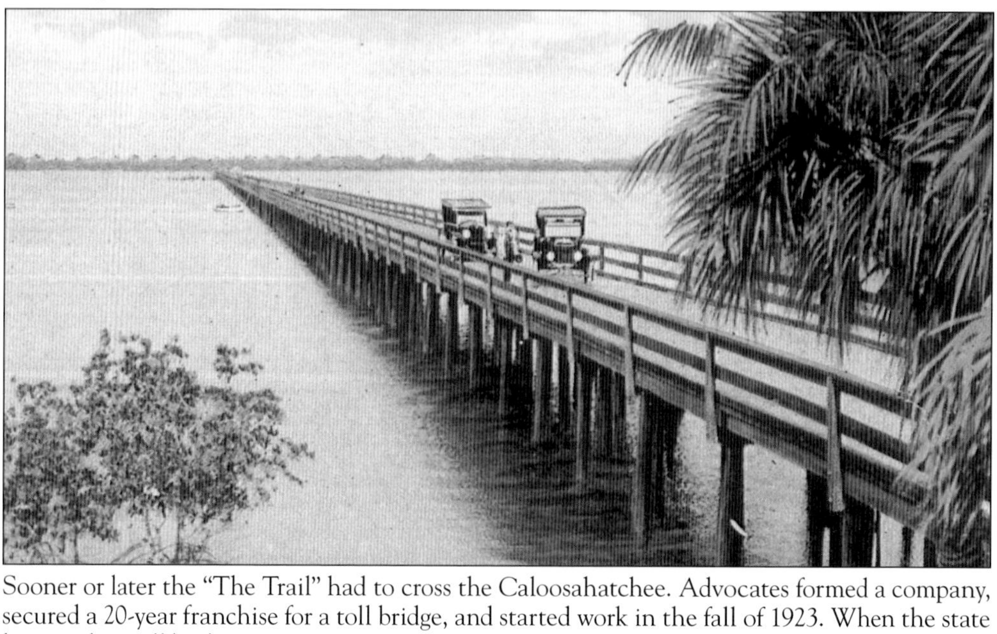

Sooner or later the "The Trail" had to cross the Caloosahatchee. Advocates formed a company, secured a 20-year franchise for a toll bridge, and started work in the fall of 1923. When the state later said no toll bridges, Lee County acquired ownership and finished the wood structure just in time for the Land Boom. In March 1924 the Fremont Street bridge opened.

The Tamiami Trail became a reality thanks to Barron Collier, but not before the Florida Legislature created Collier County from Lee County in 1923. Hendry County was carved out of Lee County at the same time. Once done, the advertising tycoon helped fund Trail construction through his fiefdom. Collier himself was once the biggest landowner in the state.

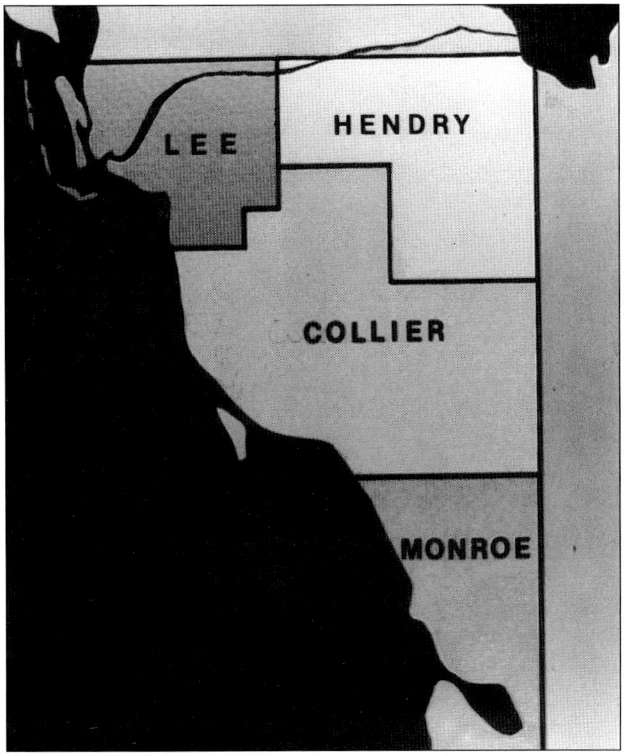

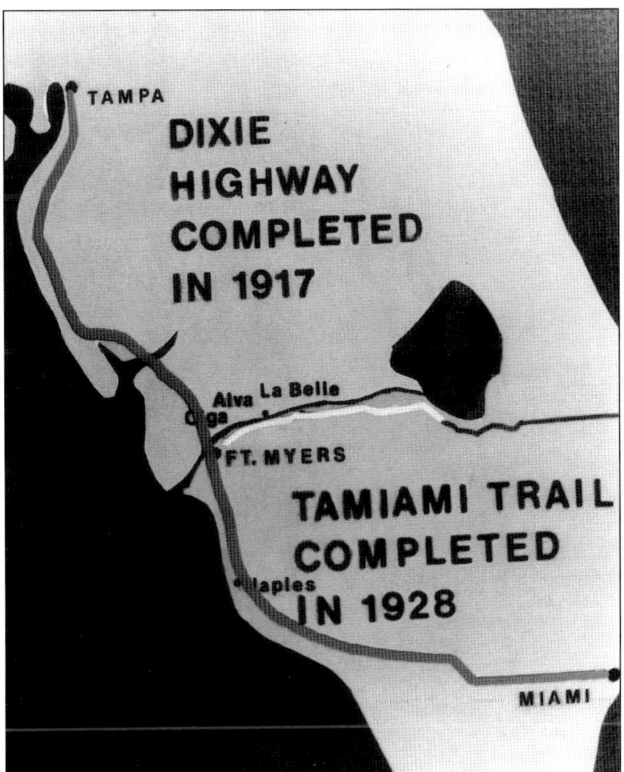

Advocates of the Dixie Highway (Arcadia-Olga-LaBelle) clashed with Tamiami Trail boosters. Surveys for the Trail began in 1915 but most work was delayed by World War I. The Tampa-Punta Gorda section opened in 1921, and Fort Myers got it in March 1924—just in time for the Land Boom. The state took control of the legendary road in 1926, and in April 1928 it opened to Miami.

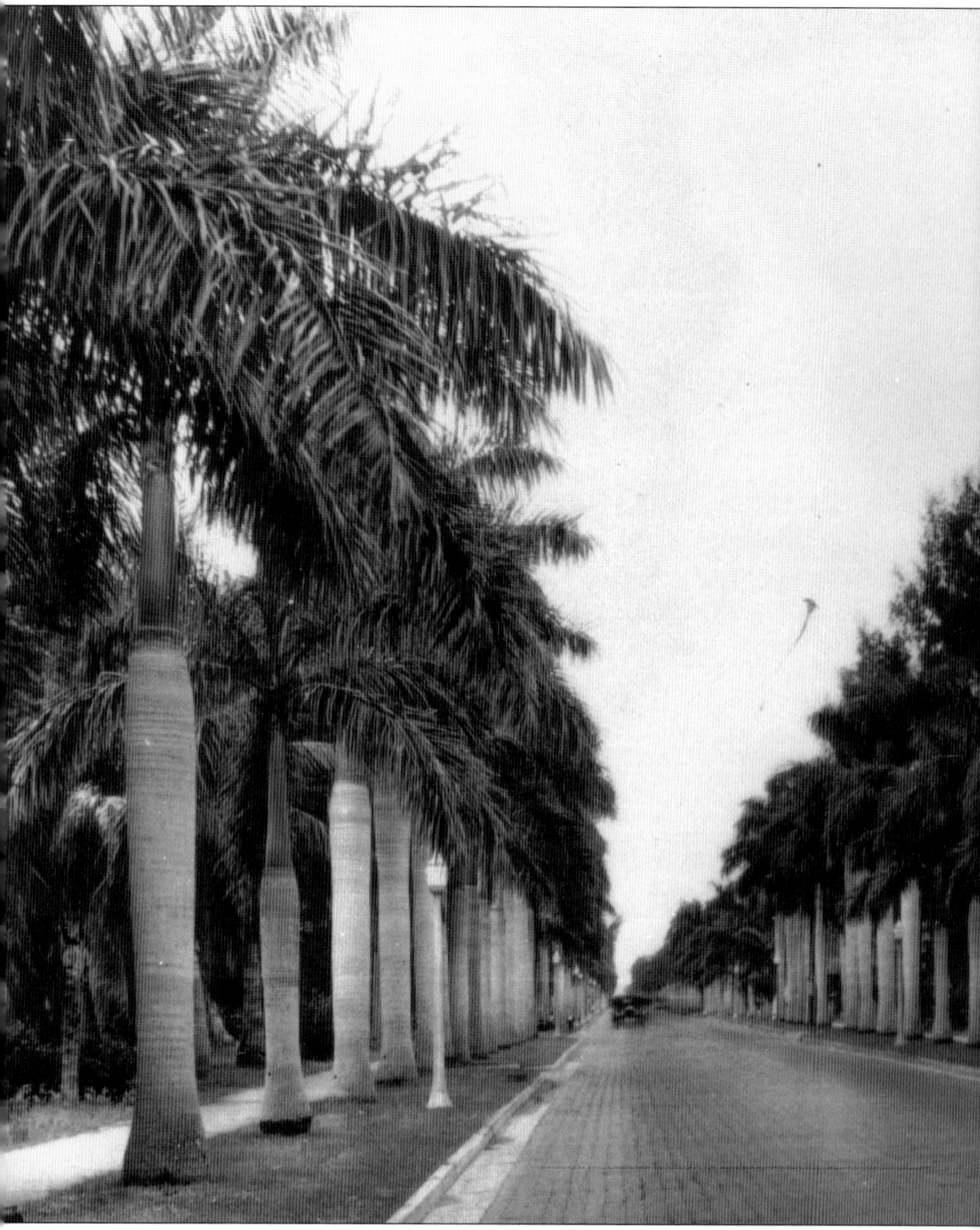

First Street was one of the more beautiful thoroughfares in Fort Myers. Several city estates were built on it; hence it became known as "Millionaires Row." The street was first built of macadam and later bricked as this image confirms. The bricks themselves lasted for many years, but the increasing weight of vehicles and higher speeds made other road materials more desirable. That

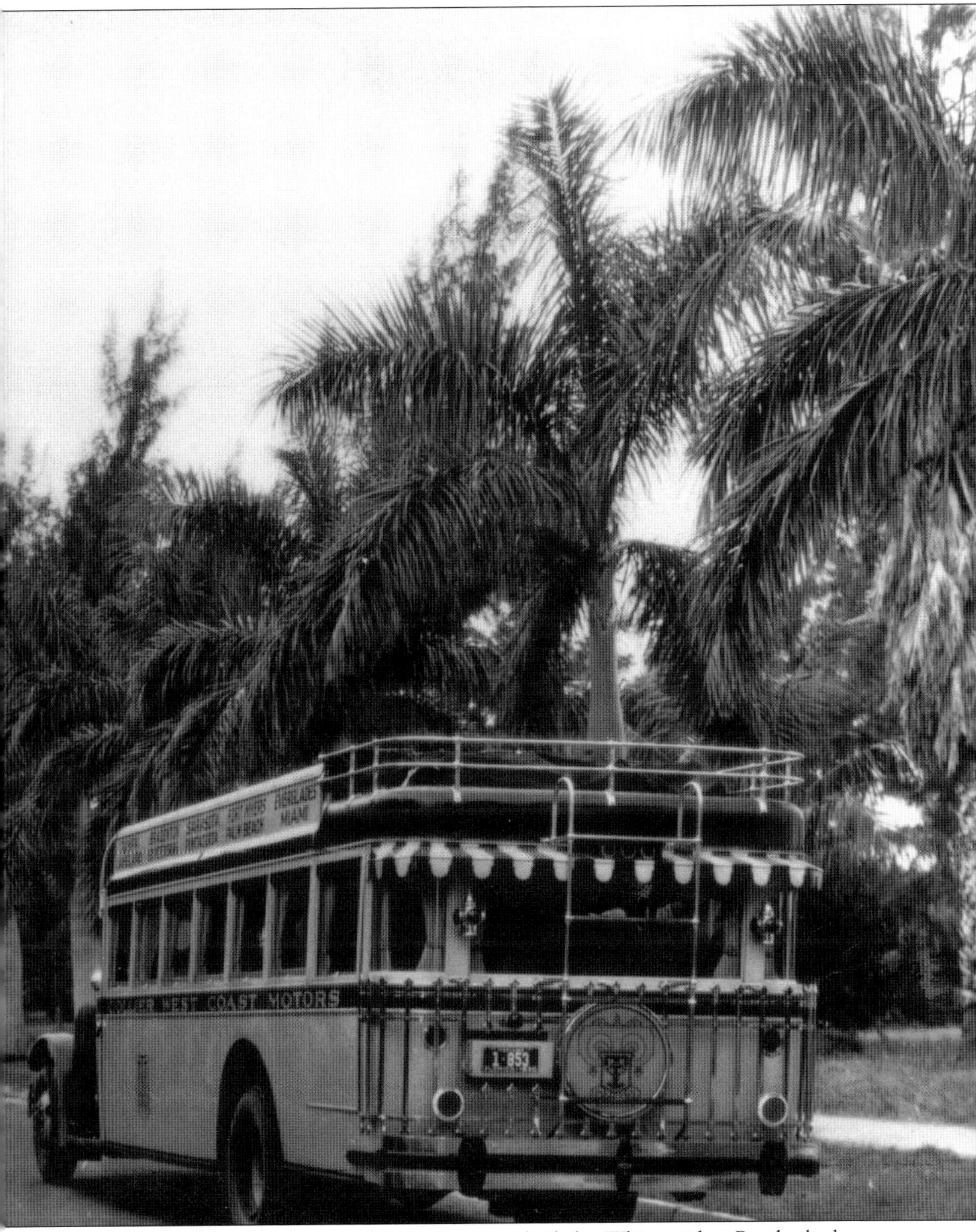

splendid motor bus whizzing past the cameraman—built by White with a Bender body—was owned by Barron Collier's Tamiami Trail Tours, which offered service from Tampa to Miami by way of Sarasota, Punta Gorda, and Fort Myers.

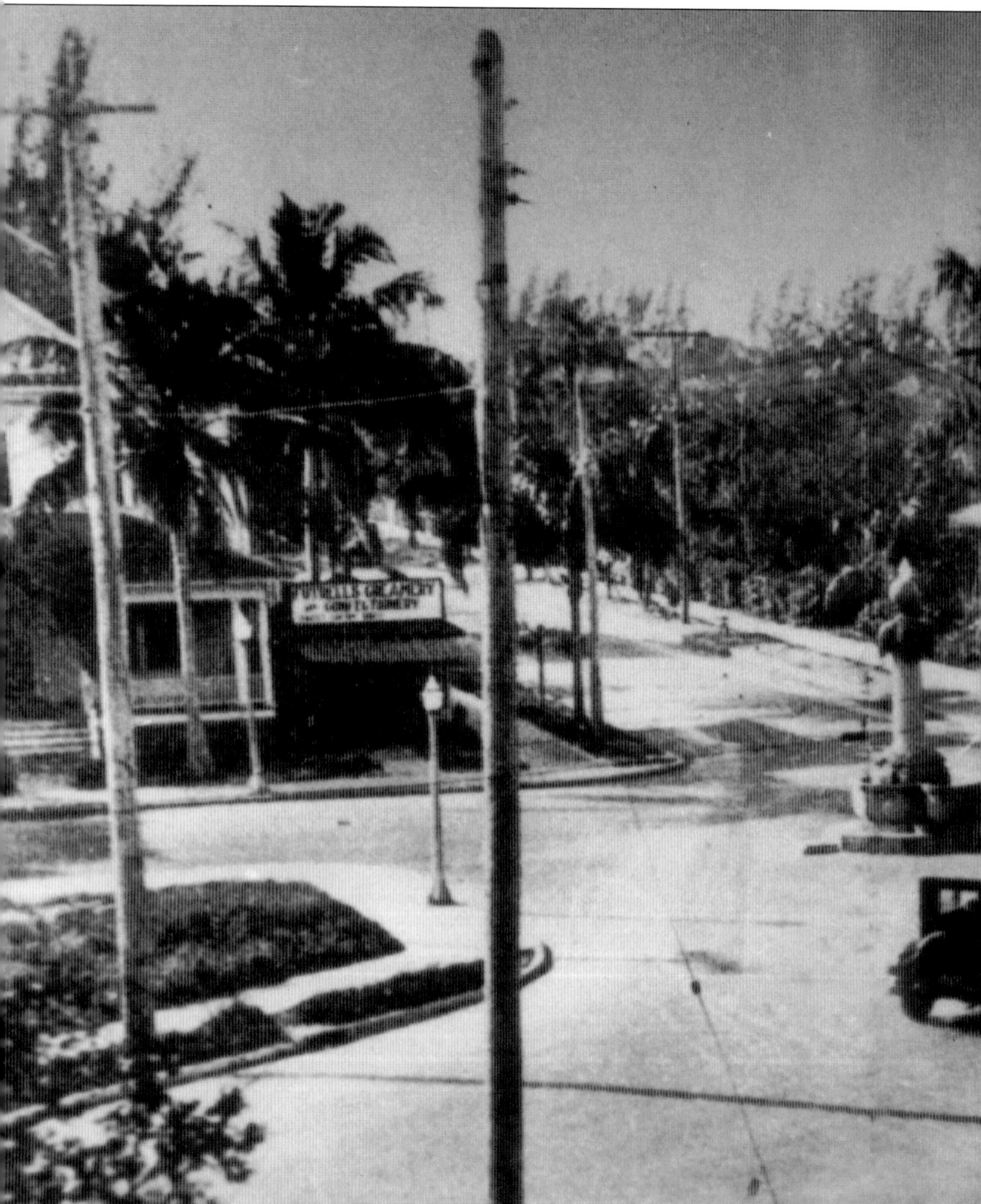

"Five Points" was an important intersection in Fort Myers. At lower left is Main Street while above it is Anderson (today Martin Luther King Boulevard). Above Anderson is Cleveland, which became the Tamiami Trail. To the right of the large frame house starts beautiful McGregor Boulevard, while in the lower right the careful reader can spot a car entering the

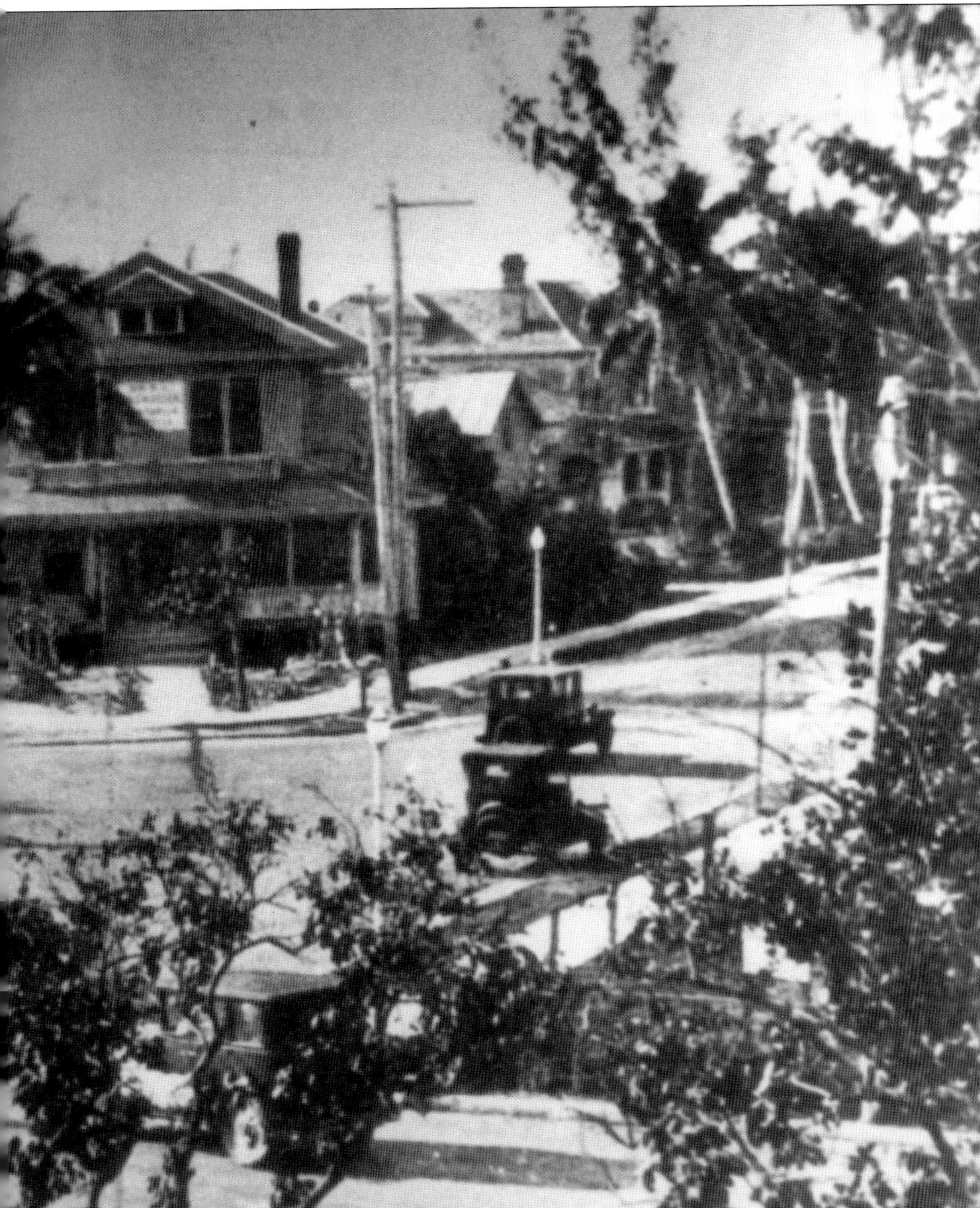

intersection from Carson Street. The famed McGregor Monument, erected in memory of city benefactress Tootie McGregor, was installed at Five Points in 1913—a glorified palm tree whose frogs and snakes jetted water. Today the monument stands in front of the Fort Myers Country Club.

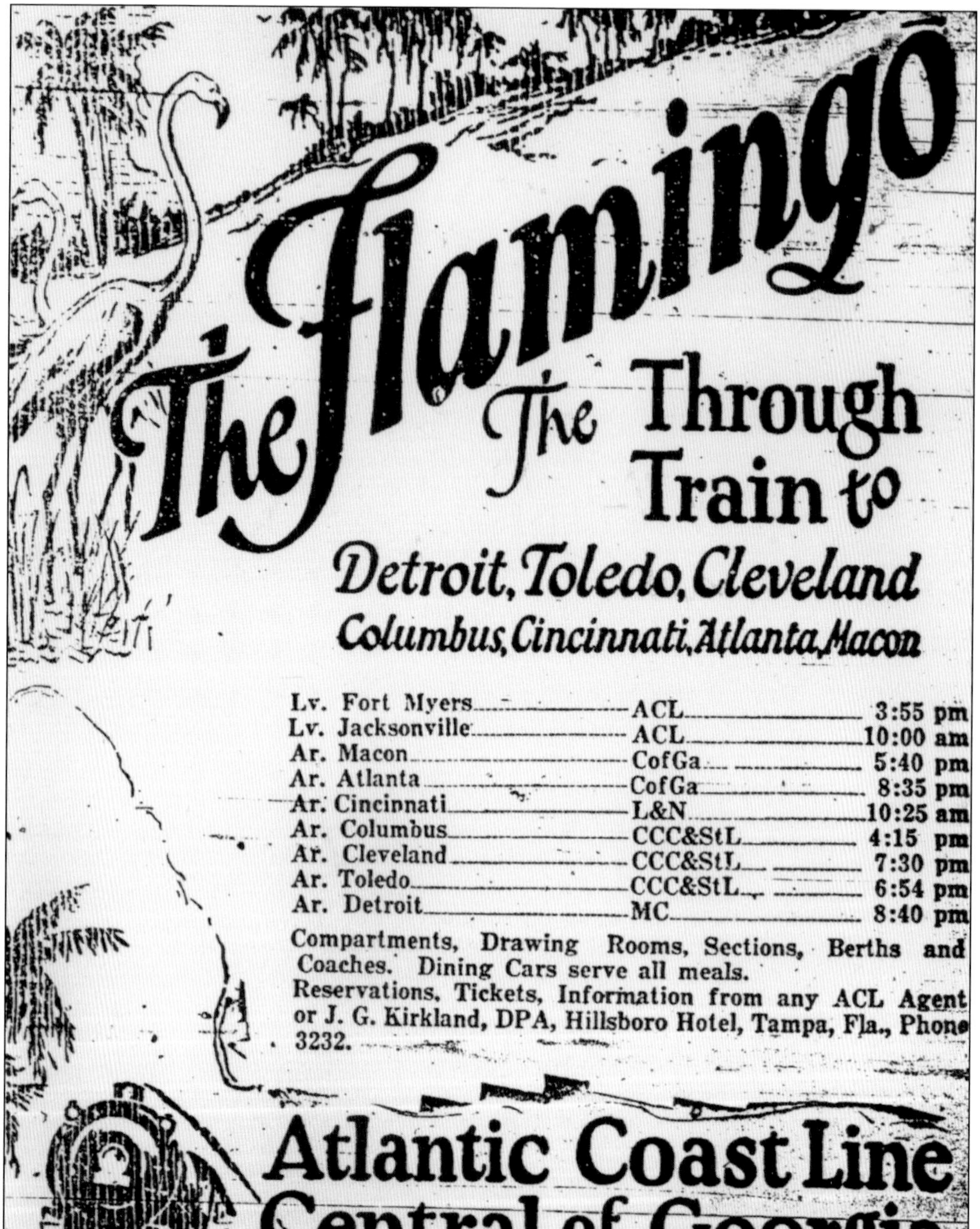

During the Roaring Twenties countless folks came and departed Fort Myers by train. Jacksonville was the railroad nerve center of the state, and virtually every through train of importance stopped there. "The Flamingo" transported patrons in style and connected "Jax" with Detroit. By reading the above ad, one would assume that the classy train began its journey in Fort Myers. Such was not the case. A connecting sleeping car or special coach was actually attached to a local Fort Myers-Jacksonville run. It was at Jacksonville that the name train was officially formed, then departed. Back then, most of the day was needed to get from Fort Myers to Jacksonville station.

Five

For Mind, Spirit, and Heart

Schools, churches, and a hospital played important roles in early Fort Myers, as the following images kindly loaned for this book confirm.

School was first conducted in a private home, and later in a multi-purpose log cabin. Eventually a real schoolhouse was built, and in 1911 the famed Gwynne Institute opened its doors. Three years later a stand-alone high school appeared. Numerous school facilities were constructed in Fort Myers during the Land Boom of the 1920s. Since then, almost continuous expansion has taken place. Today the Lee County School Board is the region's largest employer (8,500 employees) and oversees 68 schools and some 57,000 students.

The first religious service in Fort Myers was conducted by a Methodist Church "circuit rider" in the aforementioned log cabin. Methodists also erected the first church building in the Caloosahatchee region. Baptists then built a sanctuary, followed by Episcopalians, Presbyterians, and Roman Catholics. Dozens of churches of every faith now populate the greater Fort Myers area and several provided photos for this chapter.

An actual hospital helped to comprise Fort Myers when it was a military establishment. Initial steps to get a real hospital in the town started in 1912, but Robert E. Lee Memorial Hospital did not open until four years later. Lumber for the structure came from the first courthouse. Today, several hospitals serve the city, from those specializing in infant care to ones handling psychiatric needs.

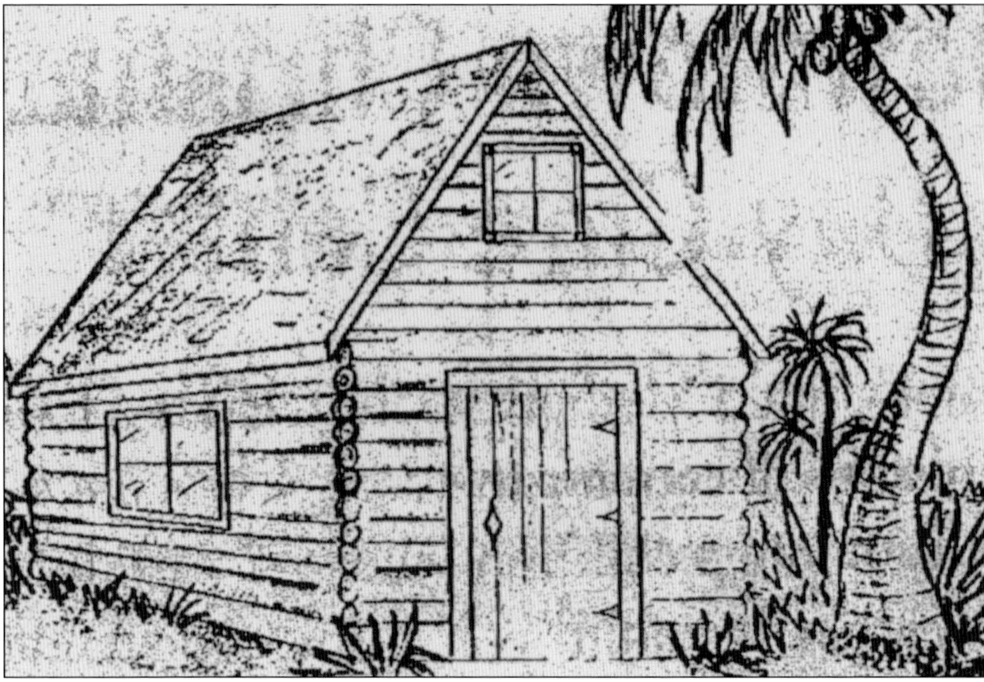

School was first taught in the home of Evalina Gonzalez, and her husband, Manuel, brought textbooks from Key West. A log cabin, like the one above, became the schoolhouse in the 1870s. Its master was Robert Bell, an Englishman, who had been hired by Capt. Francis Asbury at $25 a month. Later, Monroe County furnished $1,000 for the Fort Myers "Academy," which unruly kids likely burned down in May 1886.

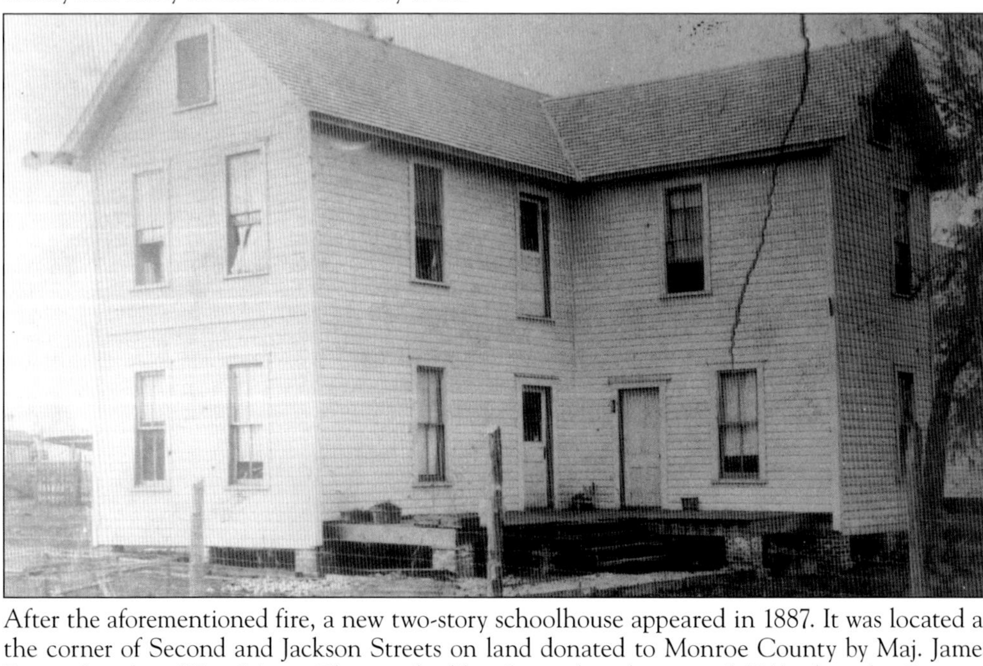

After the aforementioned fire, a new two-story schoolhouse appeared in 1887. It was located at the corner of Second and Jackson Streets on land donated to Monroe County by Maj. James Evans, founder of Fort Myers. The new building housed students until 1911 when the Gwynne Institute opened.

Kids in Punta Rassa rejoiced in their own school—an 8-foot-by-8-foot boat house on San Carlos Bay! Here, nine students and teacher Nell Gould pose for the camera in 1910. In the following year the school closed due to low pupil enrollment. Lee County would pay a teacher $40 a month as long as seven or more students were enrolled.

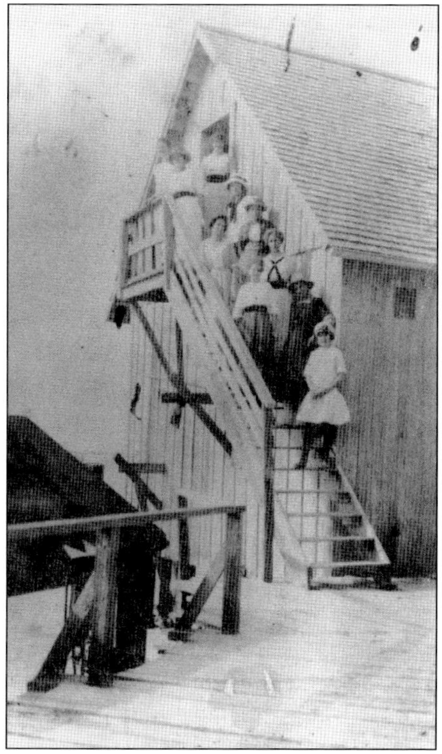

Nineteen kids have climbed aboard the Fort Myers "Edgewood" school bus in this 1914 image. We know that the prime mover was named "Joe," but why so many students hold flags has not been learned. First day? A parade? Readers with further information are asked to come forward.

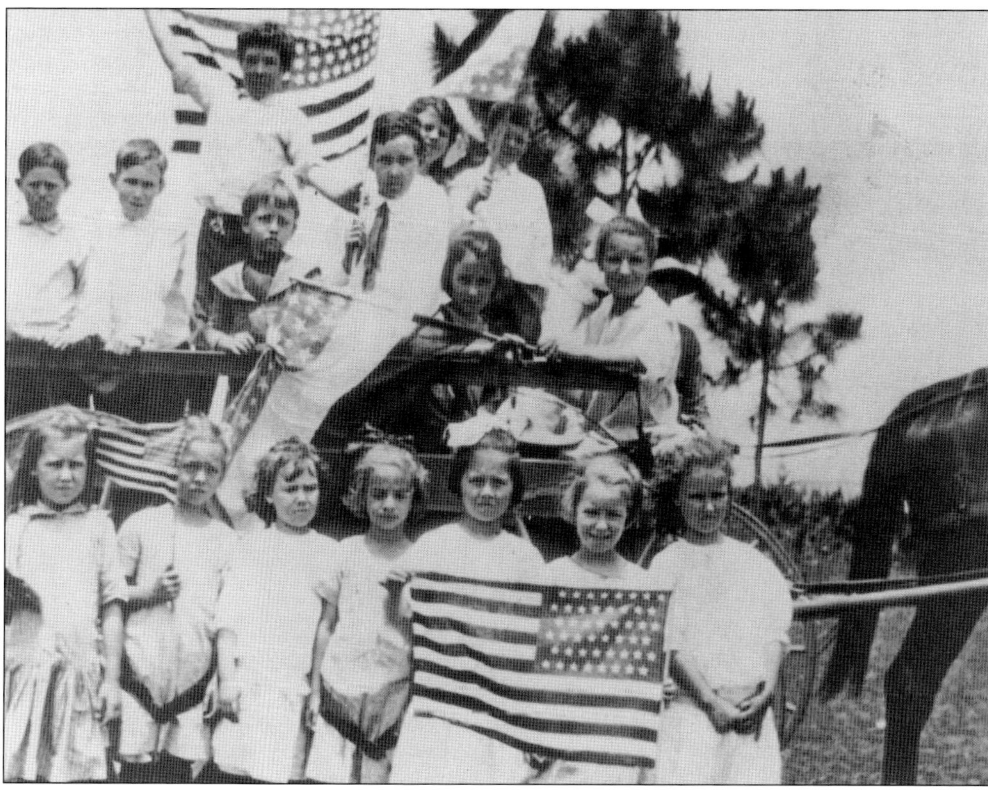

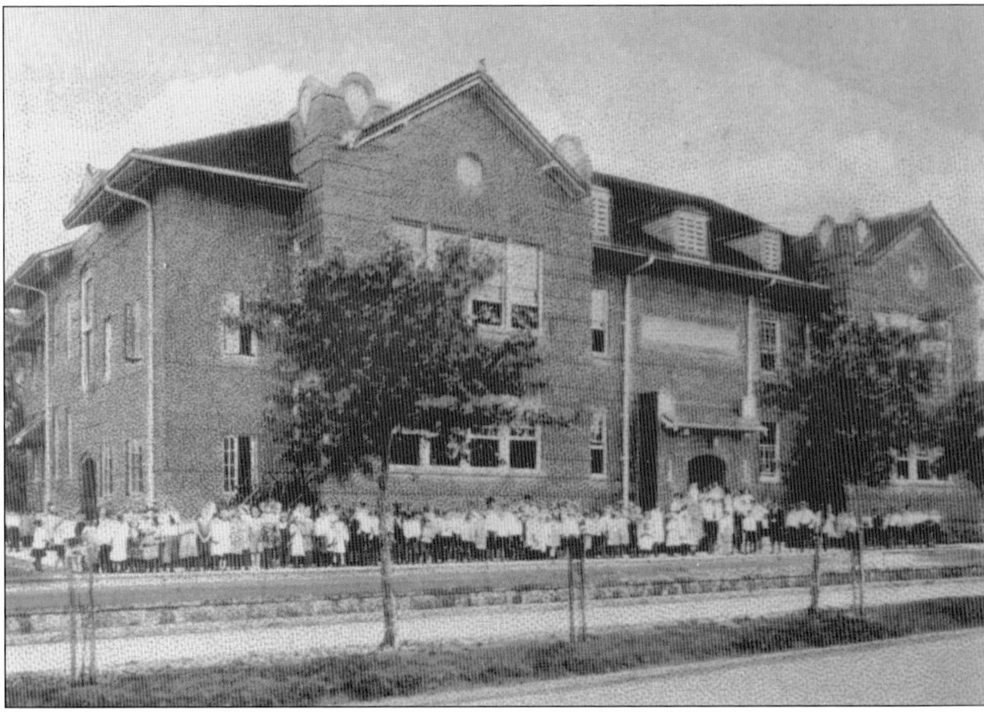

As Fort Myers grew, so did the school population. Eventually it overwhelmed the schoolhouse seen on page 74 (bottom) and a nearby barn took the overflow. This disturbed Col. Andrew Gwynne, a wealthy cotton broker and winter visitor. He died in 1909, and in his estate left a substantial gift for a new facility. Additional funds were raised, and in 1911 the $45,000 Gwynne Institute opened.

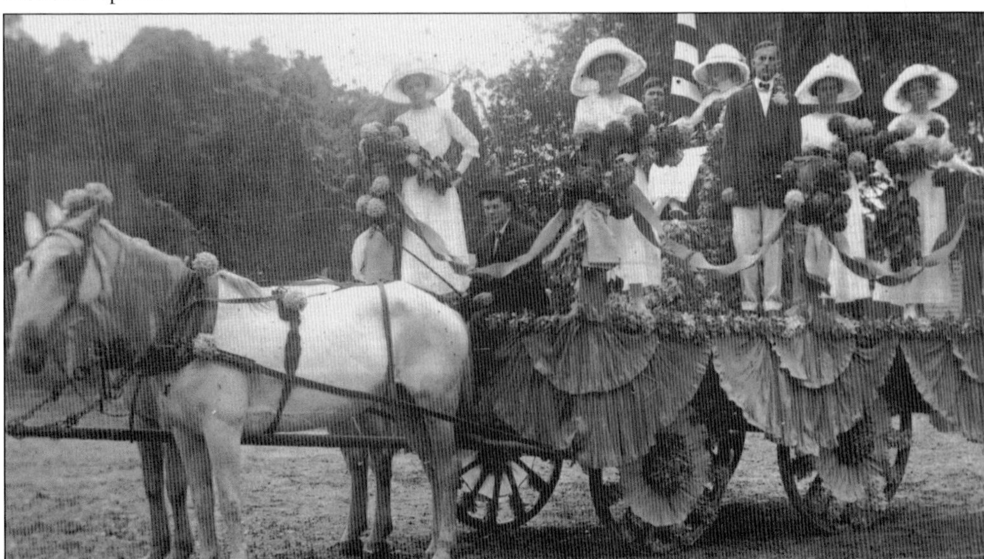

Not every moment of school was spent in the classroom. Parades were once common in Fort Myers, and here we see the 1916 senior class float of Gwynne Institute. Tropical flowers and bunting adorn the entry. And those gorgeous hats! (Courtesy of Florida State Photo Archives.)

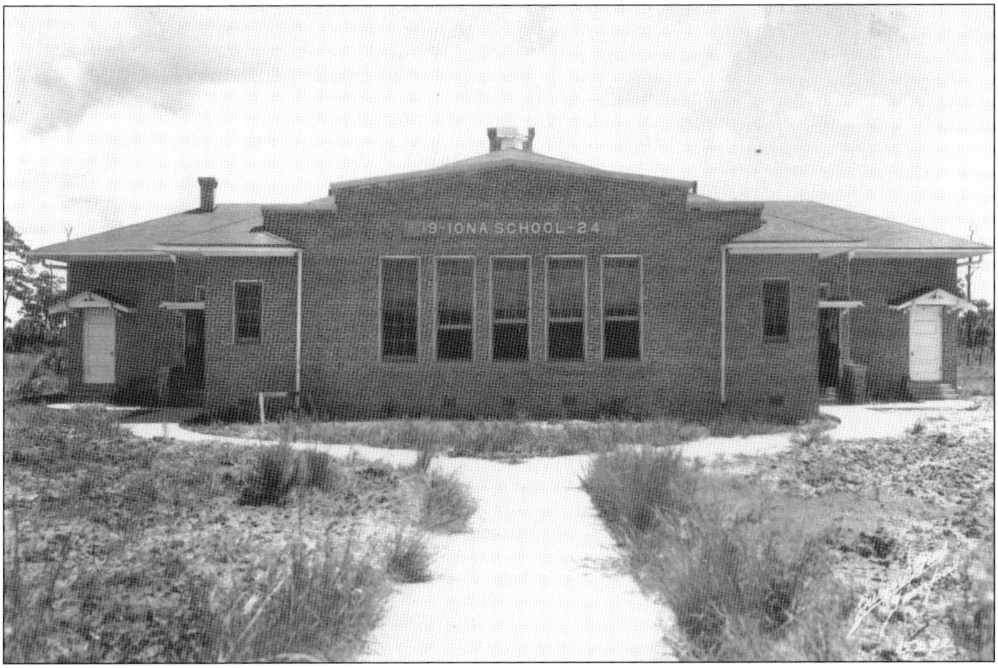

The Iona district of Fort Myers prospered in the 1920s, and the farming area demanded a better school. The one seen here opened on McGregor Boulevard in 1924 and replaced a 1909 structure. Today, it is beautifully restored and commercially occupied. Other elementary schools built during the Land Boom were Edison Park, Tice, and Edgewood. (Courtesy of Tampa-Hillsborough County Public Library System.)

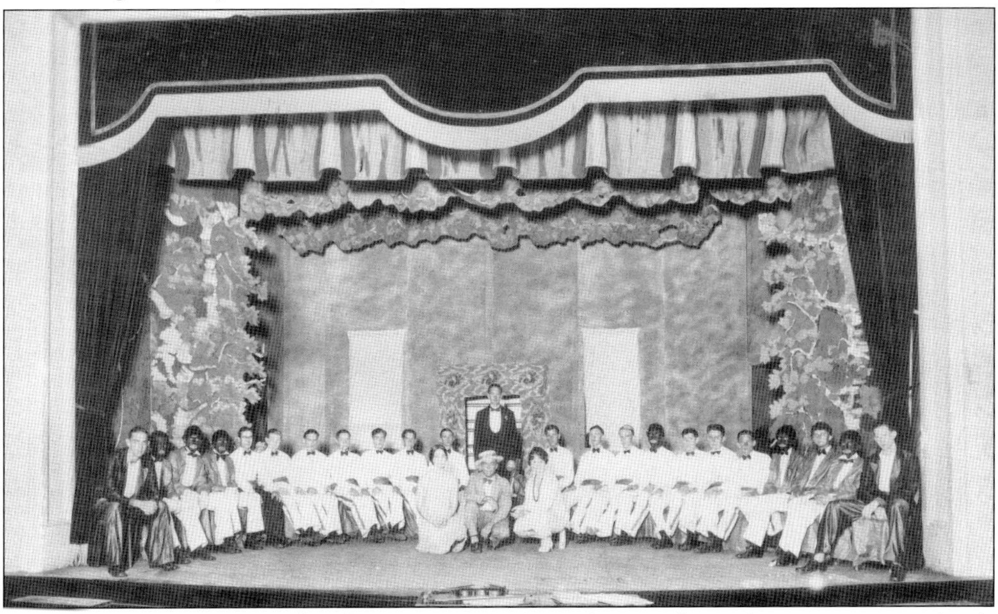

The aforementioned school at Edison Park had one feature that other Fort Myers schools envied—a real auditorium. It afforded much-needed performance space for school and social events, such as for this old-fashioned minstrel show. The trusty upright piano provided singing accompaniment.

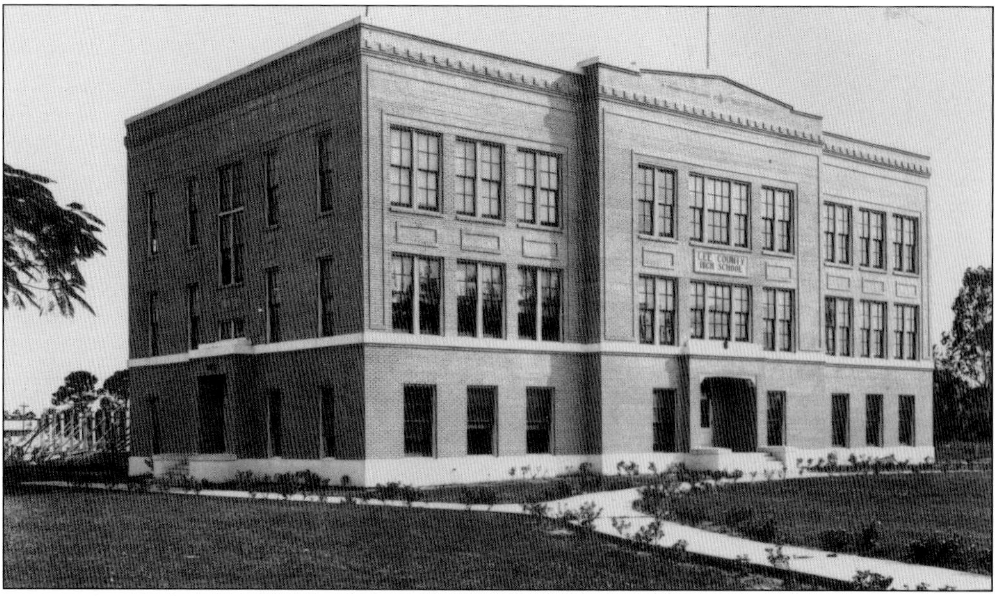

During the Land Boom a new Lee County High School opened at the corner of Thompson and Fowler Streets. It was the first to house just high school students, and many folks simply called it Fort Myers High School. The brick structure cost $224,500, and Tampa's Burgert Brothers photographed it on September 7, 1925. In 1950, an even newer complex opened on Cortez Boulevard. (Courtesy of Tampa-Hillsborough County Public Library System.)

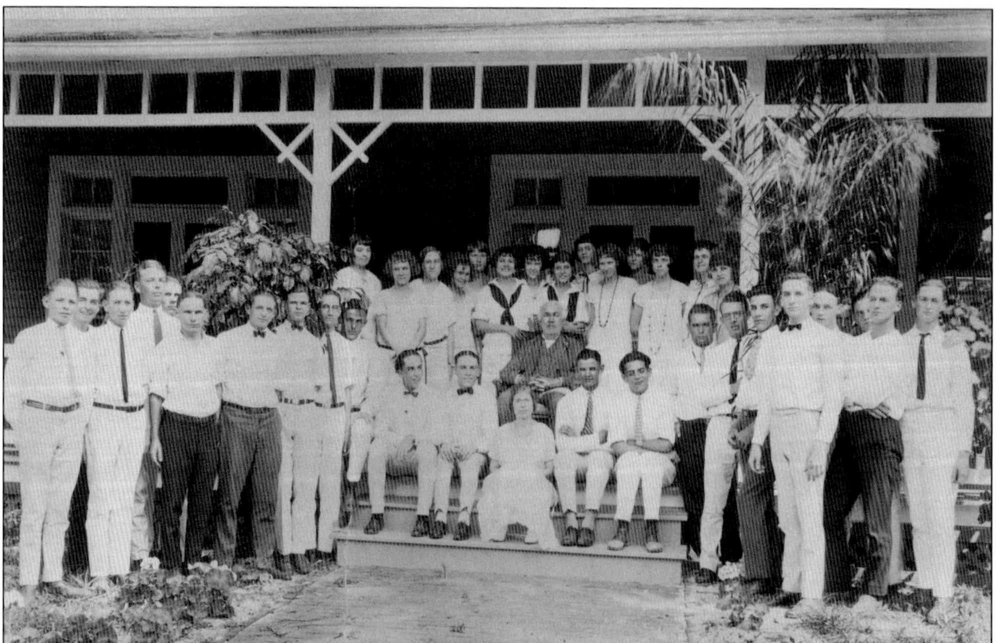

Inventor Thomas Alva Edison only had three months of formal education, but the workaholic genius took a big interest in school kids. Here, he holds court at Seminole Lodge—his winter abode on the Caloosahatchee—with the Class of 1924. Seniors relished such occasions, and if available Edison would also pass out diplomas.

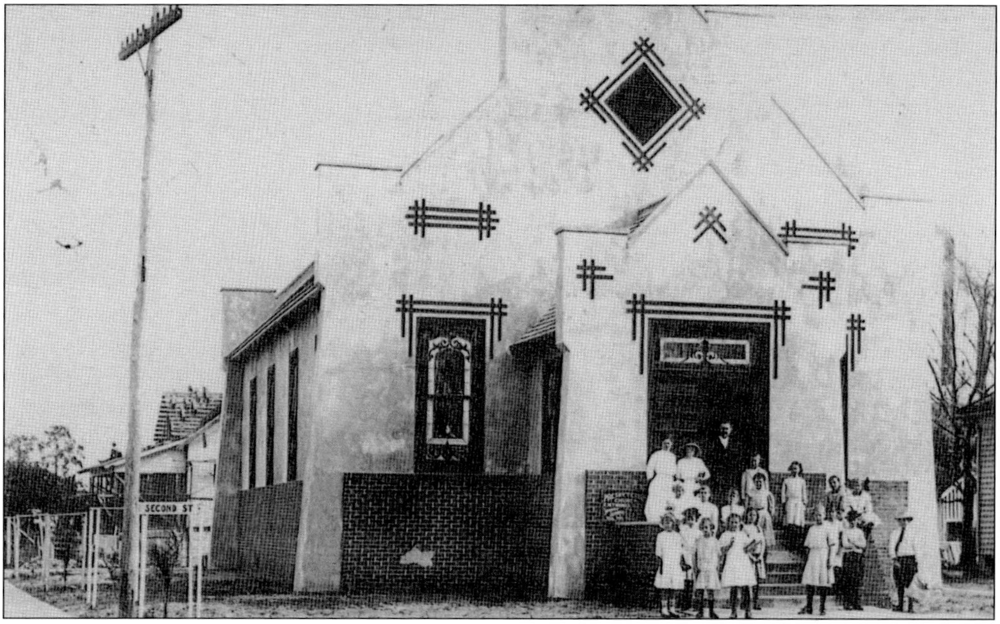

In January 1872, a Methodist "circuit rider" from Bartow conducted the first religious services in Fort Myers, in the log cabin that served as a school. In 1881, a Methodist Church sanctuary arose on First Street thanks to funds from area cattlemen. A Gothic ceiling and a cabinet organ graced the interior.

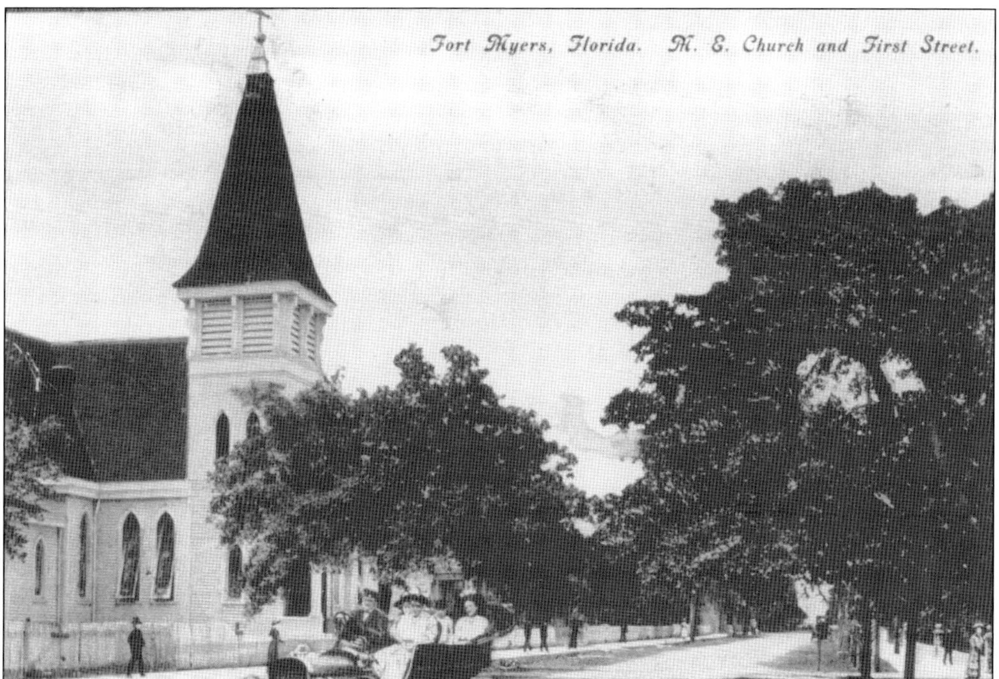

The Methodist population steadily grew in Fort Myers, so much so that a larger church facility was required. The substantial complex seen here arose on First and Royal Palm in 1903 and served the congregation for the next 50 years before being replaced.

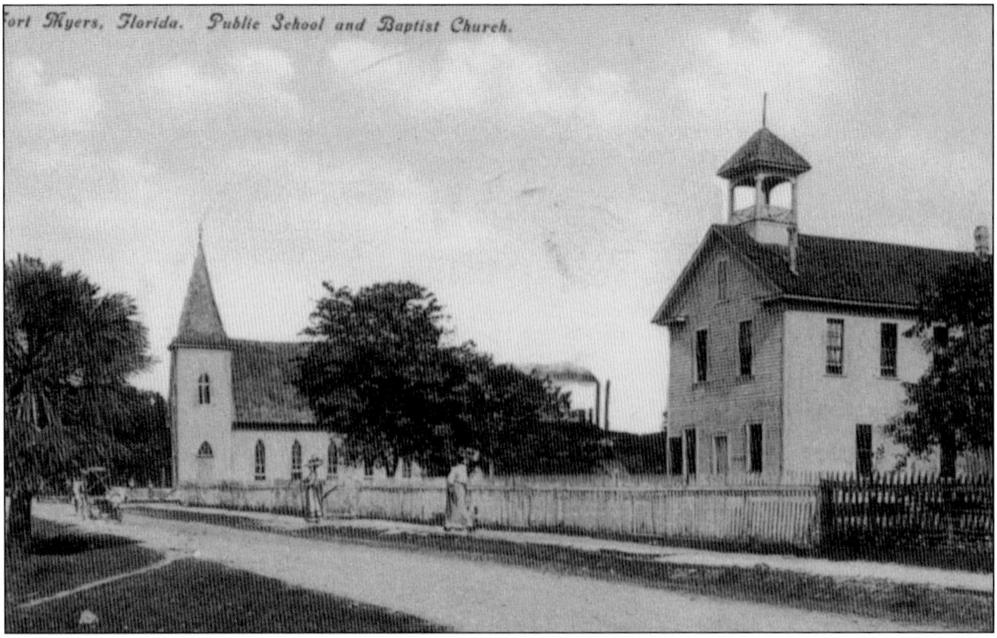

It was on Jackson Street that the First Baptist Church erected a one-room sanctuary (seen above) in 1889. In 1905, they moved the church to Jackson and Second Streets near the two-story schoolhouse (seen on page 74), then enlarged it. An even larger sanctuary appeared in 1929, and an entirely new worship facility opened in 1959.

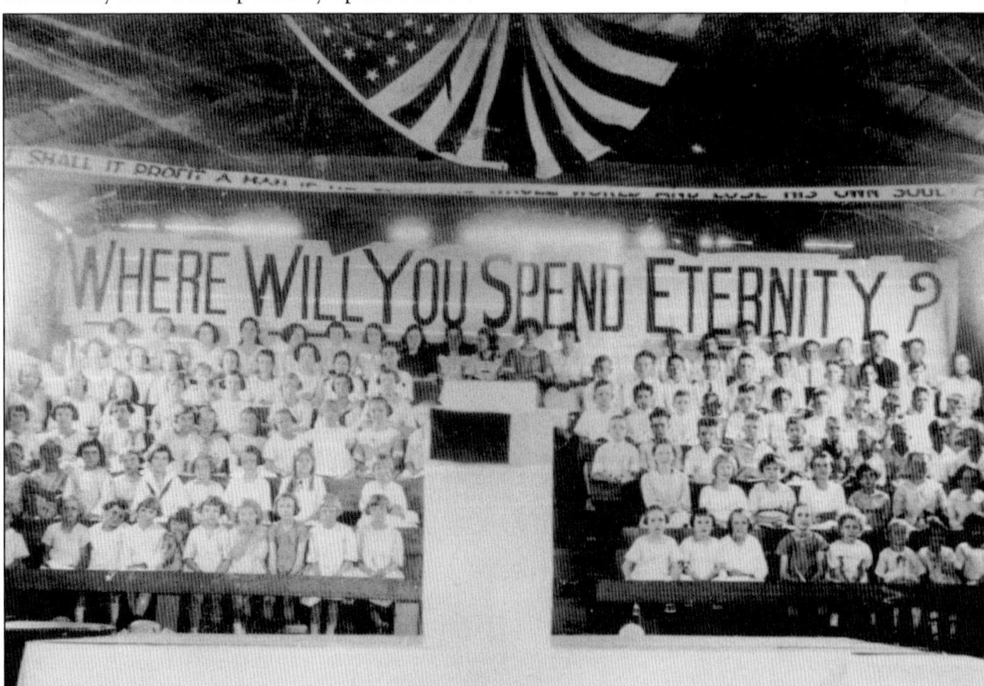

The second sanctuary of First Baptist Church had a commodious, wood interior. Evangelistic-type services were periodically held, and the one seen here involved the Sunday school. Banners and bunting were quite common.

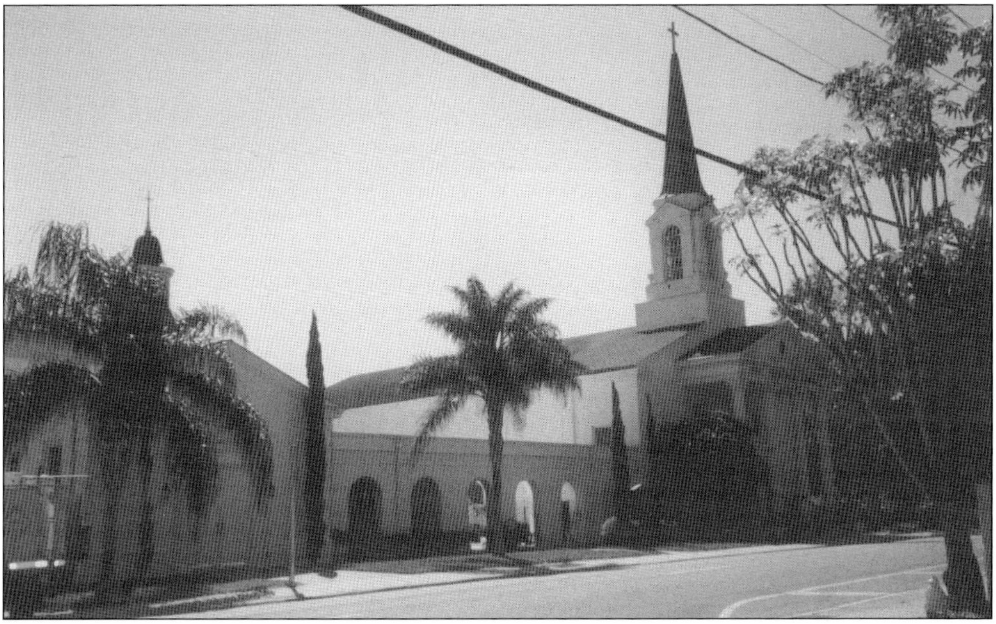

Overtures for a Presbyterian Church were heard in 1901, but the congregation's infant years proved very difficult. A decade later the first building used by the Methodists (page 79 top) was purchased and a long, upward history began for the congregation. Their 1956 facility is seen above.

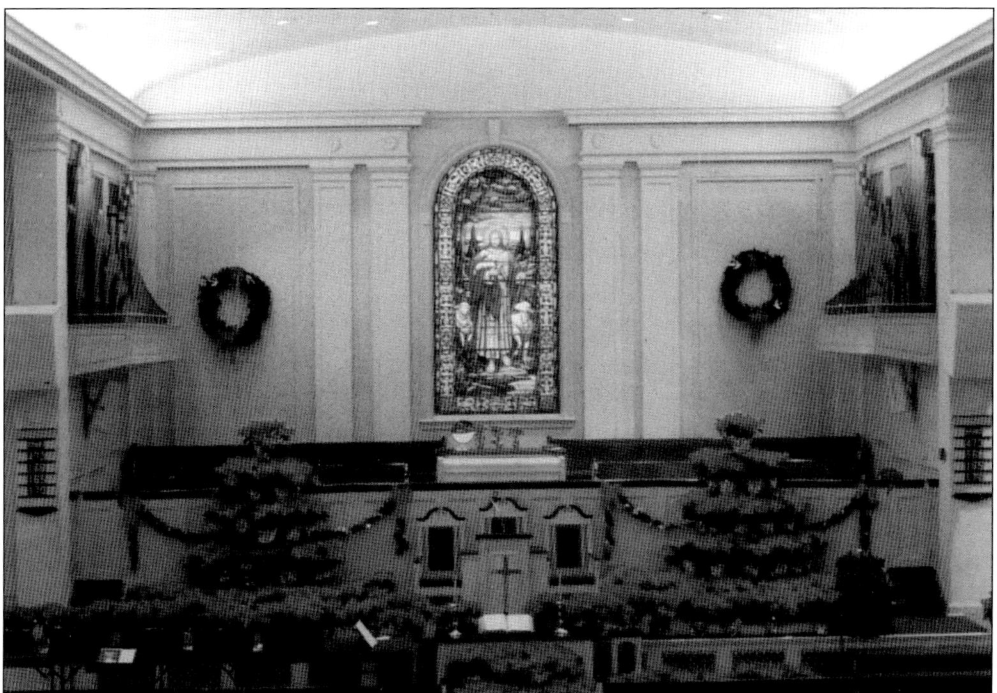

At Christmastime wreaths and trees decorate the chancel of First Presbyterian Church. The 1956 facility was a big step for the congregation, and the building debt incurred was retired in seven short years.

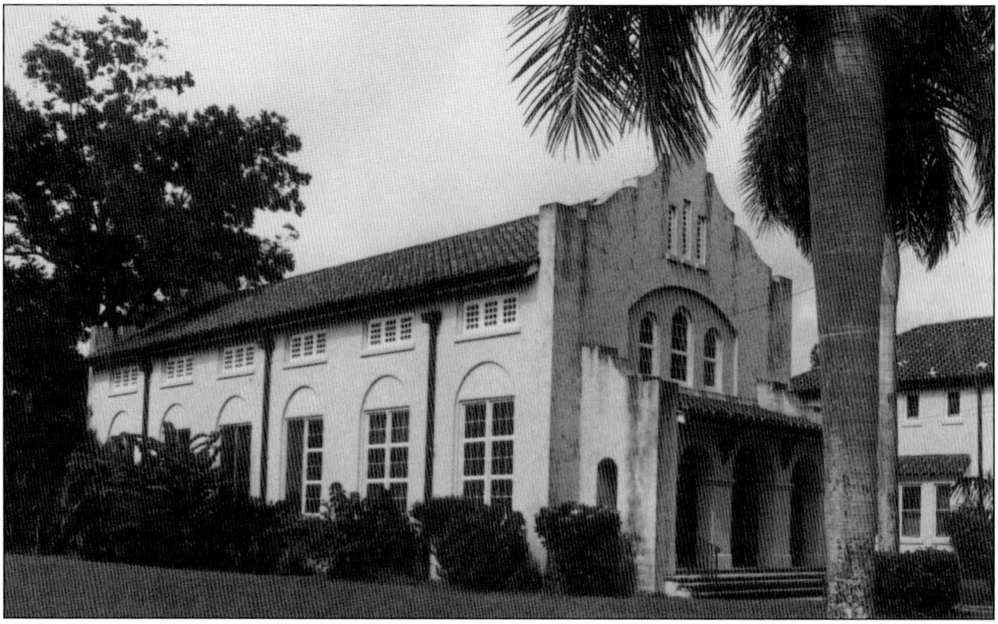

Discussions for an Episcopal parish began in 1885. Services were first conducted at the Methodist church—friend of all faiths. In 1889, parishoners of St. Luke's built a church of their own on land donated by Fort Myers founder Maj. James Evans. A substantial new facility (above) opened during the Land Boom. In 1969, a new sanctuary went up on Cleveland Avenue.

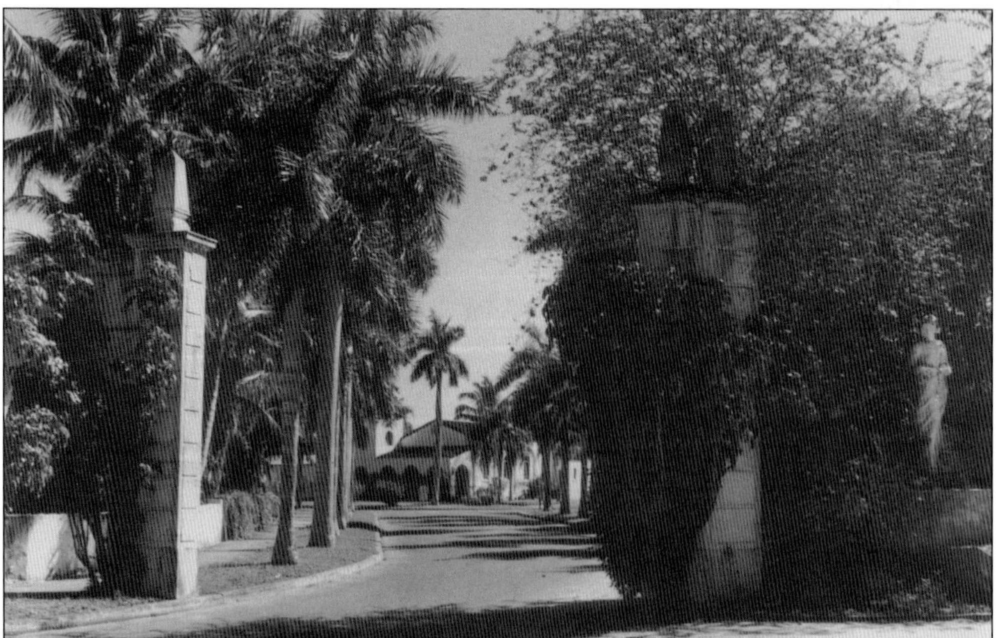

The Community Congregational Church opened in the Edison Park section of Fort Myers in 1931. The subdivision's beautiful entrance frames the church, which in 1963 was re-named Thomas Edison Congregational Church, in honor of the inventor who wintered nearby. To the right of the entrance is the famed statue that Mrs. Edison requested be draped.

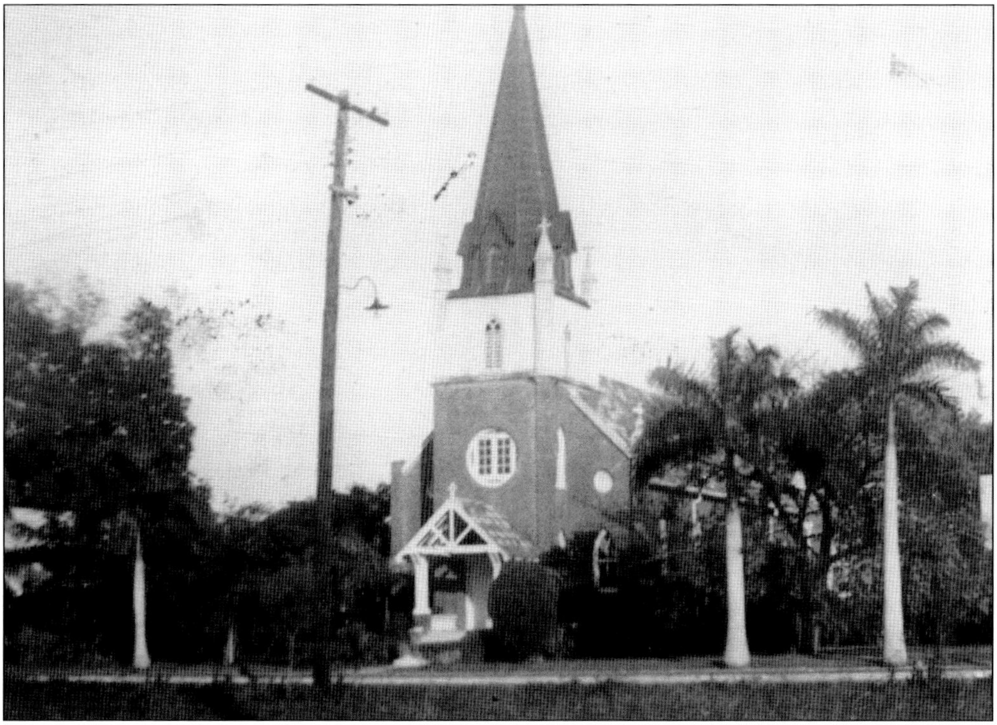

In 1878, Jesuit priests from Tampa started a mission in Fort Myers. Unfortunately, though, their visits proved intermittent because of the distance. When a regular priest was assigned in 1889, the first masses of St. Francis Xavier Parish were held in a livery stable! A $5,000 church went up in 1910.

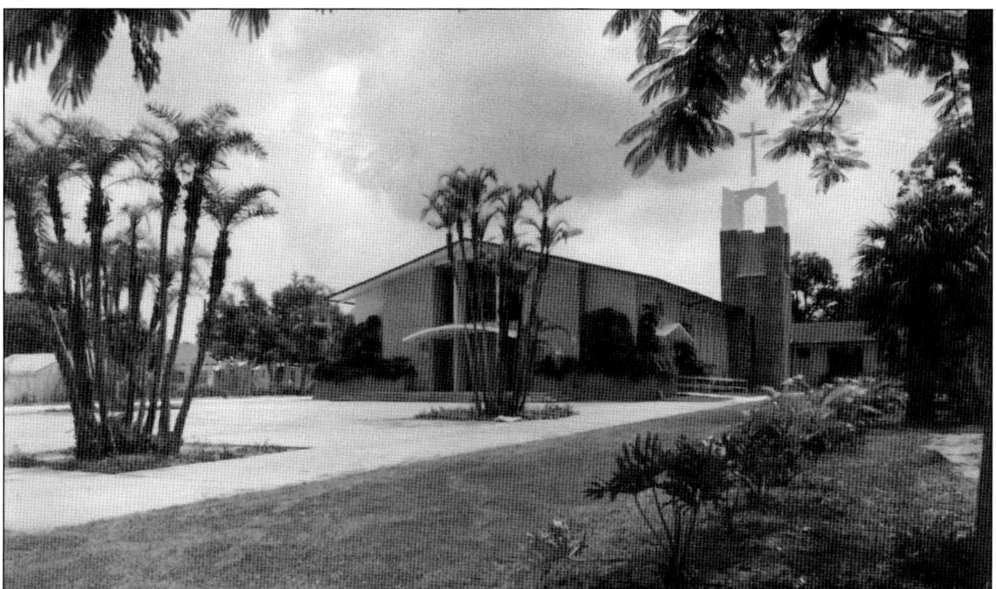

The Catholic population grew and grew as newcomers discovered the City of Palms. In 1961 parishoners of St. Francis Xavier erected this beautiful contemporary edifice on Cleveland Avenue.

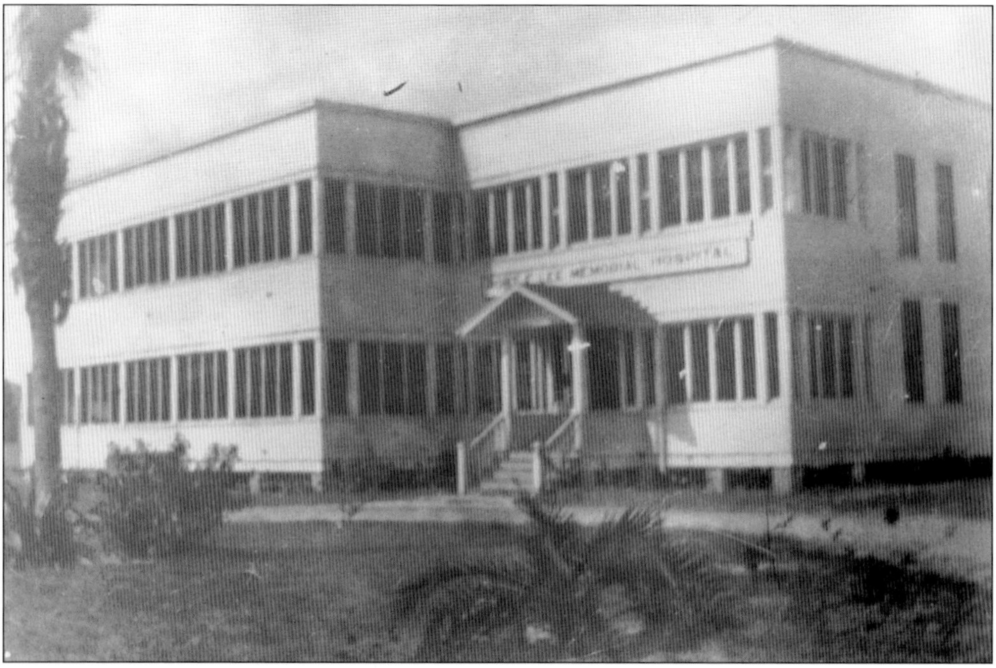

The United Daughters of the Confederacy named the Robert E. Lee Memorial Hospital, and lumber for the building came from the first county courthouse. The two-story structure, located at Victoria and Grand Avenues, opened October 1916 with four rooms for patients. In 1943, a new $200,000 facility financed by the Works Progress Administration appeared on Cleveland Avenue. Since then, continuous expansion has taken place.

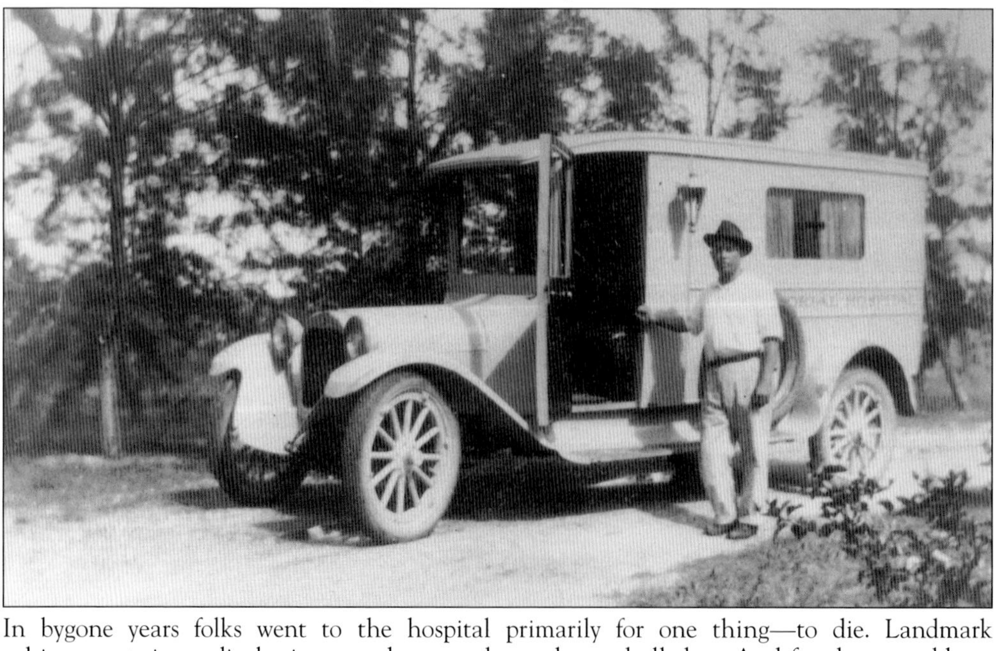

In bygone years folks went to the hospital primarily for one thing—to die. Landmark achievements in medical science and surgery have changed all that. And for those unable to make the trip, you had only to ring for the Lee Hospital ambulance, an inviting Dodge vehicle that sported no flashing lights.

Six

Growing Up

As the new century turned, important events and changes began to take place in Fort Myers. For instance, the Seminole Power & Ice Company began furnishing electricity to the town in 1898 and supplied a regular and reliable source of ice three years later. Also, Gilmar Heitman got the town's first telephone exchange opened in 1900, while in 1910 a water and sewer system was finally approved. The first motor-powered fire engine, replacing a hand pumper, was purchased by the town in 1915. Later, in 1924, housewives rejoiced when gas stoves replaced ones of wood and kerosene.

After World War I came the state's historic Land Boom. Real estate prices soared in the 1920s, and the construction of homes and buildings in Fort Myers reached dizzying proportions. The Seaboard Air Line Railway also came to town in the Roaring Twenties as did two destructive hurricanes. Then came the stock market crash of 1929.

A national depression gripped America during the 1930s, and Fort Myers could not escape it. Jobs were desperately needed, and several government projects helped, such as the Edison Bridge across the Caloosahatchee, a new post office building, and a beautiful Yacht Basin.

During World War II two important military installations opened in Fort Myers, and after the war many service personnel returned to live in the City of Palms, as well as many tourists and retirees. The photographs that follow can only hint at what happened in those five busy decades.

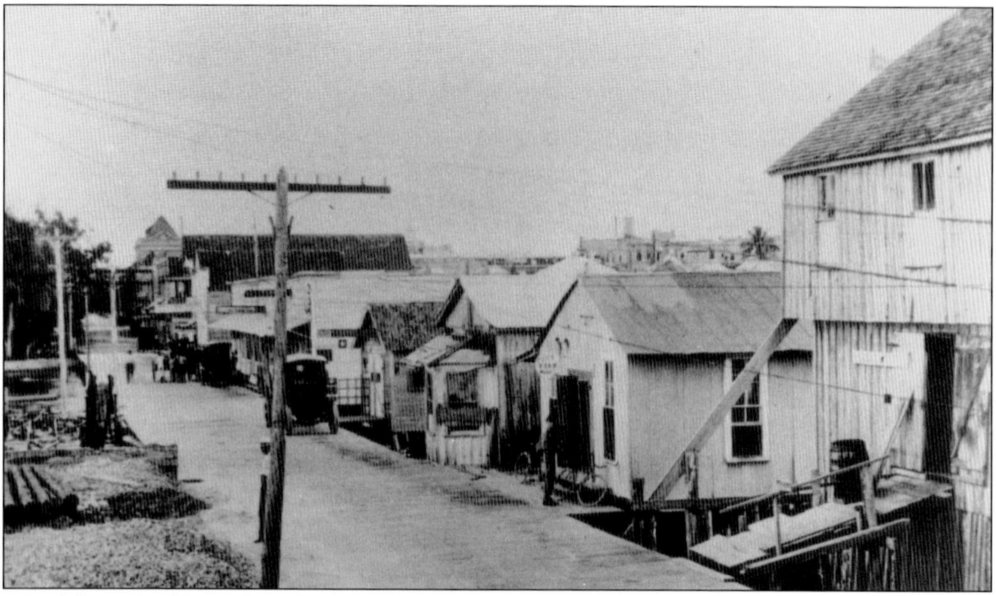

Wood frame buildings dotted the Jackson Street pier in Fort Myers. Businesses like the Chinese laundry and city fish market sat on pilings. Motorists could reach a merchant's front door by driving along a shaky plank road, as this *c.* 1915 image reveals. But the buildings blighted the otherwise beautiful waterfront. Gradually they all disappeared, including that lowly but necessary appendage—the outhouse.

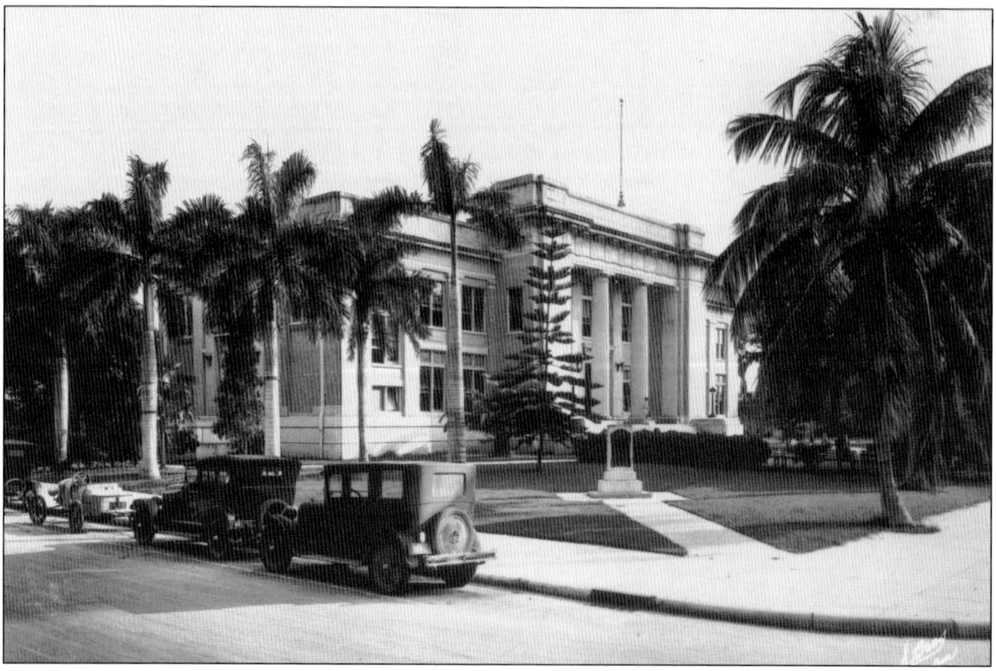

The Lee County Courthouse, a yellow brick structure conceived in the Neoclassical Revival style, opened on April 13, 1915, and cost $100,000. The famed Burgert Brothers photographic firm of Tampa composed this view of it on September 7, 1925. (Courtesy of Tampa-Hillsborough County Public Library System.)

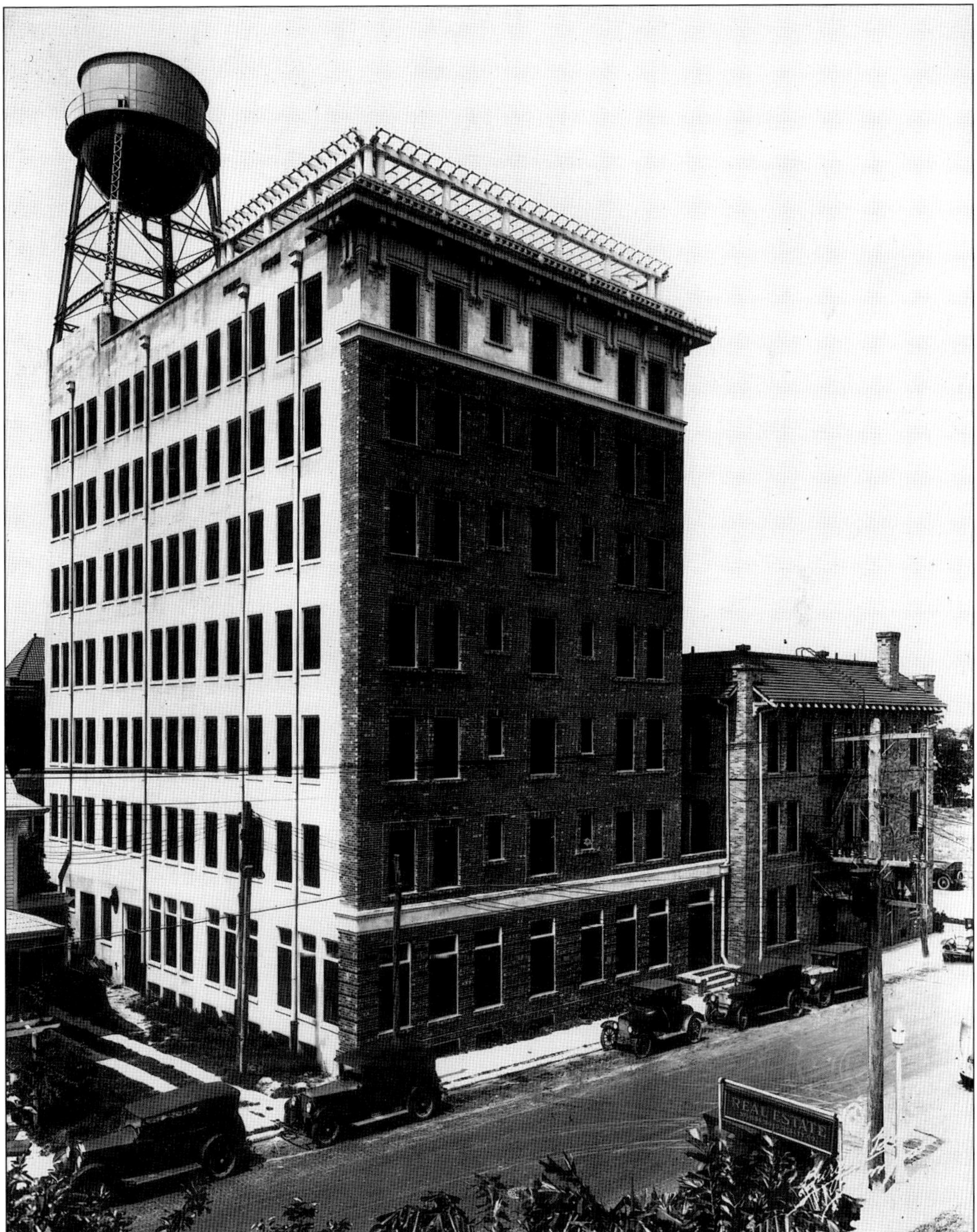

Tampa's Burgert Brothers snapped this backside view of the Franklin Arms Hotel. In 1924, an eight-story addition was constructed, making the 102-room structure the city's first "skyscraper." During the crazy Land Boom of the 1920s, a "human fly" ascended the hotel's exterior, who stopped at each floor and told folks to buy land in a new Fort Myers subdivision, Palmlee Park. (Courtesy of Tampa-Hillsborough County Public Library System.)

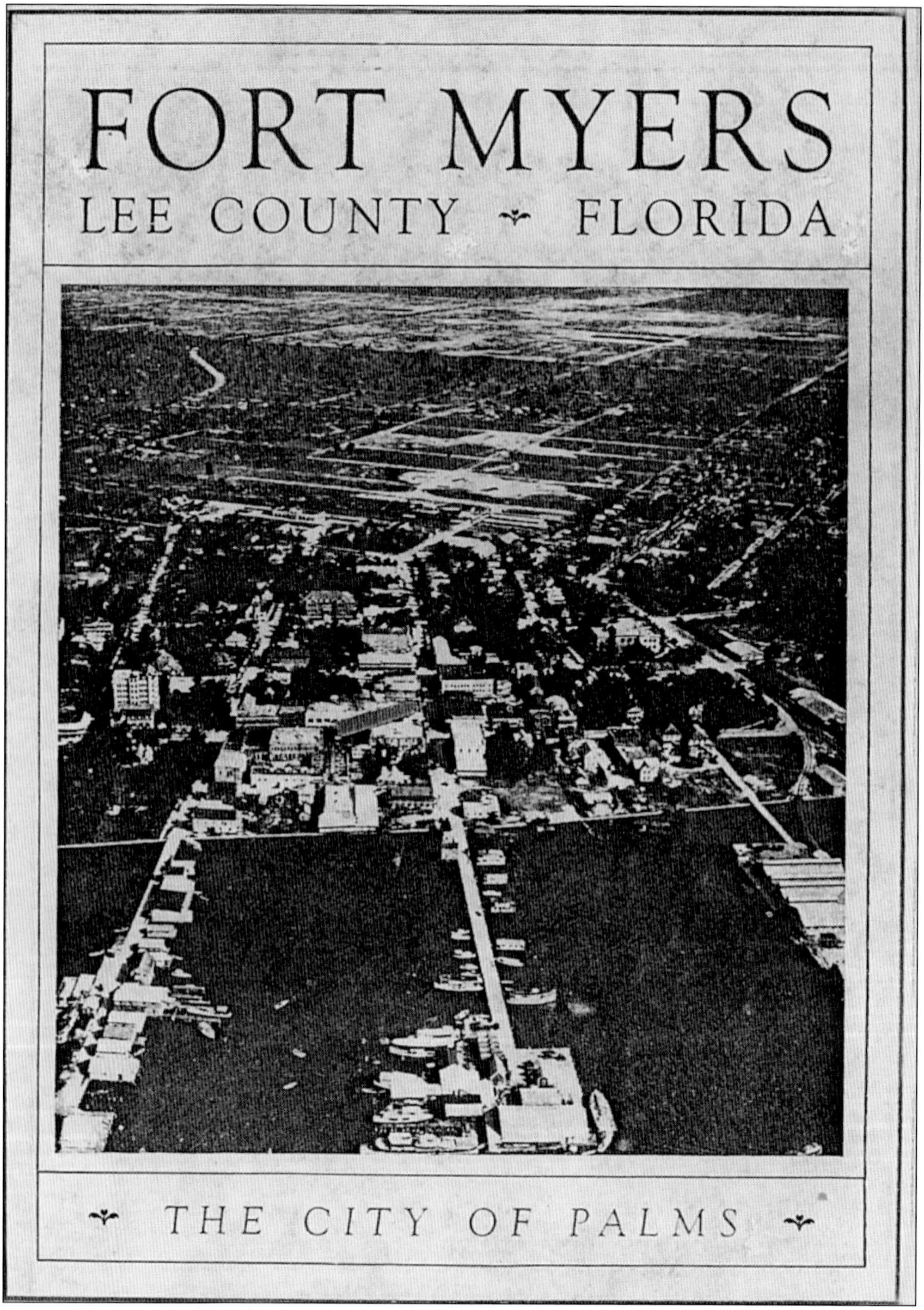

Tropical flowers and shrubbery add a special touch to the landscape of Fort Myers. But what really intrigued tourists and newcomers was the great variety of palm trees. During the 1920s a prominent nurseryman, James E. Hendry Jr., suggested to city fathers that Fort Myers be nicknamed the City of Palms. Soon, literature appeared with the new slogan.

As noted, the abundance of palm trees amazed visitors to Fort Myers, especially the Royal Palm variety that marched down McGregor Boulevard. During the 1920s, a ballad about the city was released by Rudy and Fred Rudisill of Charlotte, North Carolina. Before long, every city pianist wanted a copy.

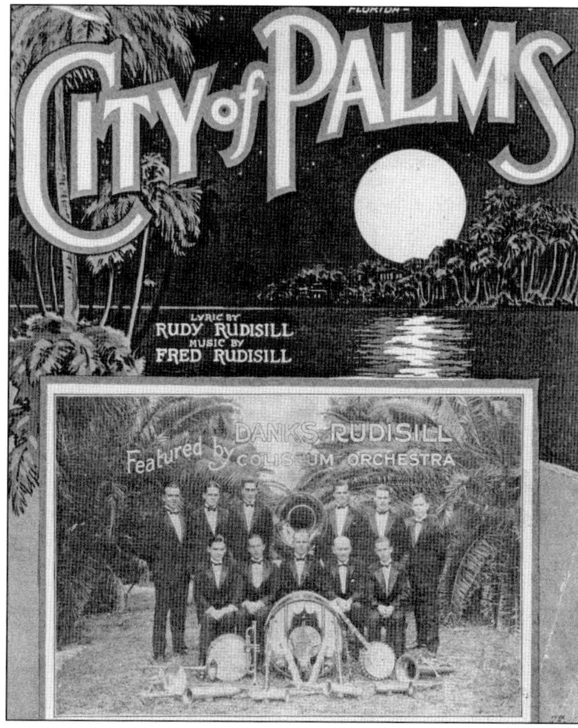

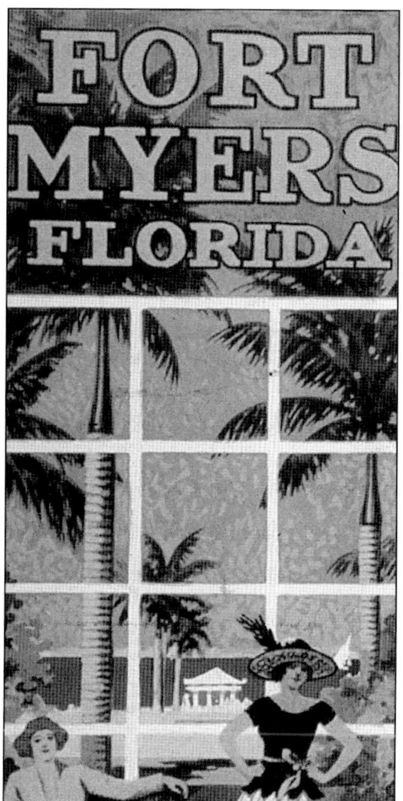

The Land Boom was a remarkable period in Florida history. Twenty-four new communities surfaced along its coastline, including nearby Venice. Real estate sales soared, and countless subdivisions appeared. Because Fort Myers had the Tamiami Trail and good rail service, Northern folk came by the droves. Colorful brochures like this one described the City of Palms.

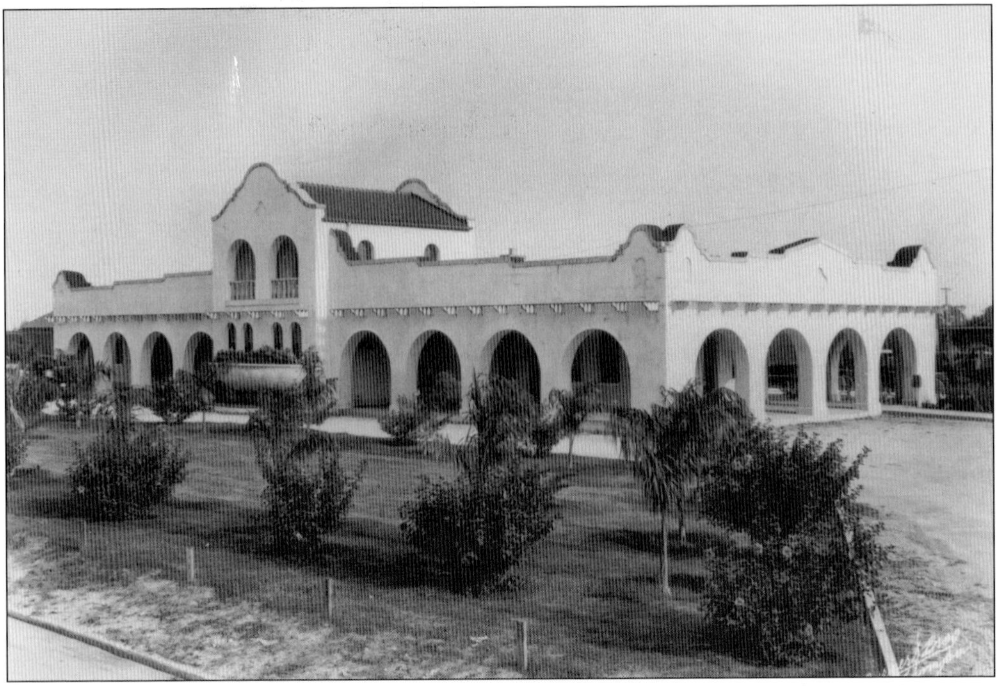

Beautiful buildings also went up in Fort Myers during the Land Boom. In February 1924, a new Atlantic Coast Line Railroad station opened on Peck Street. The Spanish-inspired structure (almost a twin of Sarasota) cost $48,000. It had dual waiting rooms (white and "colored"), fireplaces, a baggage area, and telegraph office. Today it houses the Fort Myers Historical Museum. (Courtesy of Tampa-Hillsborough County Public Library System.)

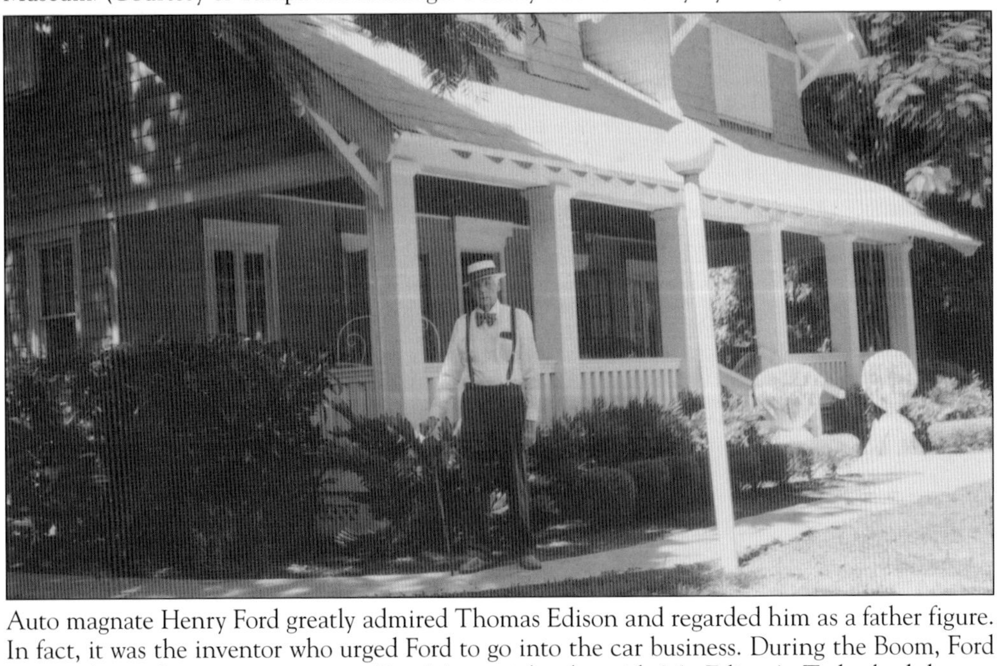

Auto magnate Henry Ford greatly admired Thomas Edison and regarded him as a father figure. In fact, it was the inventor who urged Ford to go into the car business. During the Boom, Ford acquired a modest winter retreat in Fort Myers, right alongside Mr. Edison's. Today both homes are open to the public.

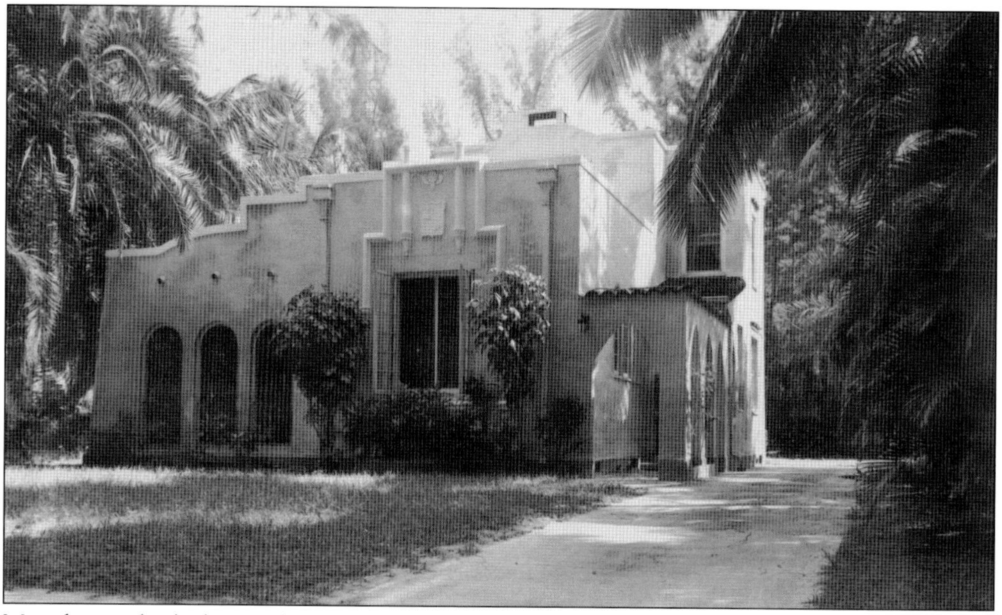

Most homes built during the Boom had a Mediterranean Revival flavor, such as this example on Providence Street in Dean Park. Tiled roofs, arched openings, heavy wood doors, and loggias were common. Other area subdivisions included Edison Park, Valencia Terrace, Alabama Grove, Palmwood, Russell Park, Carlton Grove, Edgewood, and Seminole Park. (Courtesy of Harmon Photo & Video.)

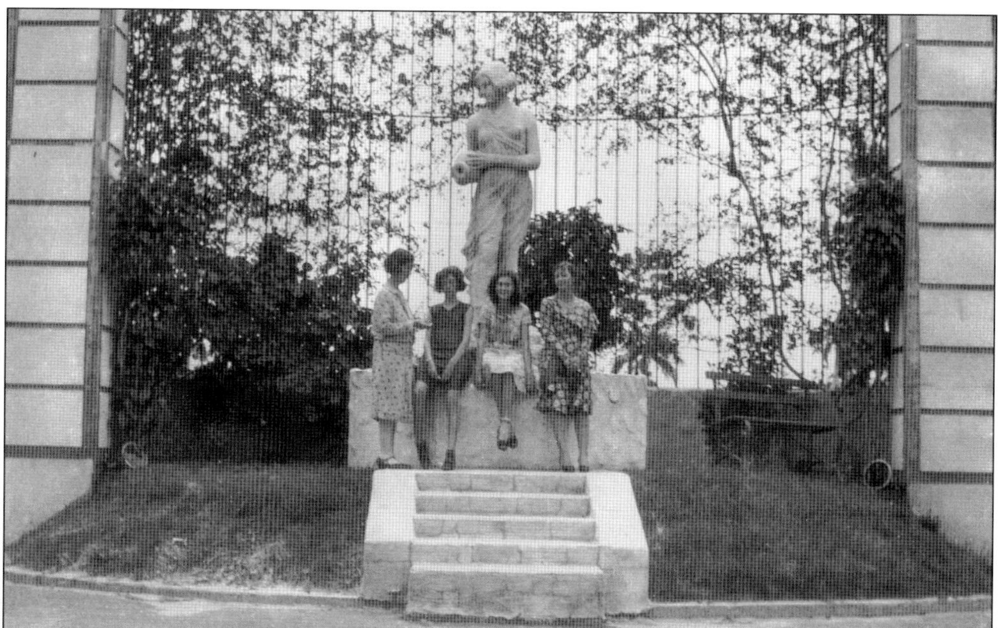

The Snell Brothers platted Edison Park, and among its builders and developers was a youthful James Newton. Beautiful railings and columns graced the subdivision's McGregor Boulevard entrance, and in 1926 a suitable statue was commissioned. Mrs. Thomas Alva Edison, who wintered across the street, found the nude result offensive. She and other women asked that it be draped with a toga, and Newton obliged.

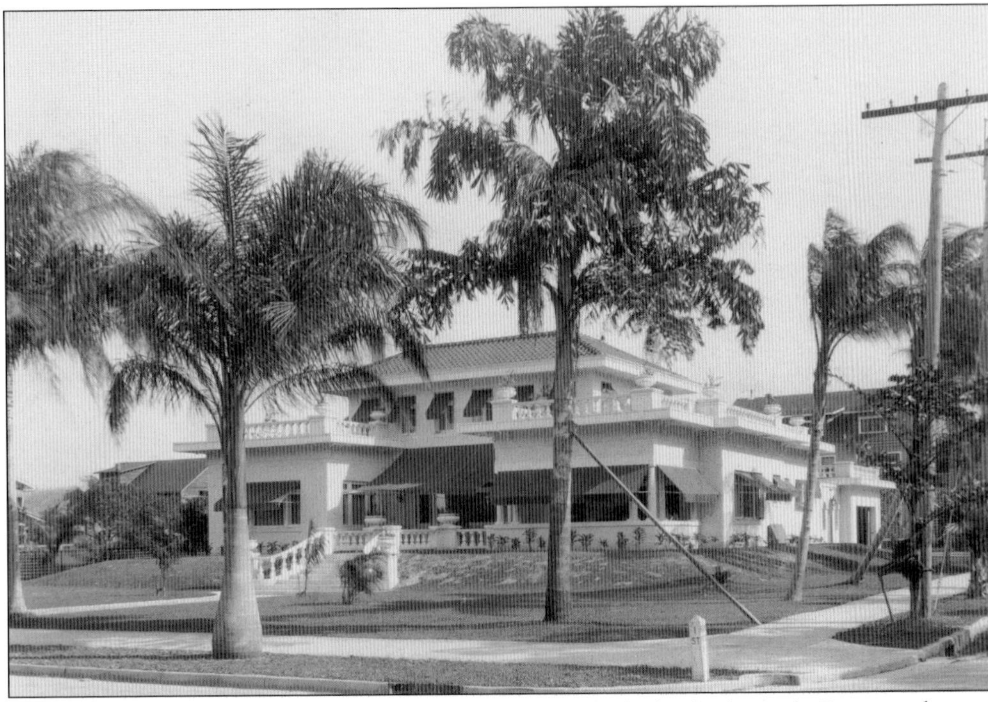

Clarence E. Chadwick invented forgery-proof paper for bank checks; his wife, Rosamond, was a nationally known concert singer. In 1925, they moved into this superb residence on First Street. The house boasted 12-inch walls of reinforced poured concrete, hardwood floors, knotty cypress woodwork, and big picture windows. Today the embankment home is occupied by a law firm.

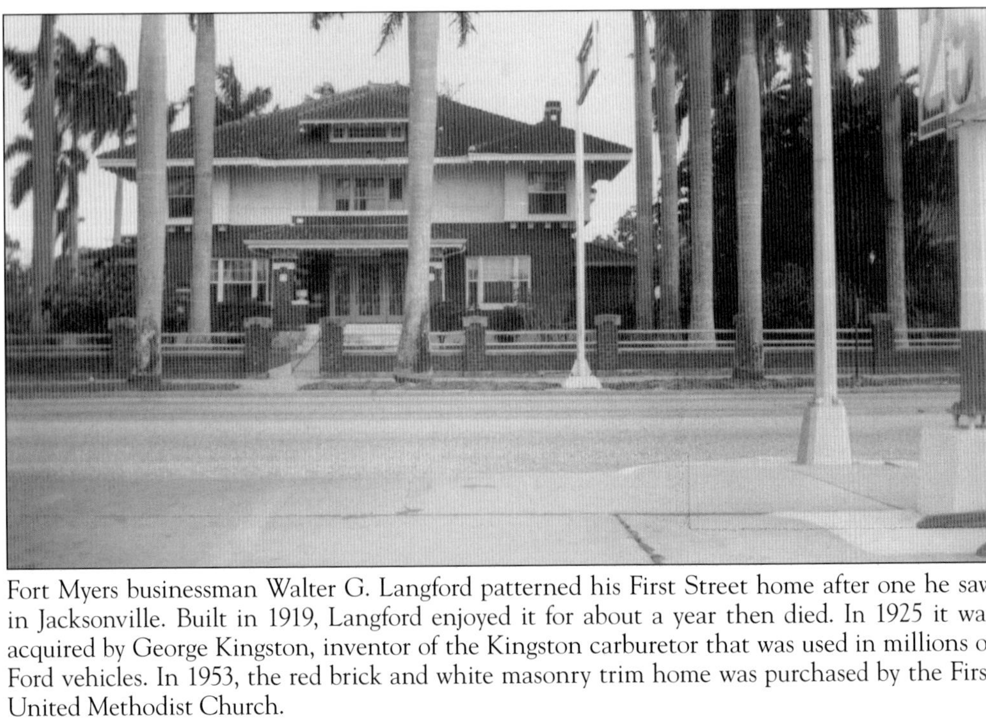

Fort Myers businessman Walter G. Langford patterned his First Street home after one he saw in Jacksonville. Built in 1919, Langford enjoyed it for about a year then died. In 1925 it was acquired by George Kingston, inventor of the Kingston carburetor that was used in millions of Ford vehicles. In 1953, the red brick and white masonry trim home was purchased by the First United Methodist Church.

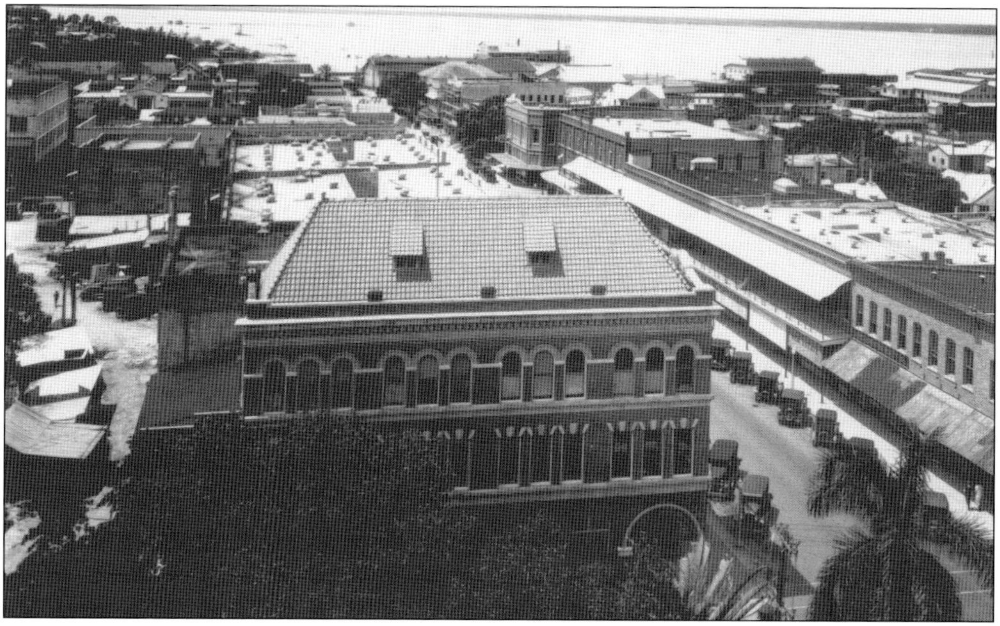

Land Boom photographs of Fort Myers survive thanks to Tampa's Burgert Brothers. This view, taken atop the Franklin Arms Hotel, looks westerly down First Street. In the center foreground is the hipped-roof Bank of Fort Myers building. Across the street (cornering Jackson) is the Heitman Building. (Courtesy of Tampa-Hillsborough County Public Library System.)

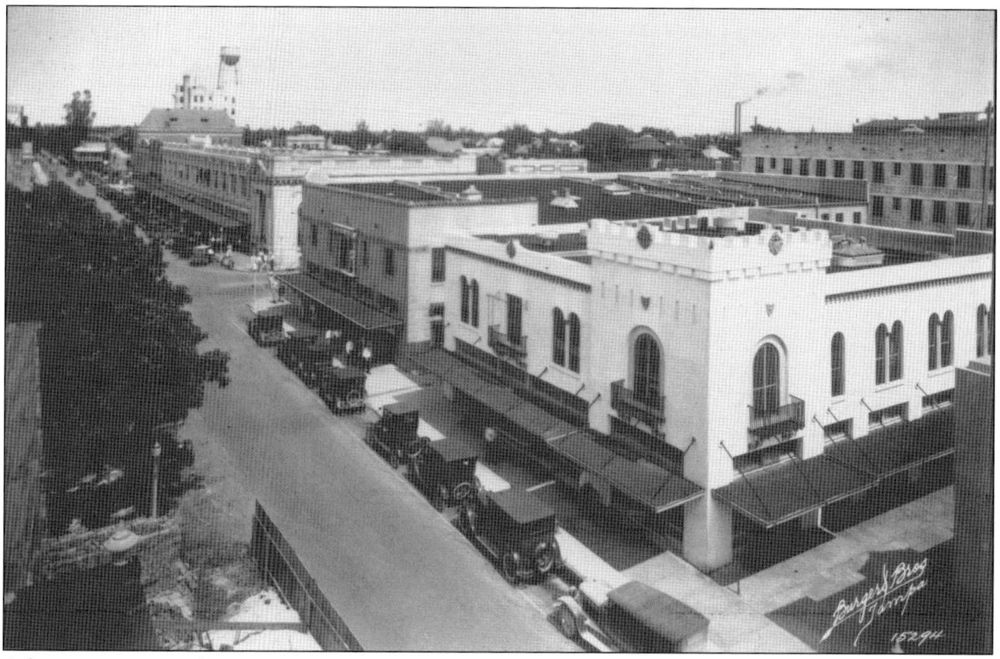

After composing the previous image, a Burgert staffer dashed down First Street and snapped this scene looking east while standing atop the Morgan Hotel. In the right foreground is the Patio de Leon, then Hendry Street, followed by the First National Bank, the Earnhardt Building, and the hipped-roof Bank of Fort Myers. In the distance is the water tower atop the Franklin Arms Hotel. (Courtesy of Tampa-Hillsborough County Public Library System.)

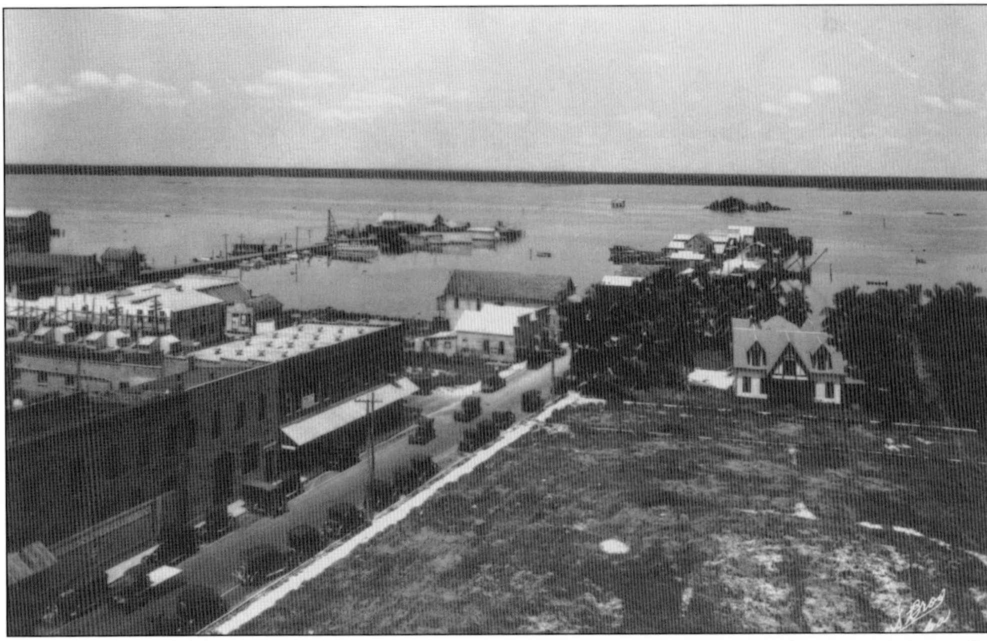

This 1925 view of the waterfront shows Jackson Street and the City Dock. To its left, at the foot of Hendry, is the Ireland Dock. The lone house (right center) was one of the fort's officers quarters; it was later used by early settlers, and eventually became known as the town library. (Courtesy of Tampa-Hillsborough County Public Library System.)

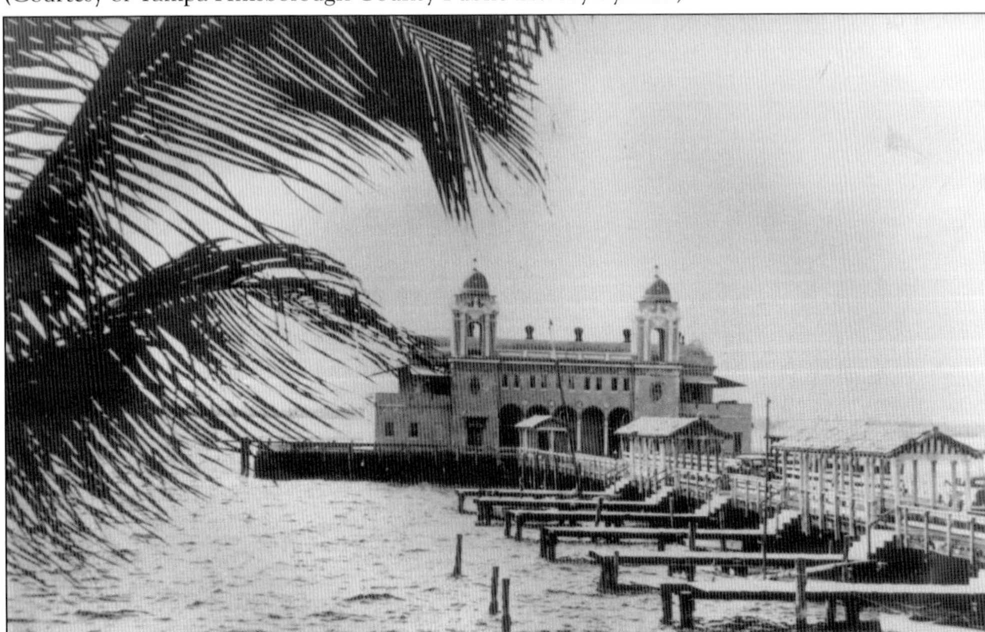

Young and old came to the Pleasure Pier for dancing, concerts, political rallies, and shows. The popular Moorish-style structure was completed in 1927 at city expense. When its piers fatigued in 1943, the auditorium was dismantled, brought ashore, and installed on Edwards Drive. During World War II, area servicemen used it as a social center. Today it is known as the Hall of Fifty States.

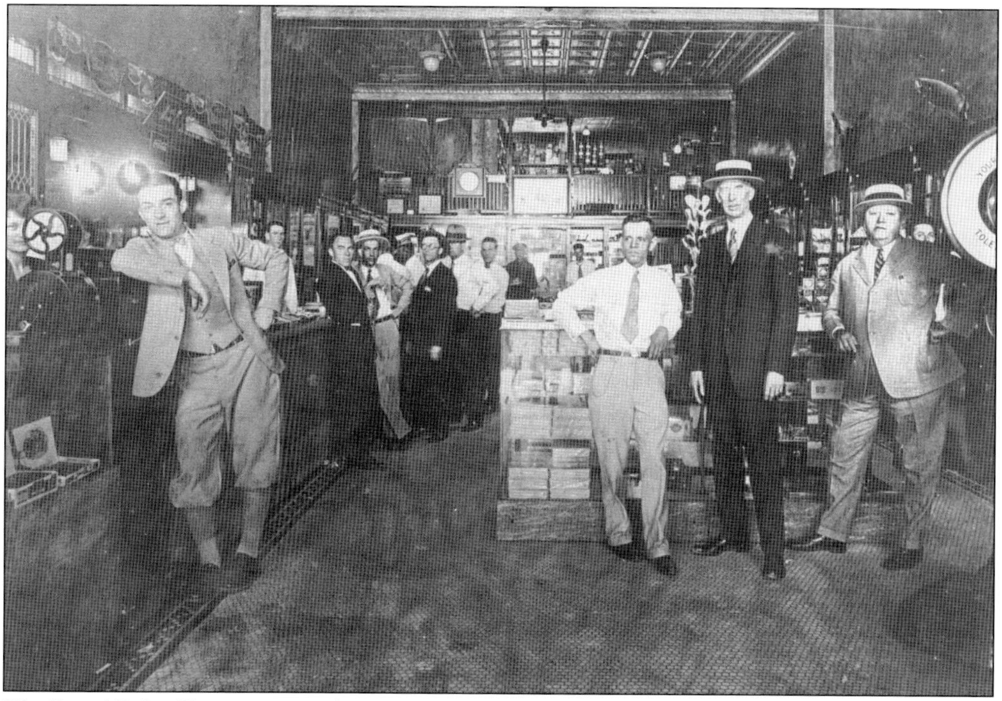

The Royal Palm Pharmacy stood on First Street. Its owner, R.Q. Richards, and the local Kiwanis Club got Connie Mack, owner of the Philadelphia Athletics baseball team, to conduct spring training in Fort Myers starting in 1925. Here, Richards faces the camera (white shirt and tie), while Mack stands to his right. The Toledo Scale (far right) weighed players, often to the delight of fans. Mack was the grandfather of Florida senator Connie Mack.

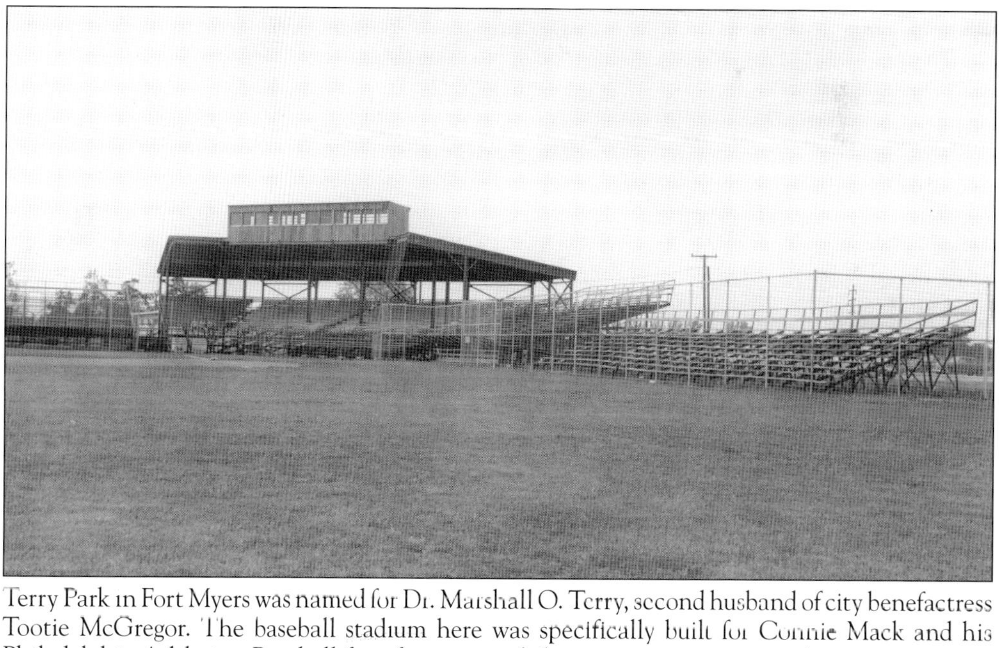

Terry Park in Fort Myers was named for Dr. Marshall O. Terry, second husband of city benefactress Tootie McGregor. The baseball stadium here was specifically built for Connie Mack and his Philadelphia Athletics. Baseball fans from around the country came to see the spring training and games, just as they do today for the Boston Red Sox and Minnesota Twins.

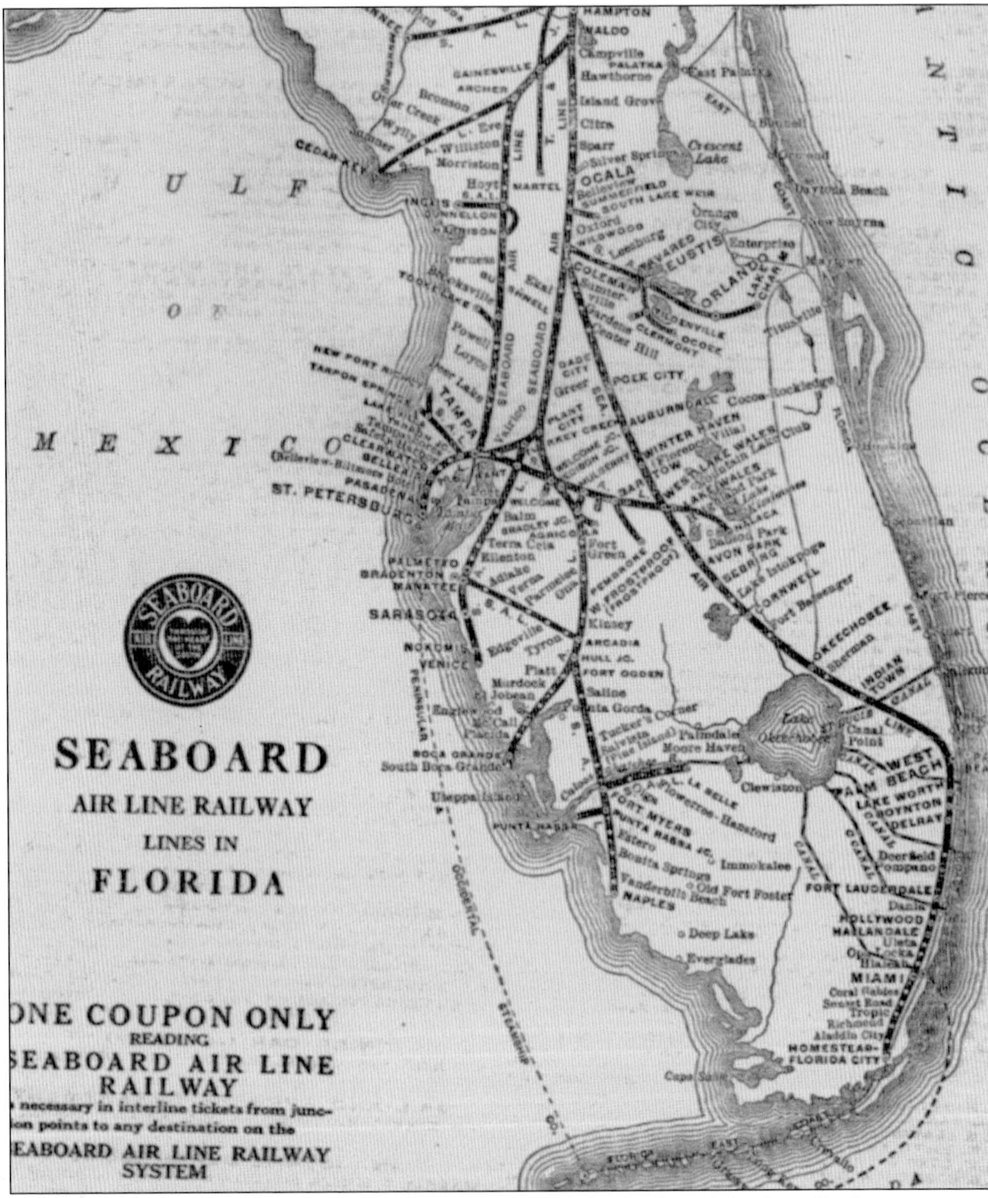

The Atlantic Coast Line monopolized Fort Myers until the Seaboard Air Line Railway appeared during the Land Boom. Its Fort Myers-Naples Extension, begun in January 1926, ran from Fort Ogden to Naples by way of Fort Myers and Bonita. Branches departed the City of Palms for Punta Rassa (Truckland) and eastward to LaBelle. James E. Hendry Jr., a prominent Fort Myers realtor and nurseryman, quietly obtained right-of-ways for the Seaboard and caught rival Coast Line by surprise. Most noteworthy was the Seaboard's long drawbridge across the Caloosahatchee. Its big freight house went up on Michigan Avenue (today Gully's Discount Store Fixtures) and a passenger station was erected on East Riverside Drive. The Seaboard dearly wanted the traffic of Southwest Florida, and countless manifests of timber were shipped plus citrus and vegetables; however, trucks made in-roads on much of the business and slowly the entire extension was dismantled. In 1952, the Seaboard vanished and the Coast Line resumed its monopoly.

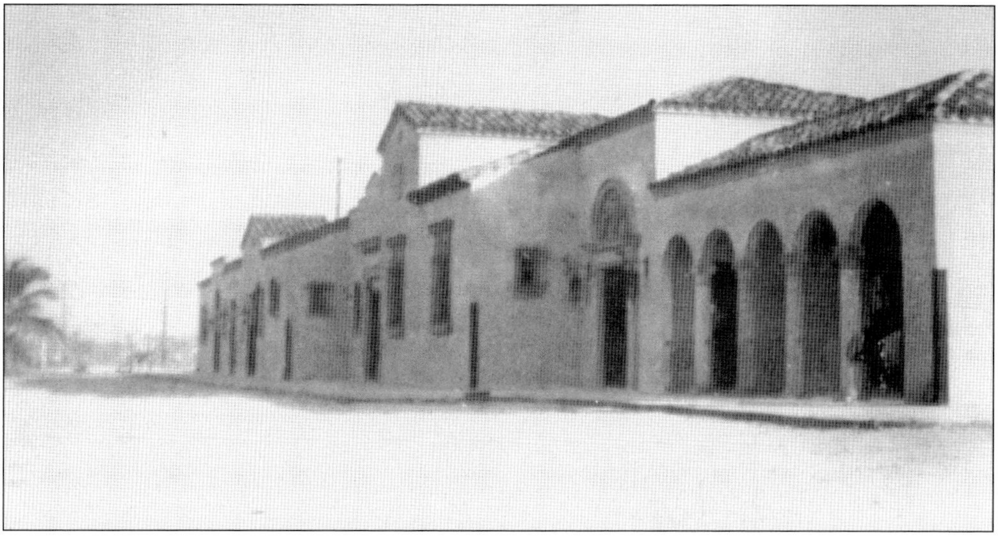

The Seaboard erected a beautiful passenger station on East Riverside Drive. Conceived in the Spanish Mission style by architects Wiley & Clarke of West Palm Beach, the $75,000 structure was 200 feet long. Interior walls and ceilings were finished in mottled cream stucco with ivory trim. Today it houses Reilly Brothers, a building supply firm. (Courtesy of The Railroad Museum of South Florida.)

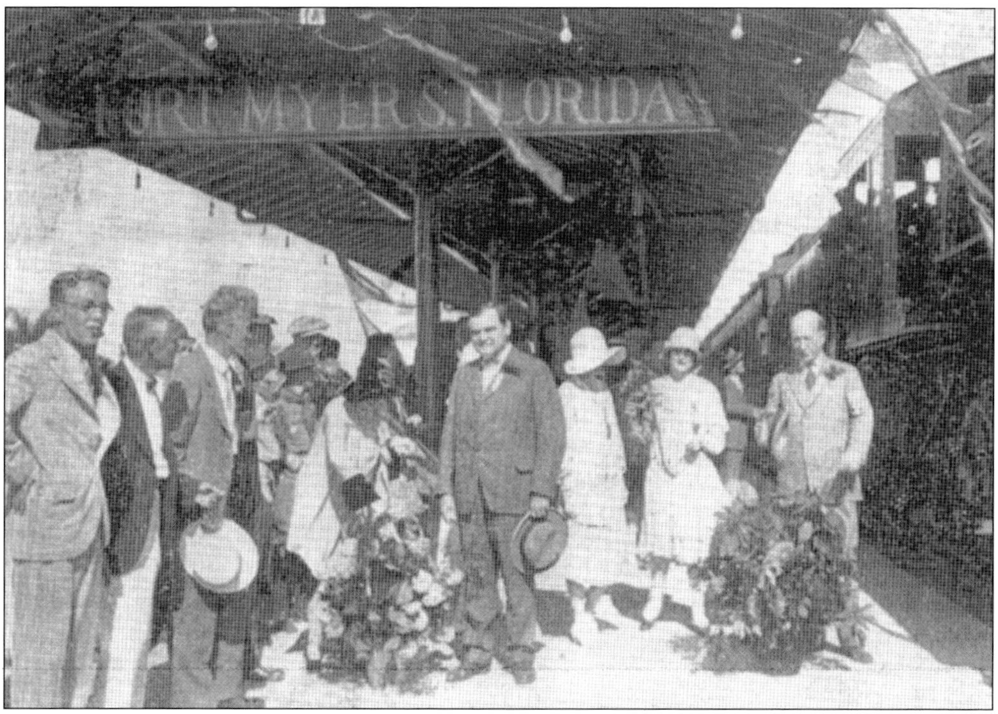

Seaboard passenger service began January 7, 1927, when five sections of the famed Orange Blossom Special pulled into town. This celebratory run included Gov. John Martin (facing camera with hat) and Seaboard president S. Davies Warfield (far right). The entourage of some 600 souls continued on to Bonita and Naples, returned to Fort Myers, then journeyed to Miami for more celebrations.

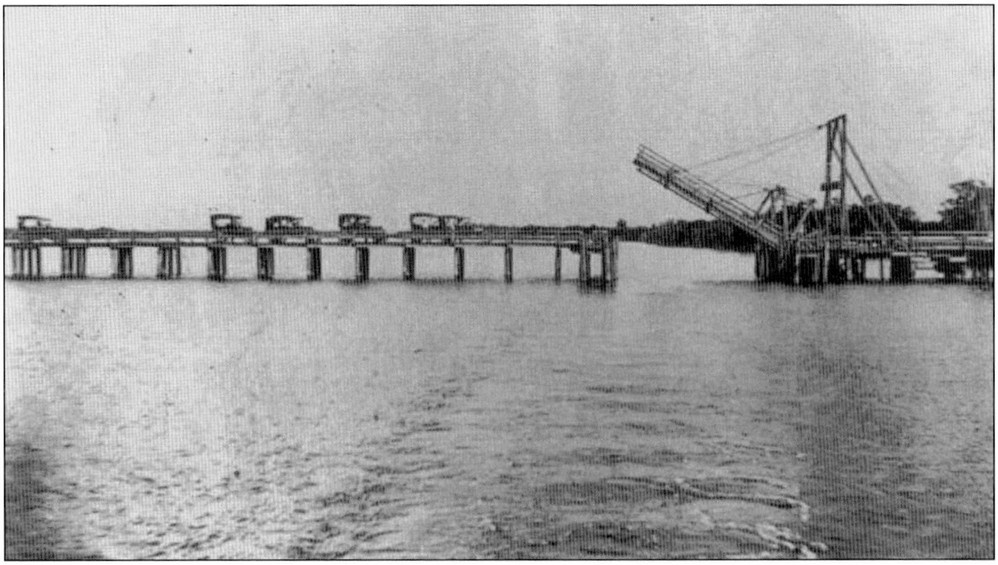

A wooden drawbridge over Matanzas Pass linked Crescent Beach (today Fort Myers Beach) with the mainland. The Crescent Beach Road & Bridge Company opened the toll bridge in 1921 and charged drivers 54¢. Later, a graded road was built from the drawbridge north to McGregor Boulevard, which is today known as San Carlos Boulevard. (Courtesy of Florida State Photo Archive.)

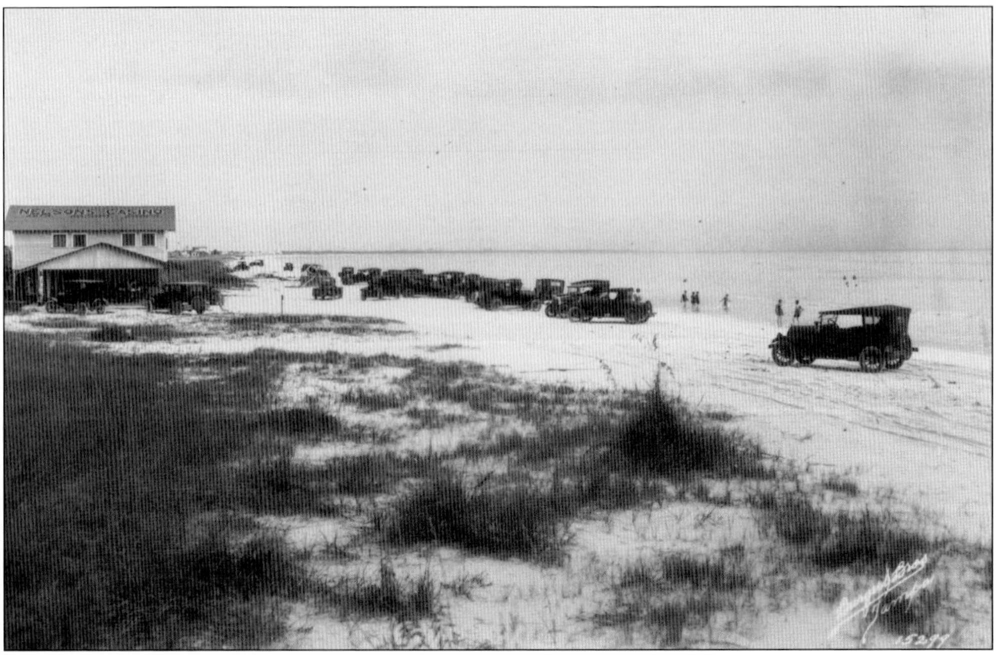

For many years the only thoroughfare down Fort Myers Beach was the beach itself. Driving on the packed sand was fun, though many cars got stuck. Then, as now, beachgoers delighted in a day's outing, and cars by the drove appeared on weekends. For those who did not bring eats, grub and grog awaited at Nelson's Casino. The scene here was snapped by Tampa's Burgert Brothers on September 7, 1925. (Courtesy of Tampa-Hillsborough County Public Library System.)

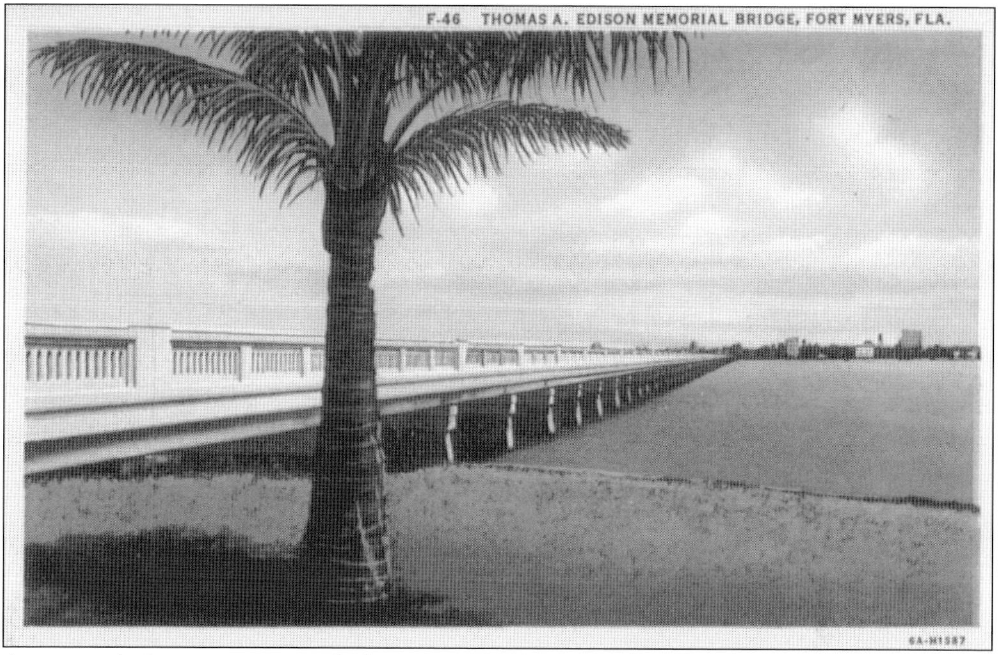

A national depression gripped the country when the Edison Bridge opened across the Caloosahatchee in October 1930. Formal dedication ceremonies, however, were delayed until February 11, 1931, on the occasion of Edison's 84th birthday. The concrete structure cost $300,000 and provided jobs. That the bridge first lacked lights—an Edison invention!—made fodder for *Ripley's Believe-It-Or-Not.*

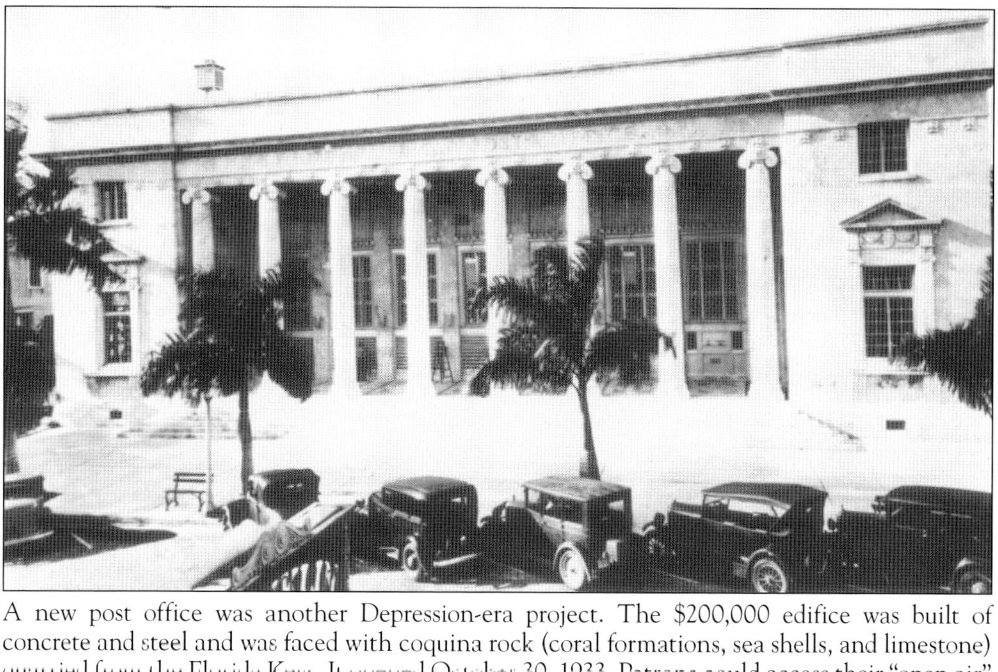

A new post office was another Depression-era project. The $200,000 edifice was built of concrete and steel and was faced with coquina rock (coral formations, sea shells, and limestone) quarried from the Florida Keys. It opened October 30, 1933. Patrons could access their "open air" lock boxes (seen beyond the columns) day or night. In 1965 the structure became the Federal Building. (Courtesy of Florida State Photo Archive.)

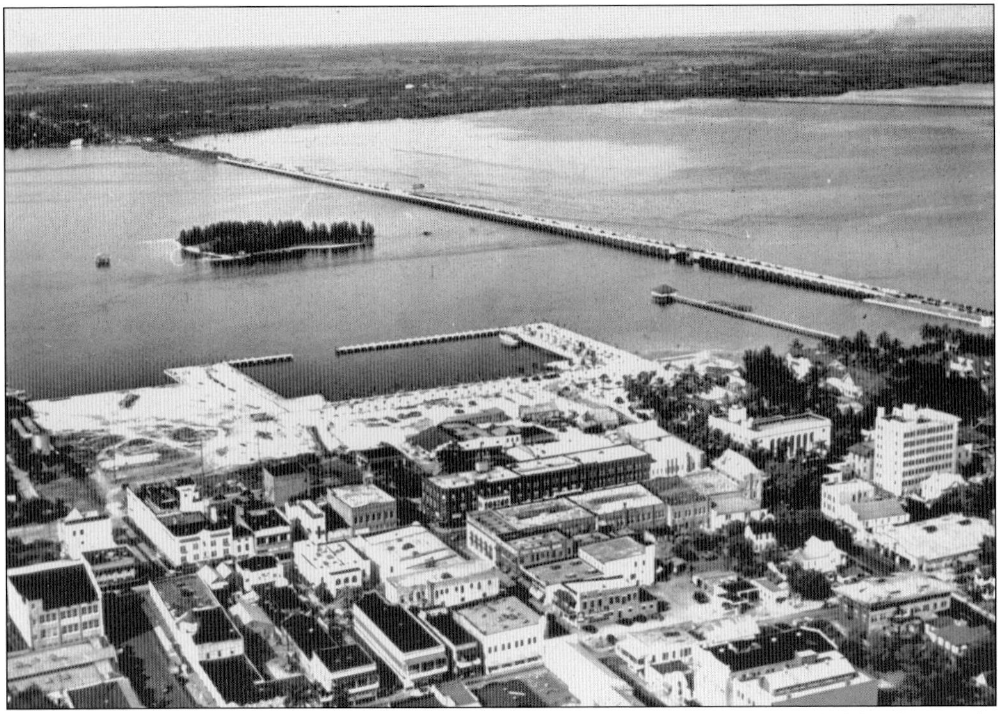

Another job generator during the Depression was a new city yacht basin. Funded by the Works Project Administration, the undertaking eliminated rickety docks, crumbling seawalls, and derelict buildings. The $300,000 project began New Years Day 1937, and lasted some two years. In this view, palm trees have just been planted around the basin's perimeter. The Edison Bridge is visible, and to its left is Lofton Island. (Courtesy of Florida State Photo Archive.)

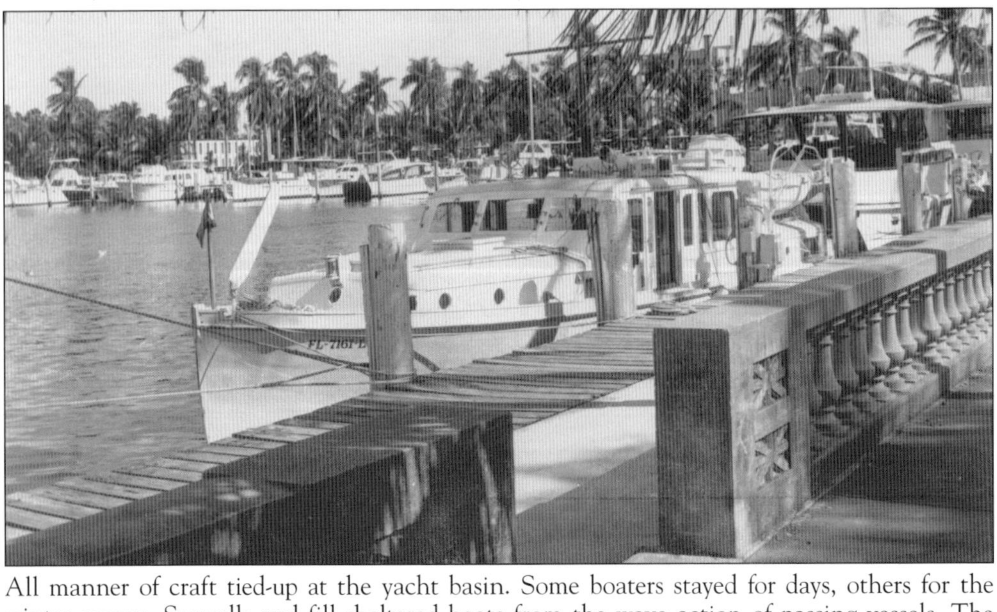

All manner of craft tied-up at the yacht basin. Some boaters stayed for days, others for the winter season. Seawalls and fill sheltered boats from the wave action of passing vessels. The Royal Palms seen in the previous image have now reached maturity, and a bevy of wooden yachts are visible. The basin remains a treasured possession of the city and has tripled in size.

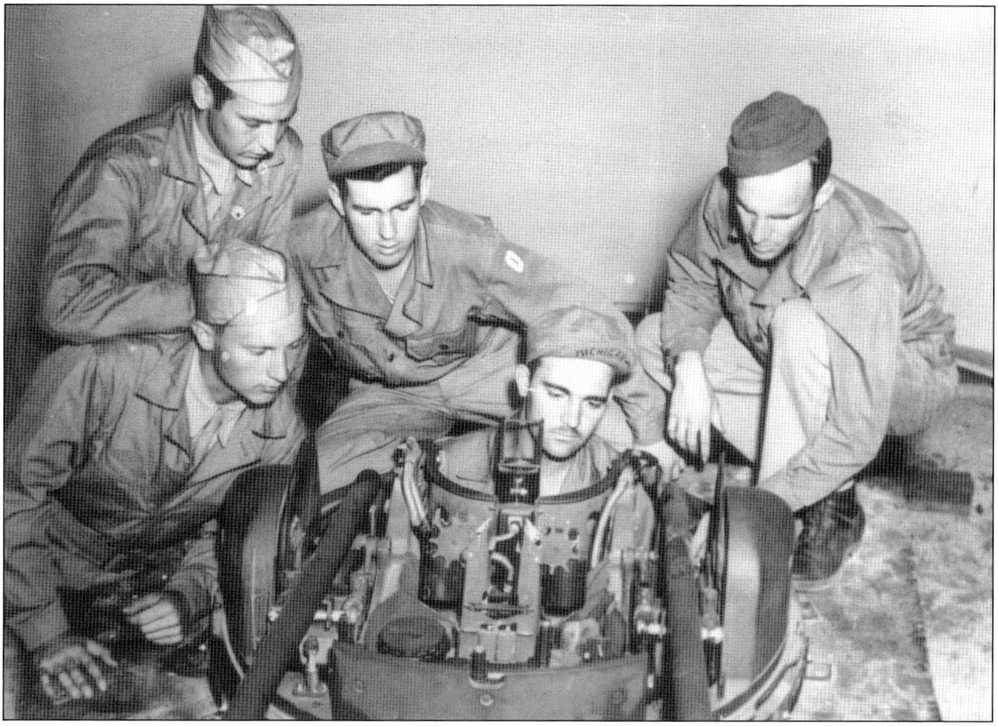

Florida was home to dozens of military installations in World War II. In nearby Buckingham, a huge flexible gunnery school was created in 1942. Runways were built as well as hangars, barracks, and shops. On-hands training took place, and at its peak over 16,000 service personnel were connected to the facility.

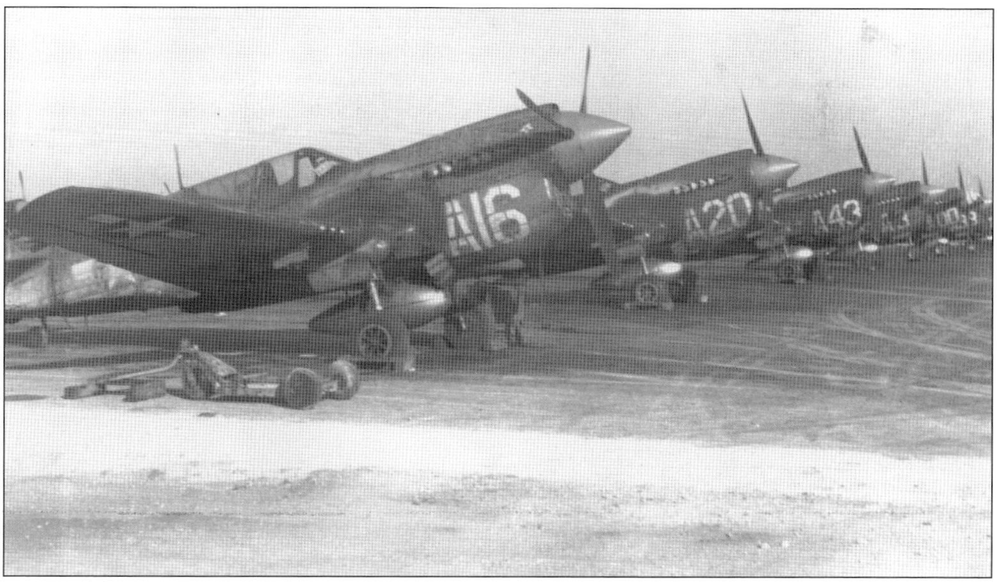

Page Field in Fort Myers was named for local World War I flying ace Channing Page. In 1942, the facility was taken over by the the Army Air Corp and greatly expanded. Various detachments trained at Page, including the 53rd Fighter Group which used P-40s (above). At its peak, some 4,000 personnel were stationed here.

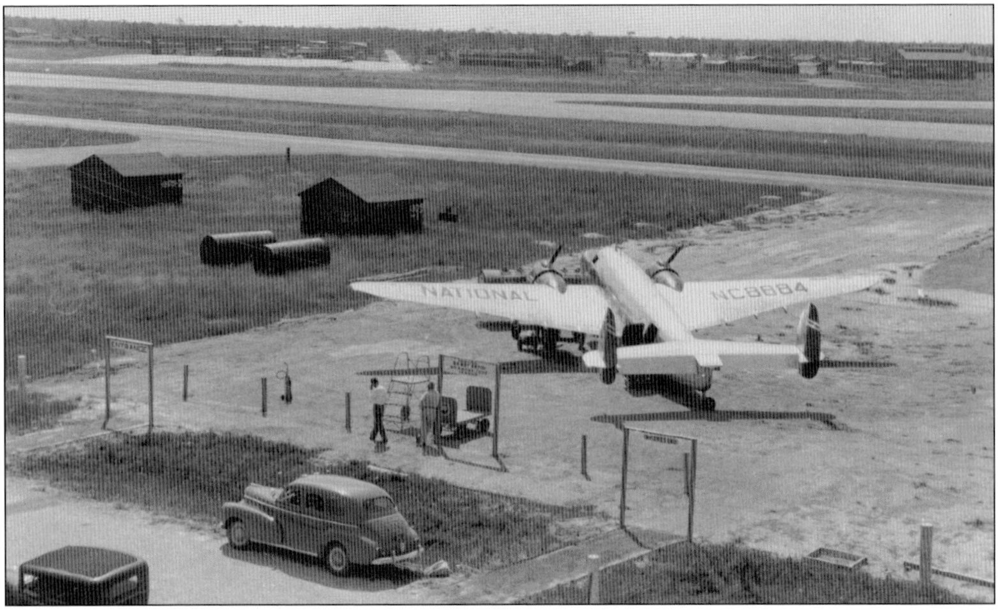

Fort Myers converted a former golf course into an airport with sod runways in 1927. Commercial service began in August 1937, when National Airlines stopped en route from St. Petersburg to Miami. Eventually a lack of concrete runways halted service. Thanks to the Works Project Administration, the problem was corrected and service resumed in 1940. In this post–World War II scene, a National Airlines prop flight prepares to taxi.

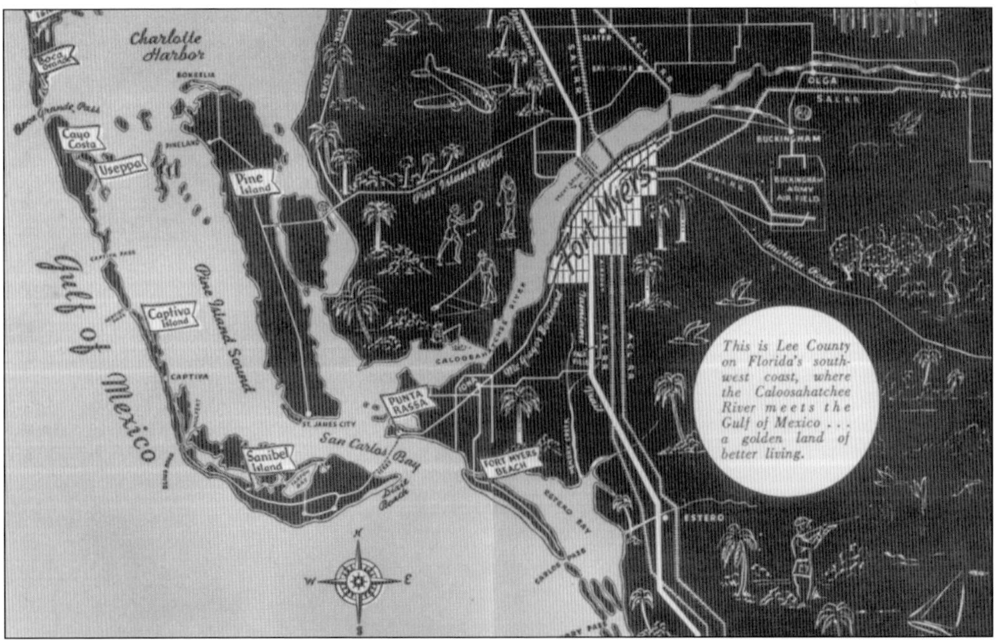

Many World War II servicemen married locals or returned to Fort Myers after the war. Tourists and visitors also began to appear, then the first wave of Social Security retirees. Brochures helped attract newcomers and most contained a map of the area, like the 1950s one above. When finally the mosquito was controlled and air-conditioning was widely installed, an economic uptick took place.

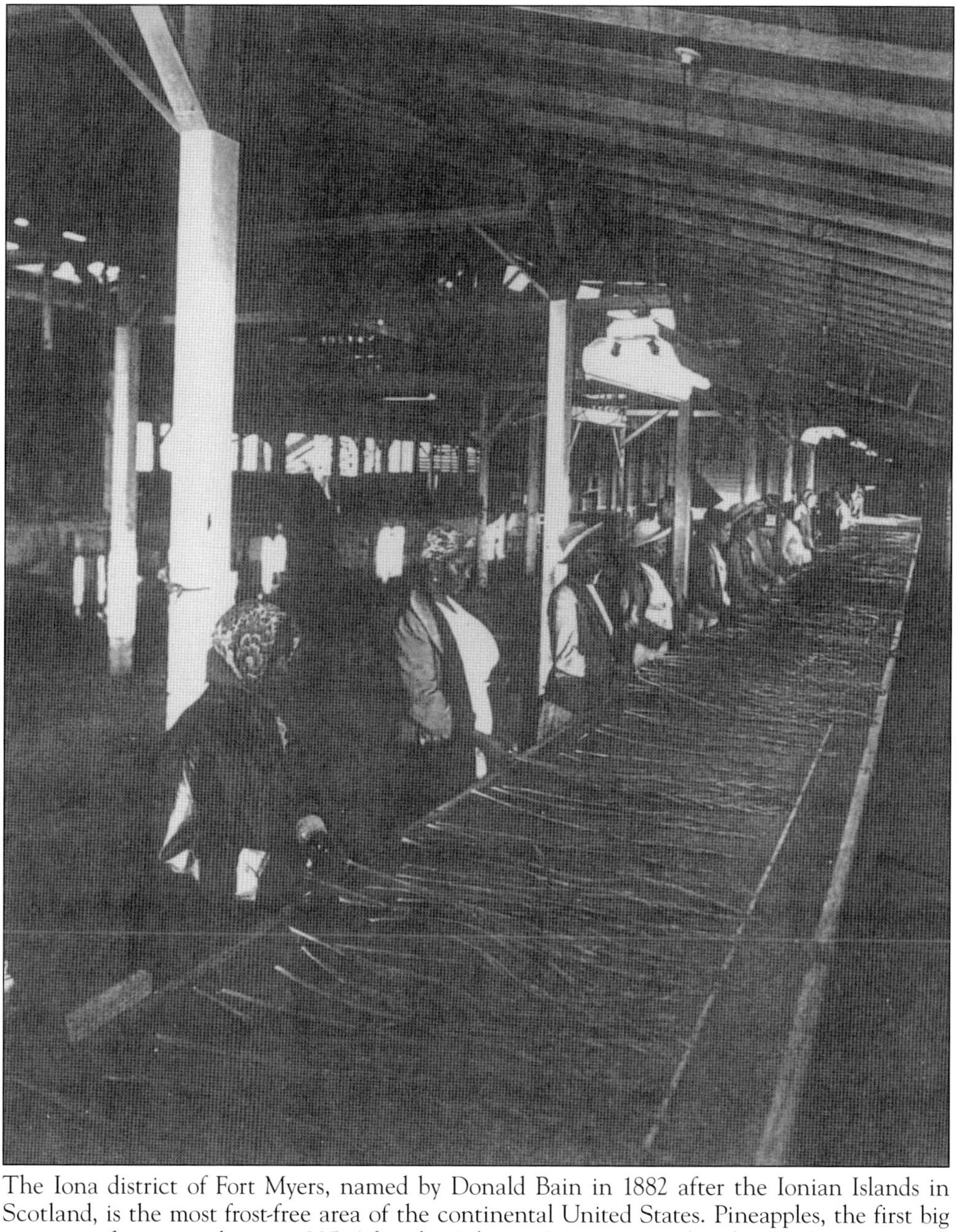

The Iona district of Fort Myers, named by Donald Bain in 1882 after the Ionian Islands in Scotland, is the most frost-free area of the continental United States. Pineapples, the first big crop, were first grown here in 1885. After the Atlantic Coast Line Railroad arrived in Fort Myers (1904), the area was settled by truck farmers. Dr. Franklin Miles, founder of Elkhart Laboratories in Indiana, greatly experimented with winter vegetables grown in Iona. During the Land Boom, thousands of acres were planted with tomatoes, cucumbers, egg plant, green beans, and squash. Also, some 83 miles of drainage ditches were dug. In 1935, a completely new industry arrived—gladiolus. Packing houses were built for the harvest, and in this January 1945 image women are sorting examples at the A&W Bulb Company. Today, only a small amount of farming occurs in the area. New homes, condominiums, and riverside subdivisions have become the order of the day. (Courtesy of Tampa-Hillsborough County Public Library System.)

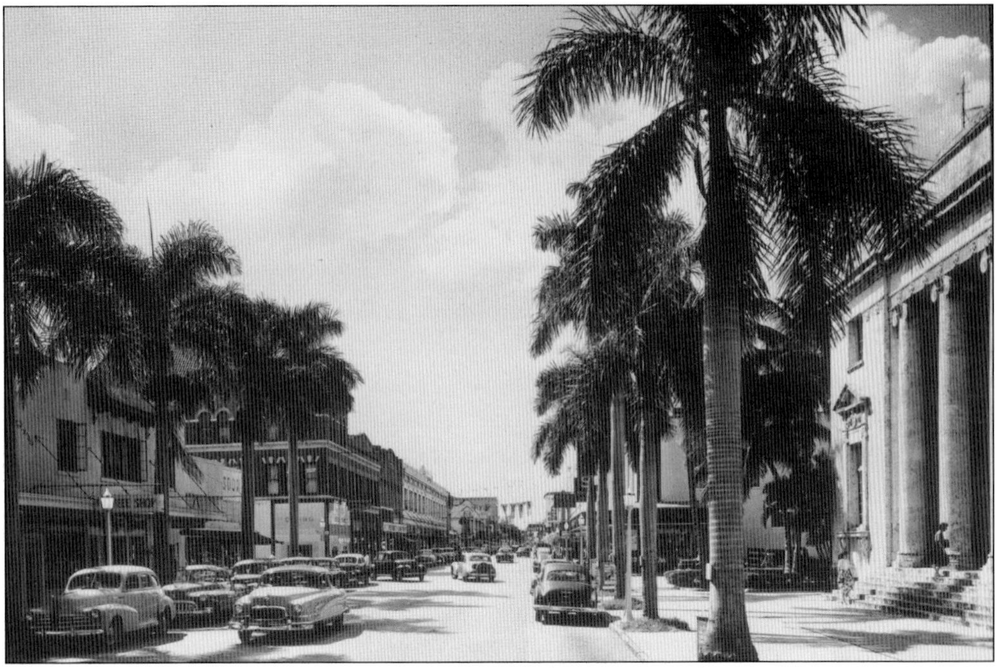

We close this chapter with two retrospective photos. The above image is First Street on October 28, 1950. (Turn to page 93 for the same scene 25 years earlier). The "open air" post office (right) is now almost 20 years old. Beyond it is Sears, which took up residence in the Heitman Building. The Bank of Fort Myers edifice is across the street, and beyond it stands the Earnhardt Building followed by the First National Bank. (Courtesy of Florida State Photo Archive.)

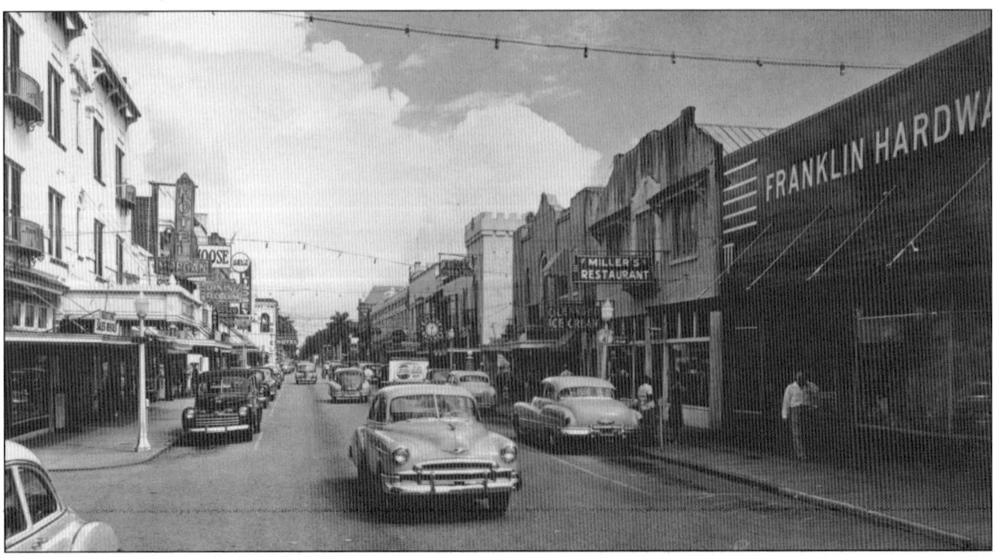

Our photographer has dashed down First Street and points the camera east (the same view 25 years before on page 93). Car traffic has increased not to mention business signage. Once vacant building lots now embrace stores. Buicks and Chevys abound, and a "woody" station wagon (mid-left) is parked in front of the Hotel Morgan. Your authors ask: were these the golden years? (Courtesy of Florida State Photo Archive.)

Seven

SAFETY HILL

When Fort Myers was active during the Civil War, several Union "colored" troops helped man the facility. Later, when Fort Myers was first being settled, both blacks and whites lived in the same neighborhoods.

Readers will recall Nelson Tillis, the first black settler of Fort Myers, who arrived on Christmas Day, 1867. At one time he and his family lived near the Thomas Edison estate on McGregor Boulevard. Tillis earned a living as a fisherman, fishing guide, and carpenter. As other black families began to settle in, the darker side of Southern toleration became visible. By the 1900s, newly arriving whites did not want blacks living in the same neighborhood.

Thus, the community of Safety Hill arose. While hills themselves seem scarce in Southwest Florida, the land itself may have been just high enough to free the area of drainage problems. Others say the area was the only place blacks could feel safe. In those distant times, "Jim Crow" laws forbade any person of "color" from crossing the railroad tracks after dark, and similar ordinances remained on the books long after they ceased to be enforced.

In 1927 the first all-black high school opened in Safety Hill; it was named after Paul Laurence Dunbar, a renowned black writer of an earlier time. Dunbar High School also became a social and activities center of the black community. In the 1940s, the name Safety Hill was dropped and "Dunbar" became the new neighborhood identity. Most of the images that follow about this important area of Fort Myers were kindly furnished by the newly formed Lee County Black History Society, Inc.

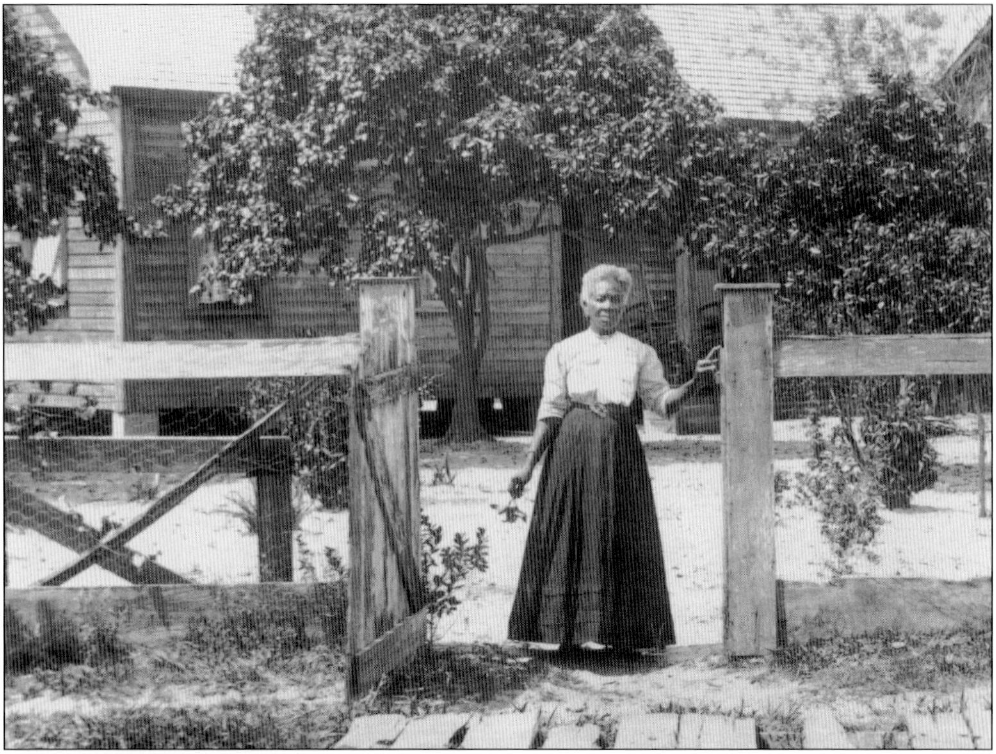

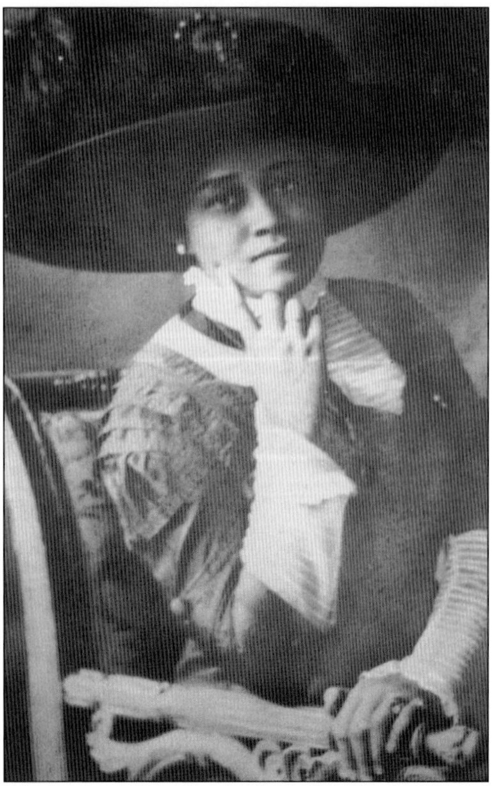

Most black families lived in Safety Hill, but not all. The lady above, Sara Williams, stands at the gate of her home, which was located on Cleveland Avenue near downtown Fort Myers. She was the mother of a prominent city figure, Dr. Ella Piper.

Born in Georgia in 1884, Ella Bailer attended Spellman College in Atlanta and then a beauty college in New York City, graduating in 1915. She later joined her mother in Fort Myers and married Frank Piper in 1920. In time Dr. Piper ran a beauty salon and a soft drink business in Fort Myers, was a community activist, a friend of Mrs. Thomas Edison, and a respected member of Safety Hill.

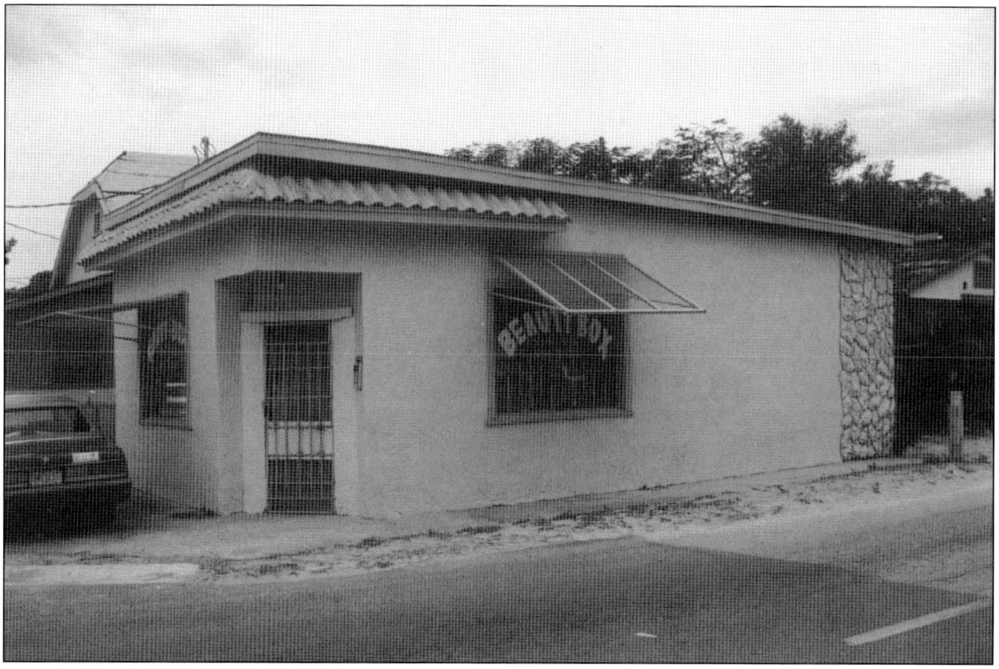

The "Beauty Box" on Orange Street was established in 1938 and was one of the first beauty salons in the Dunbar area. It is also thought to be the oldest black business establishment still in existence. The building seen here was first constructed as a residence in 1926 and later changed to commercial use.

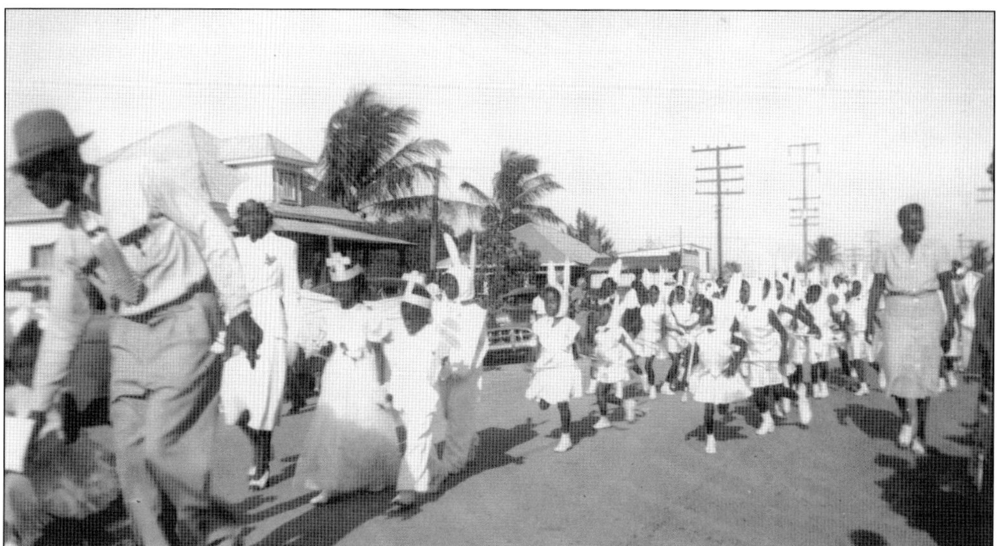

Easter parades were once quite the thing in American towns and cities, as the Irving Berlin song and movie with Judy Garland and Fred Astaire remind us. The event was eagerly anticipated and for years the Dunbar community scheduled one, as this 1950s image confirms.

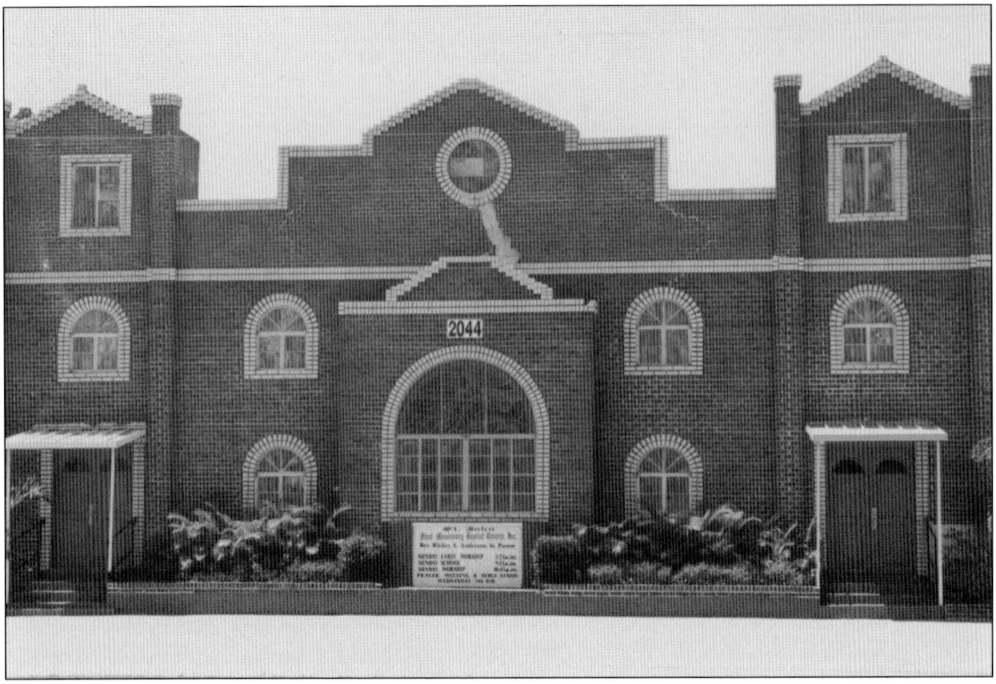

St. John First Missionary Baptist Church on Brown Street was organized as a congregation back in 1898. The two-story structure was originally a chapel at Buckingham Air Field during World War II. After the latter closed, the church acquired the building, whereupon it was moved to its present location in 1951 and improved with red brick.

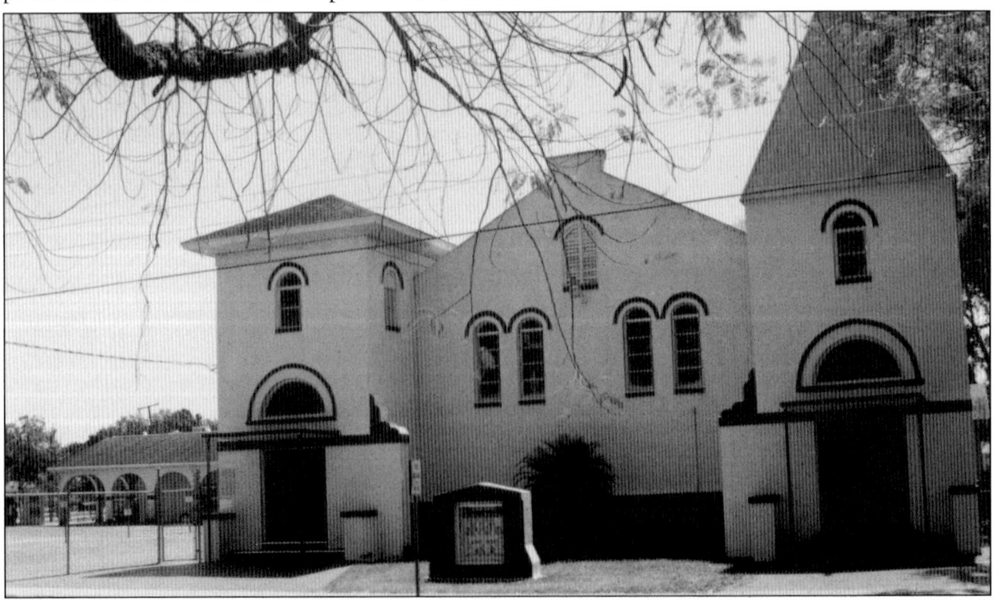

Founded in 1895, Mt. Olive African Methodist Episcopal Church is today located on Orange Street in Dunbar. Originally the congregation met in the Lee County Court House, then in a soft drink plant until a sanctuary was erected only to be destroyed in the 1926 hurricane. Another facility was built and it too suffered from fire and storm. Despite adversity, members erected the above structure in 1929.

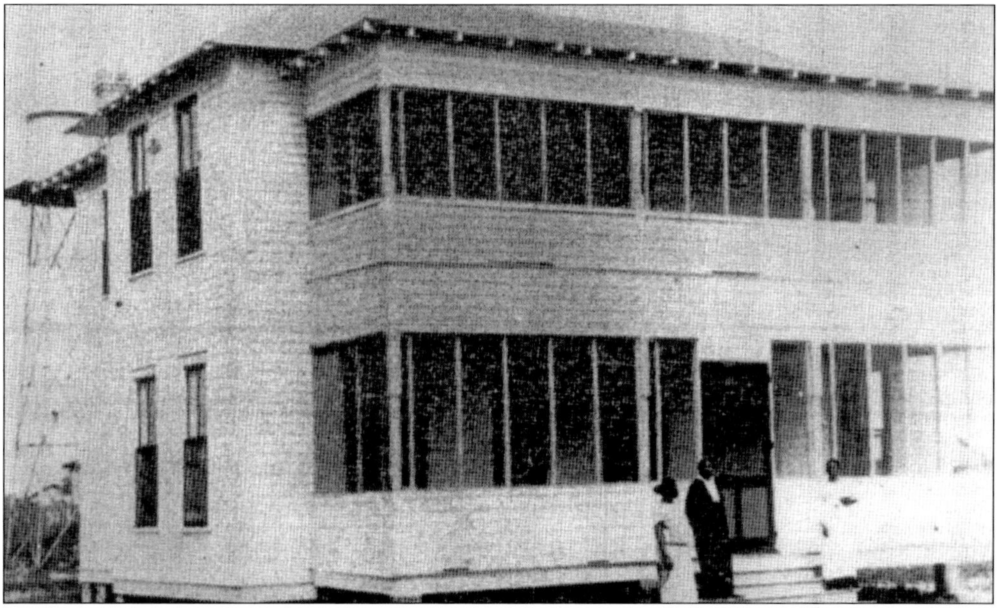

The Jones-Walker Hospital on High Street was a source of much pride in the black community of Fort Myers. For years there was no such facility for blacks. Mrs. Melissa Jones, Candis Walker, and others raised monies for the building at school and church functions, which were matched by other resources. The hospital's name honored both women. The facility became defunct with the enlightenment of the 1960s.

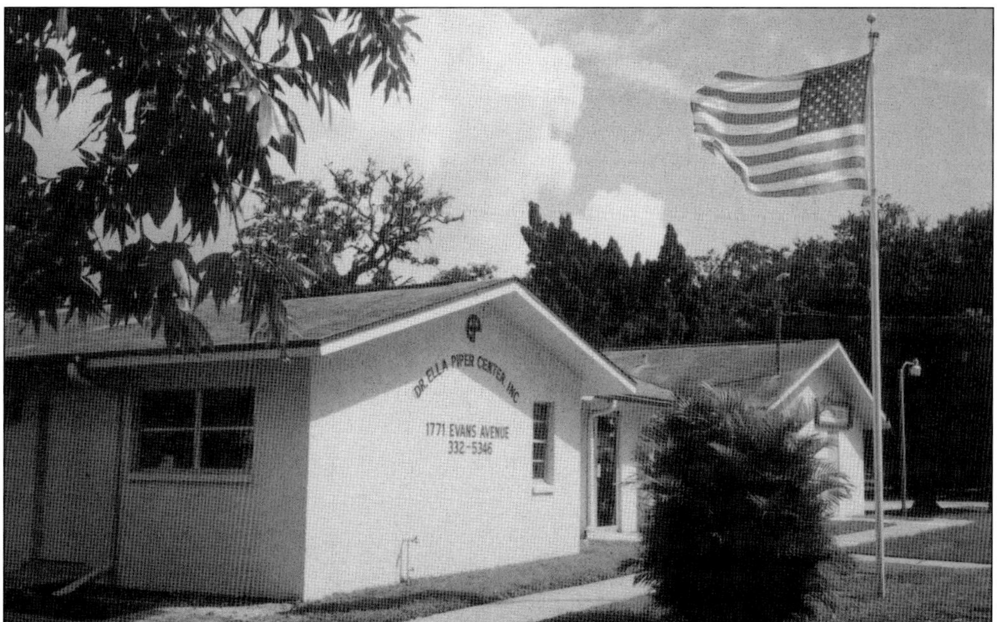

Dr. Ella Piper, who had careers as a chiropodist, beautician, and a soft drink entrepreneur, used her money and position in the black community to do good works. When she died in 1954, her home had been willed to the people of Safety Hill as a social center for the old and very young. Later, several government agencies stepped in and made possible the current Ella Piper Center (seen here).

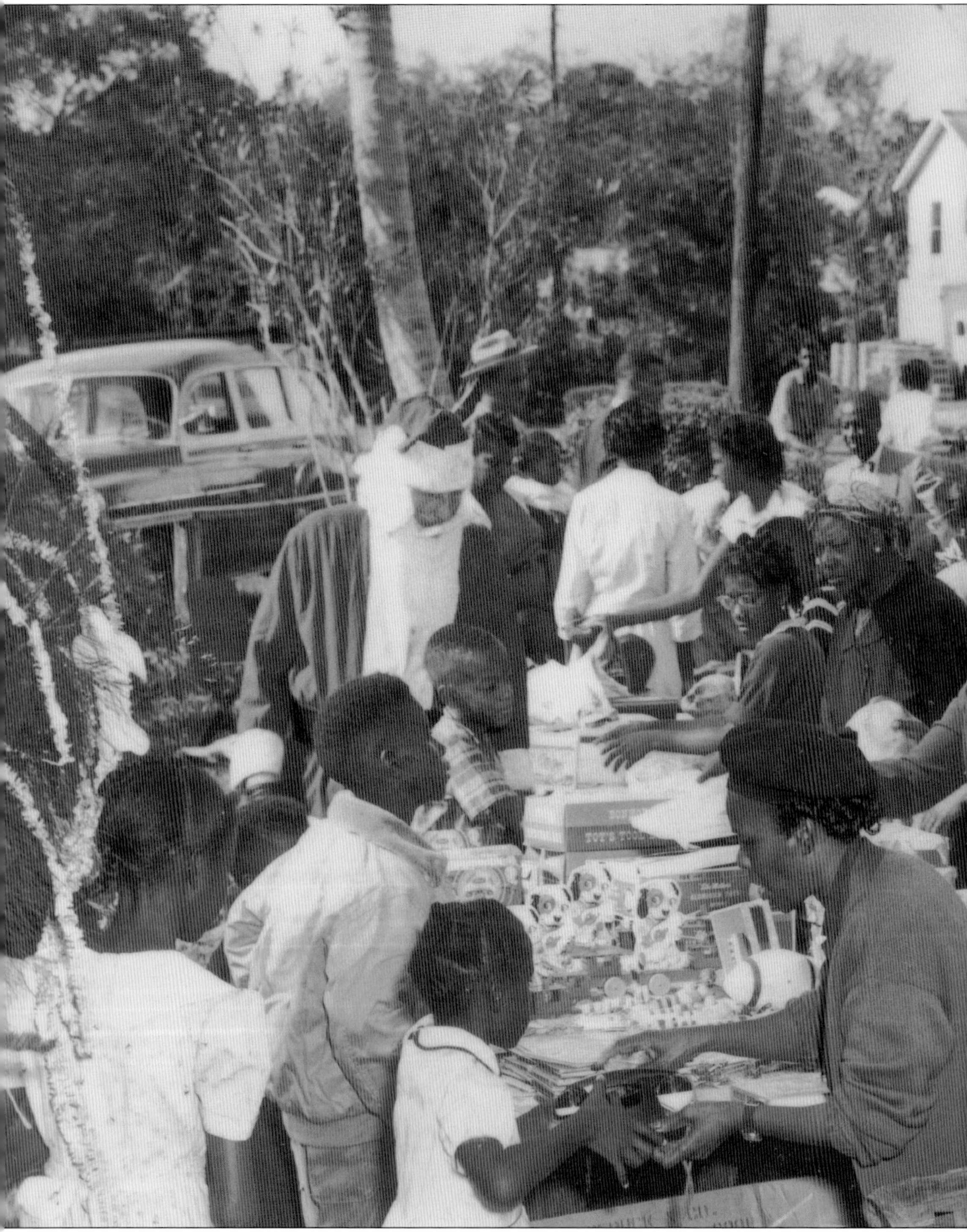

Readers will remember Sara Williams from page 106 (top). She loved to throw Christmas parties for the kids of Safety Hill. As the years rolled by the parties grew in size, and more and more citizens brought presents for the youngsters. When Sara passed on, her daughter Dr. Ella

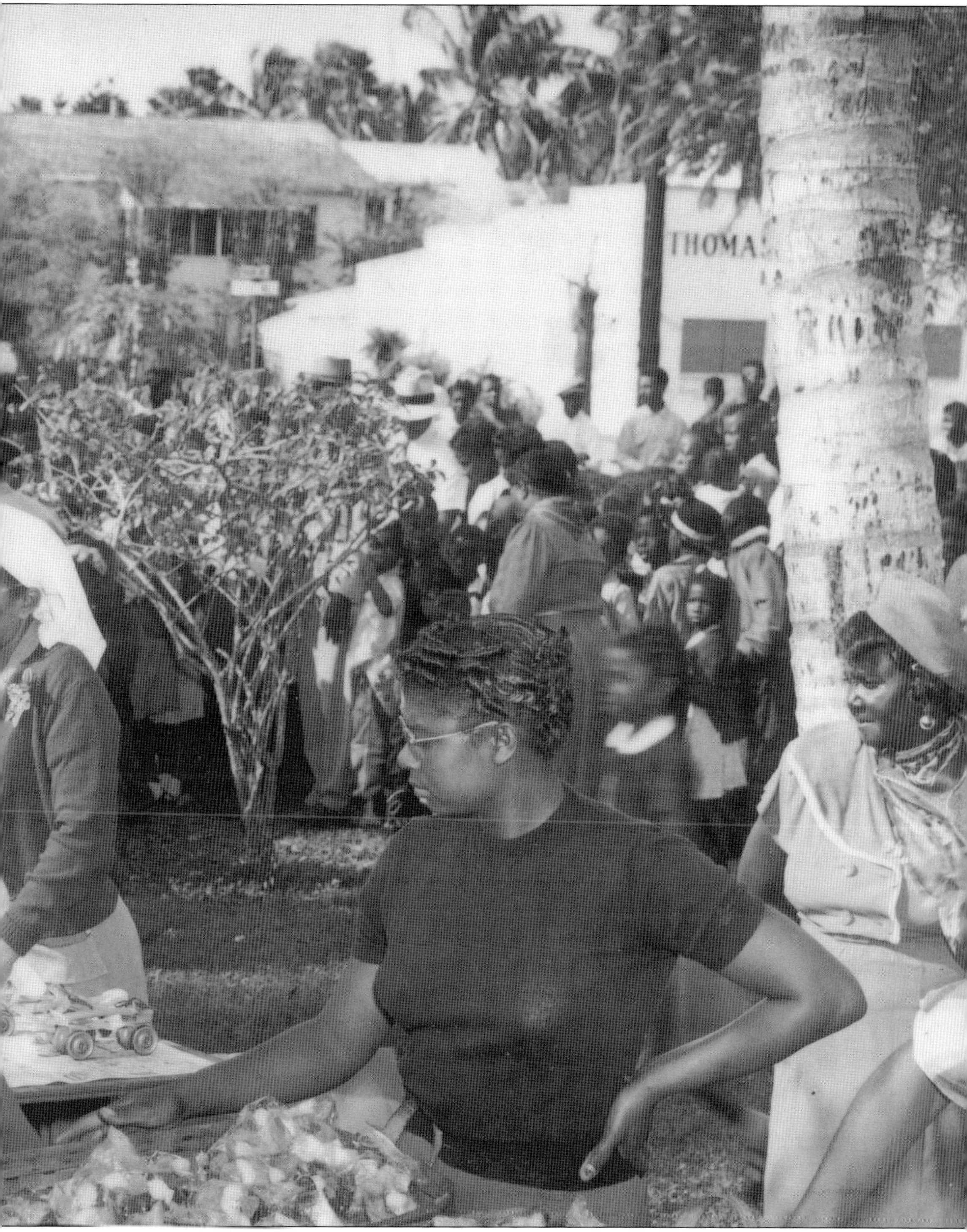

Piper continued the tradition of giving Christmas parties. This 1950s image shows an ample supply of goodies and many happy faces.

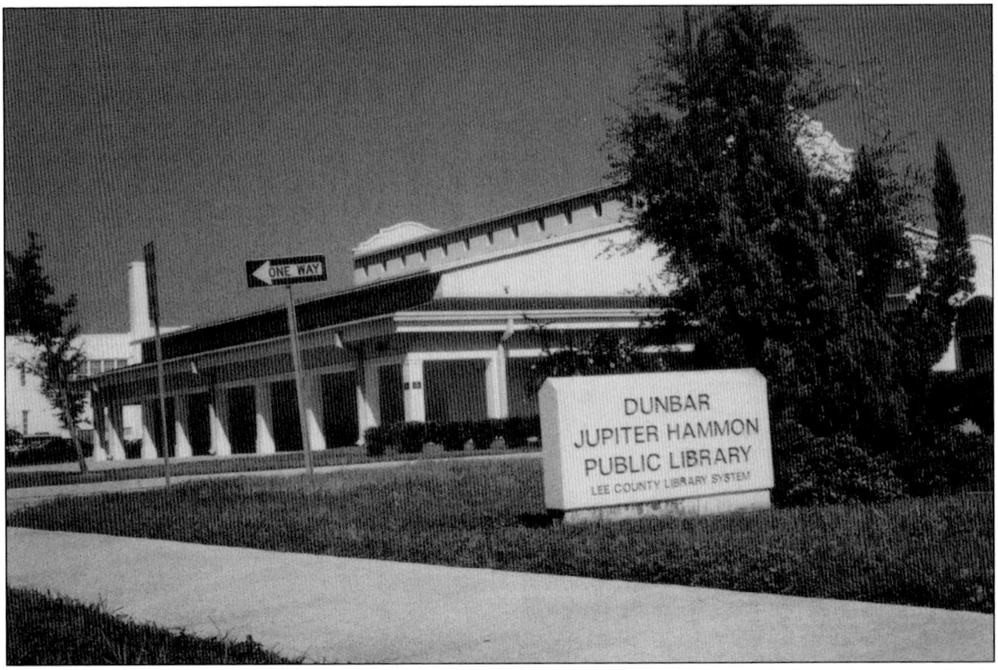

The Jupiter Hammon Public Library, named for the famed black poet of slave days, was built in 1996 and replaced a much smaller structure in Dunbar. Today over 25,000 volumes are maintained at the Hammon facility, which is run by the Lee County Library System.

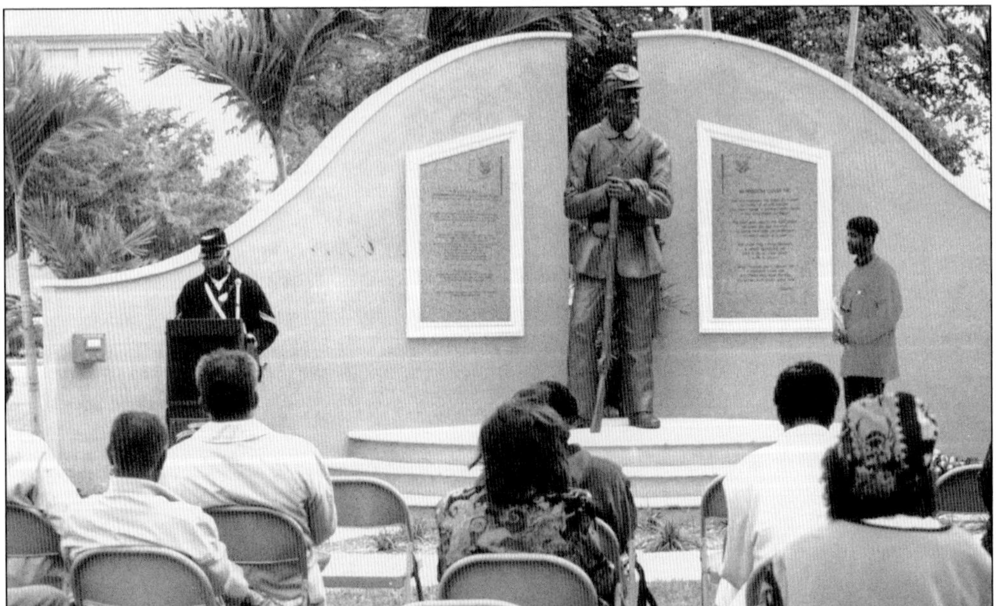

On November 11, 1998, citizens gathered in Centennial Park in downtown Fort Myers to witness the unveiling of this statue representing the 176,000 black soldiers of the Union Army who fought in the Civil War. Readers will recall that two companies of black infantry helped defend Fort Myers in the one-day battle with the Southern "Cattle Guard" on February 20, 1865.

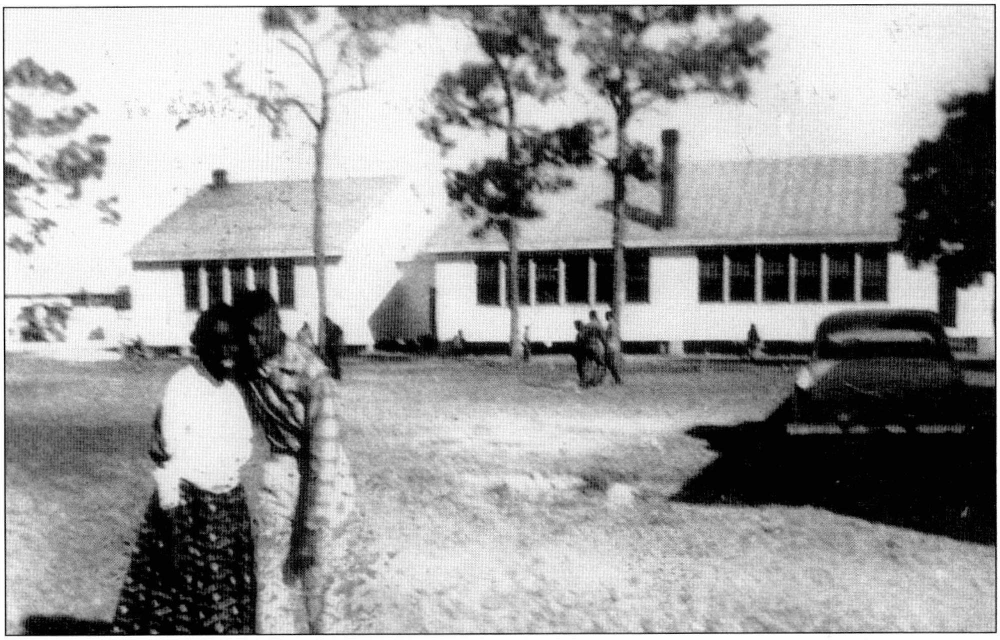

Built in 1913, Williams Academy was the first government-funded school for blacks in Fort Myers. Grades one through eight were conducted in the two-story structure, which stood at the corner of Anderson and Cranford Avenues. Later the building was moved to the Dunbar High School site in the 1930s, where it housed first and second grades.

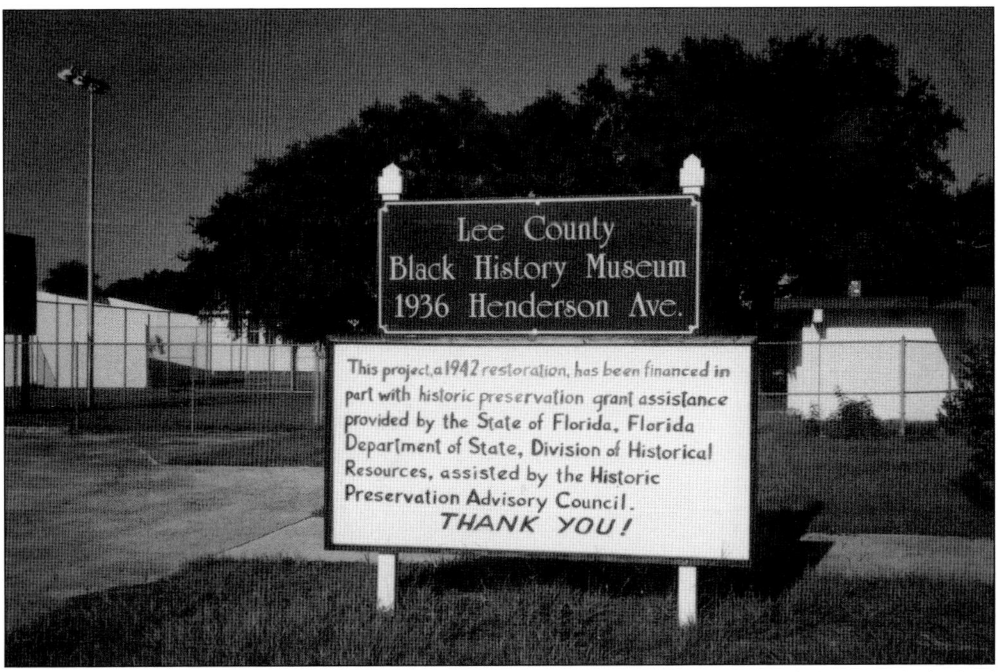

The old Williams Academy schoolhouse (previous image, left side) is currently being refurbished as the Lee County Black History Museum. In 1993, attorney Janice Cass spearheaded the Lee County Black History Society, which is dedicated to preserving the black cultural heritage of Southwest Florida.

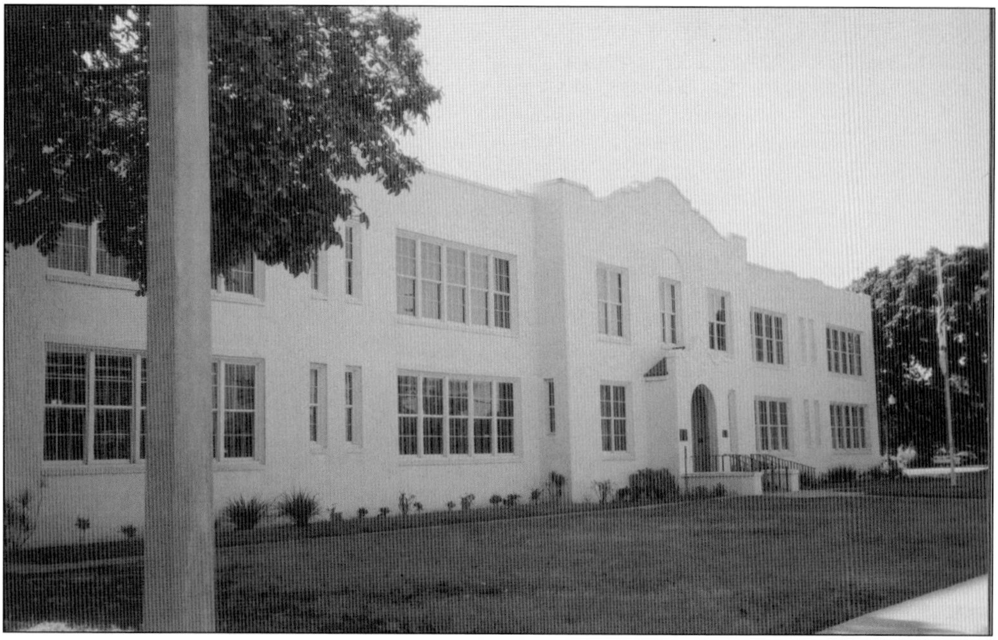

Dunbar High School, located at High and Blount Streets, was built in 1927 at a cost of $99,000. It was named for the renowned black poet Paul Laurence Dunbar, and patterned after another school in Fort Myers, Edison Park Elementary. Until 1962, black students from as far away as Charlotte and Collier Counties were bussed to Dunbar.

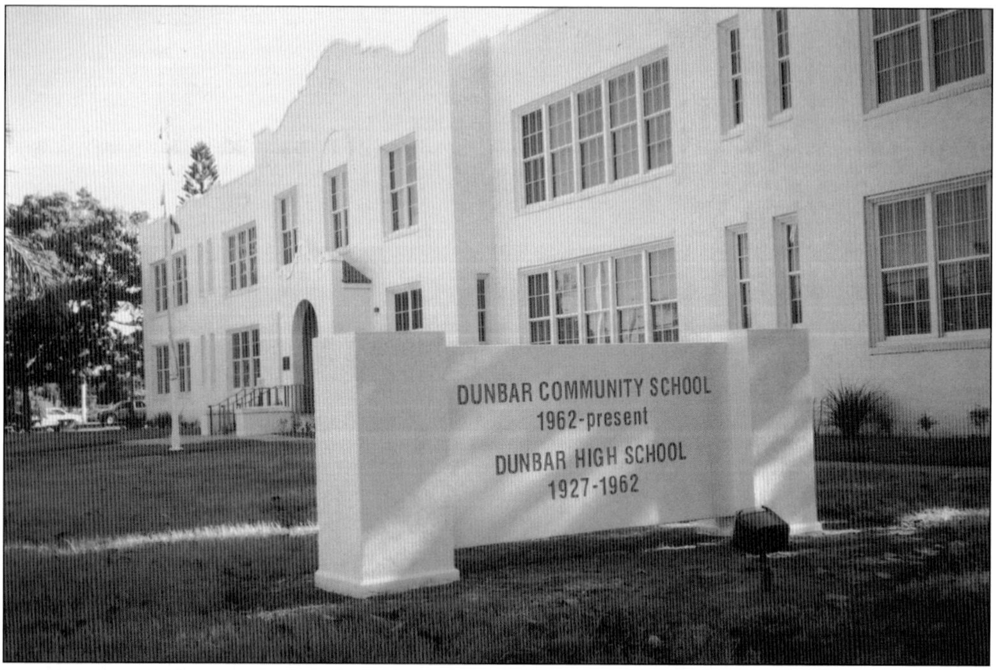

In 1977 the old Dunbar High School facility was converted to a Community Education Center. Jim Stephens, a revered community leader and one of the most popular basketball coaches of the former high school, became the first community education coordinator.

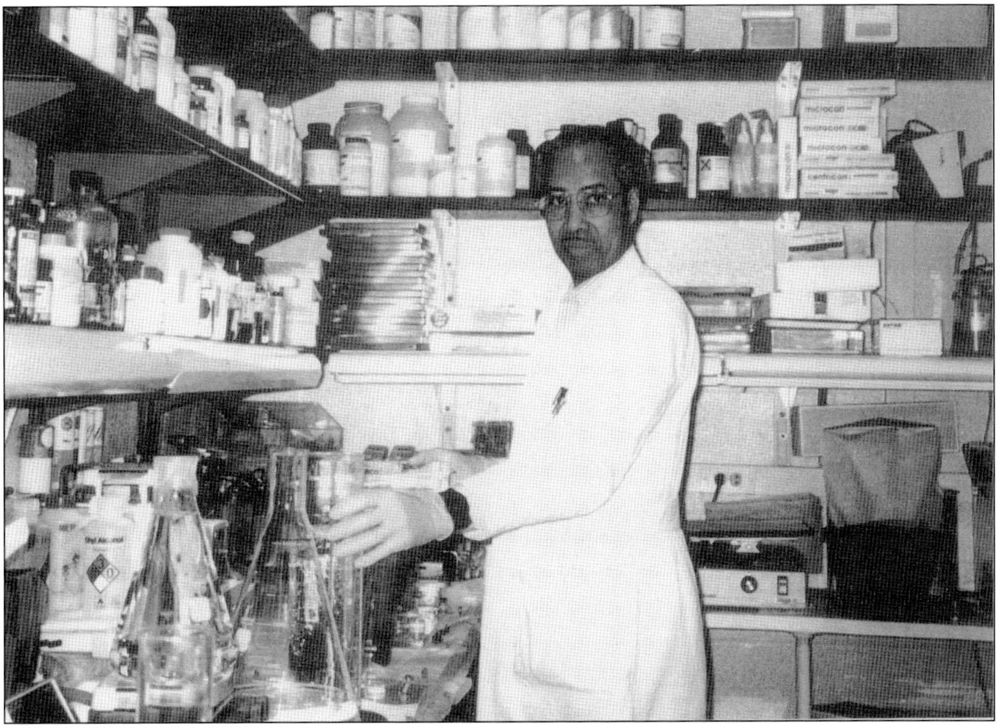

A 1960 graduate of Dunbar High School, Timothy Benjamin went on to receive degrees from Florida A&M, George Washington University, and the University of the District of Columbia. In 1968 he joined the Laboratory of Experimental Carcinogenesis at the National Institute of Health and became a cancer research scientist.

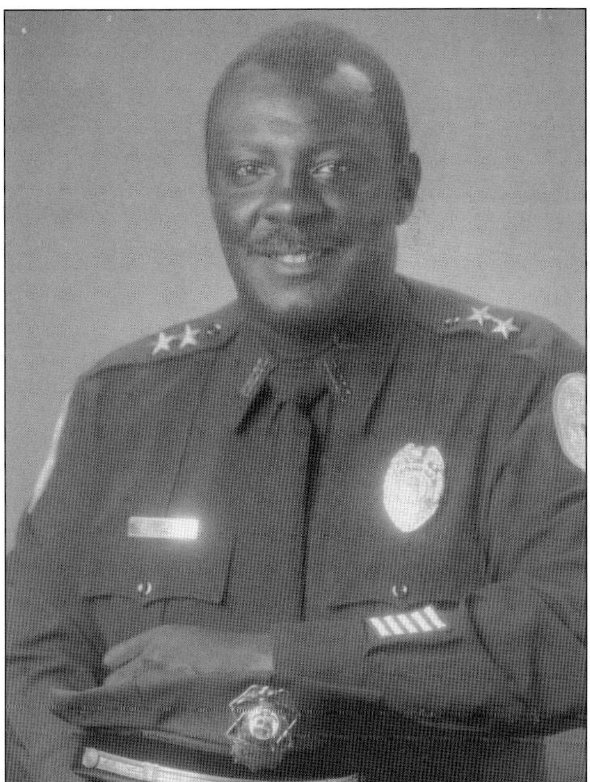

Born and raised in Fort Myers, Larry Hart became a policeman at the age of 24. Sixteen years later, on the basis of his training, experience, and outstanding leadership qualities, he was chosen to become the city's chief of police in March 1995. Hart continually receives praise from area law enforcement officials.

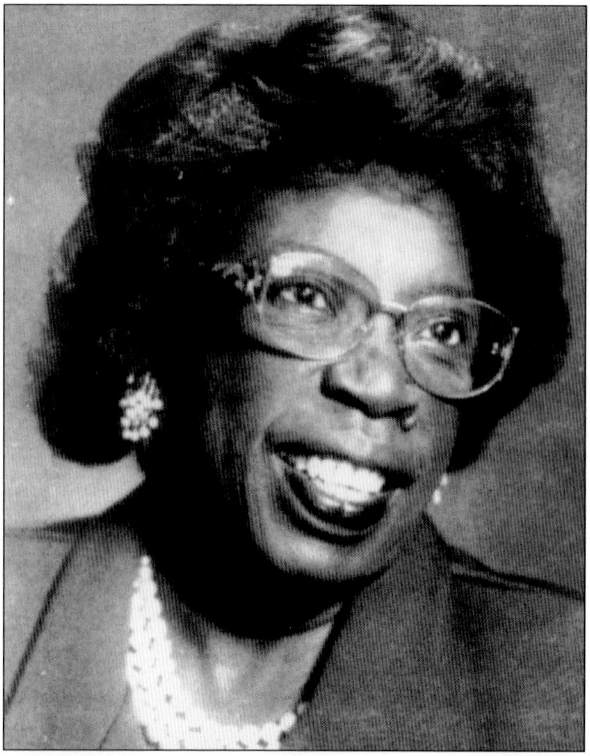

In 1982 local businesswoman Veronica Shoemaker became the first black person to be elected to the Fort Myers City Council. Eighteen years later she still serves in that capacity. Two years after her election she was joined by another black woman, educator Dr. Ann Knight, who also remains a representative of the people.

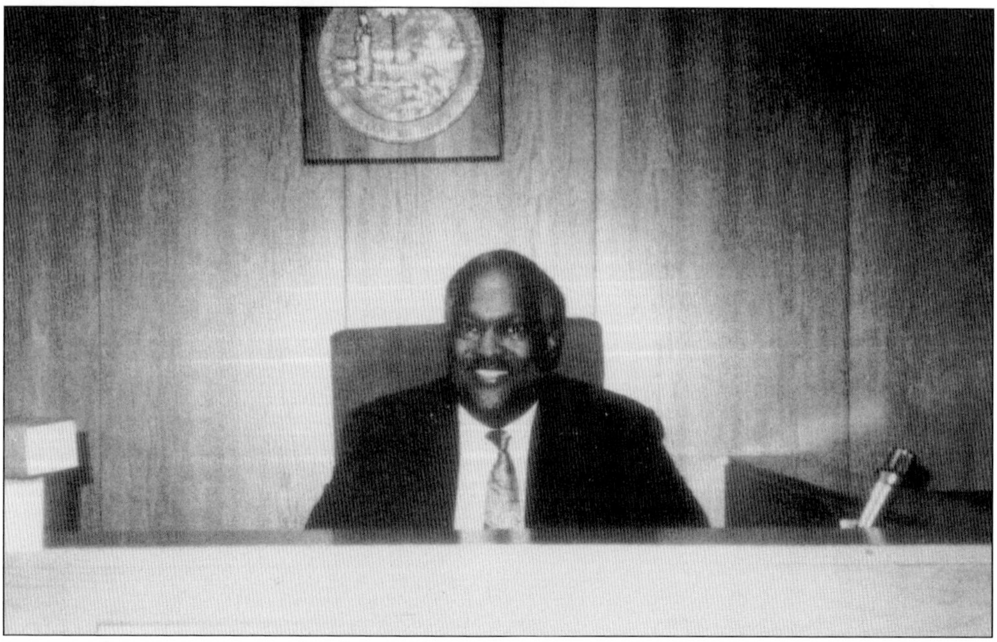

Isaac Anderson, a young and ambitious lawyer born and reared in Dunbar, was first appointed, then elected (by a huge majority) to a Lee County judgeship in the 1980s. Since then he has twice been elected as a circuit judge. Another black attorney, James Adams, has also been elected a circuit judge, which easily demonstrates the evolving era of change in which we all live.

Eight

New Horizons

Until the 1960s the only city in Lee County was Fort Myers. For almost a hundred years the City of Palms was the social, educational, and cultural center of this largely agricultural area, which is approximately 800 square miles in size.

Then, three modern "happenings" took place almost simultaneously. Science and airplanes started to control the pesky mosquito, air conditioning became economically feasible, and the first Social Security crowd came of age. Thomas Edison's prediction that 90 million people would discover Fort Myers started to come true, with help of course from developers, banks, real estate folks, promoters, and friendly politicians.

The city across the Caloosahatchee, Cape Coral, personifies the explosion of growth, and is today the largest metropolis of Lee County. But tourists and newcomers also discovered the barrier islands near Fort Myers as well as Fort Myers Beach. New housing appeared, and the flux of people meant new roads, bridges, schools, shopping, and a huge airport. Lee County's population in 1960 stood at 54,000—today that number is over 400,000. But as growth occurred, downtown Fort Myers declined. People left, and shopping centers, plazas, and the big Edison Mall drew consumers elsewhere.

Downtown Fort Myers remained, however, the center of governance. The county commissioners were located here as well as the courthouse and record buildings. As the population soared, government services rapidly increased, so it was inevitable that old commercial structures would experience rejuvenation and that new ones would be built. Further, entrepreneurs have helped transform downtown Fort Myers into an inviting entertainment and residential area. In the following pages we can only glimpse the numerous changes and transformations.

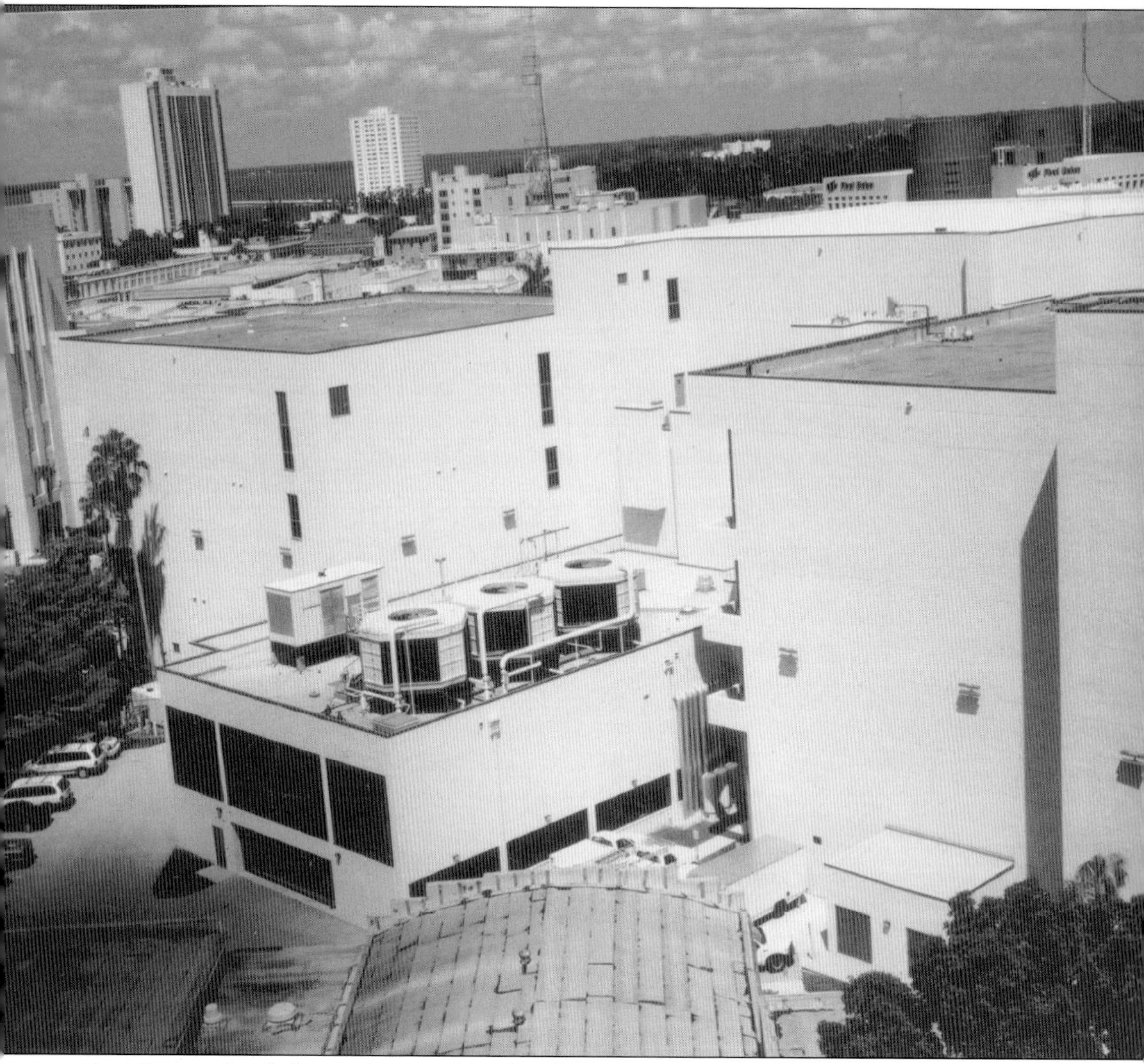

Lee County decided to replace its old jail in downtown Fort Myers in 1981. Two years later, the huge Lee County Justice Center (seen above) opened. Both city and county cases are tried here; the center boasts 11 court rooms, 22 judges chambers, hearing rooms, state attorney offices,

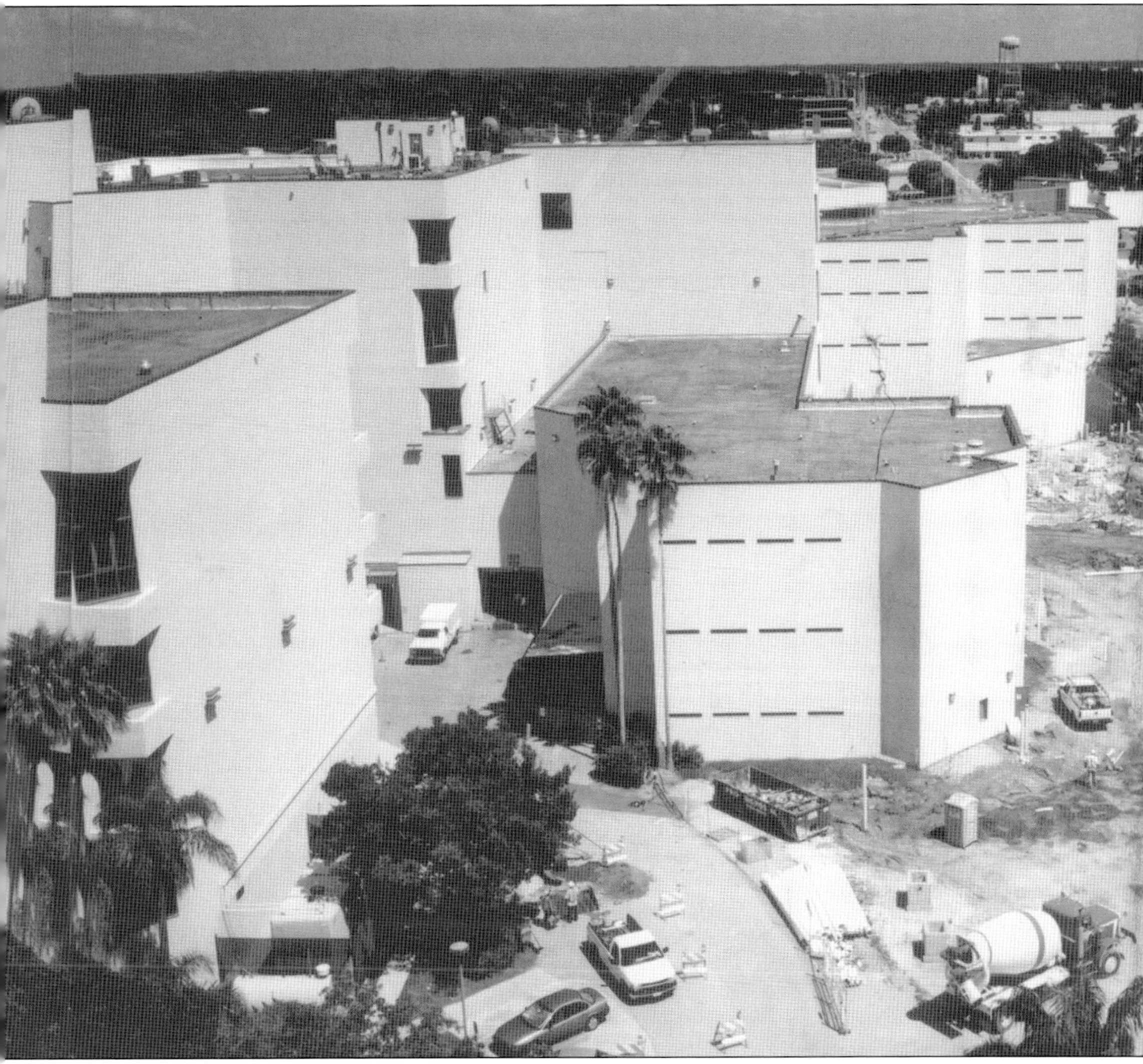

public defender offices, administrative offices, a probate court, county clerk offices, a law library, and a cafe. A juvenile detention area is currently being added to the 240,000-square-foot facility, which is one of the largest structures in the city.

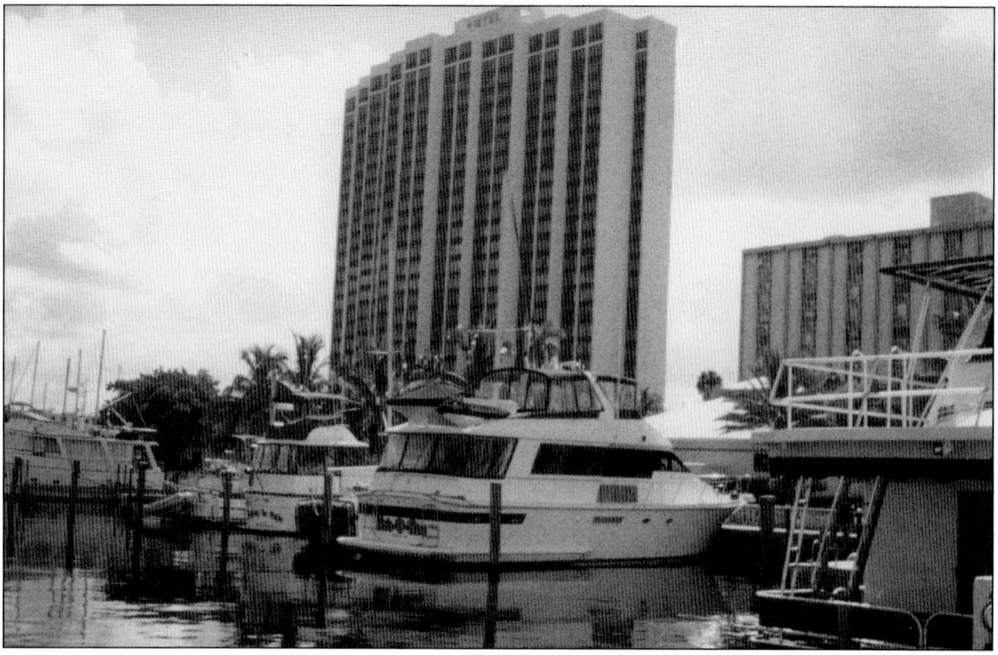

The 25-story Sheraton Harbor Place Hotel—the tallest commercial building in the city—arose near the Caloosahatchee in 1986. It featured a marina so boaters could berth their vessels and spend a weekend in one of the 452 rooms or deluxe suites. Over the years several ownership changes have occurred, and today the hostelry is operated by the Ramada Corporation.

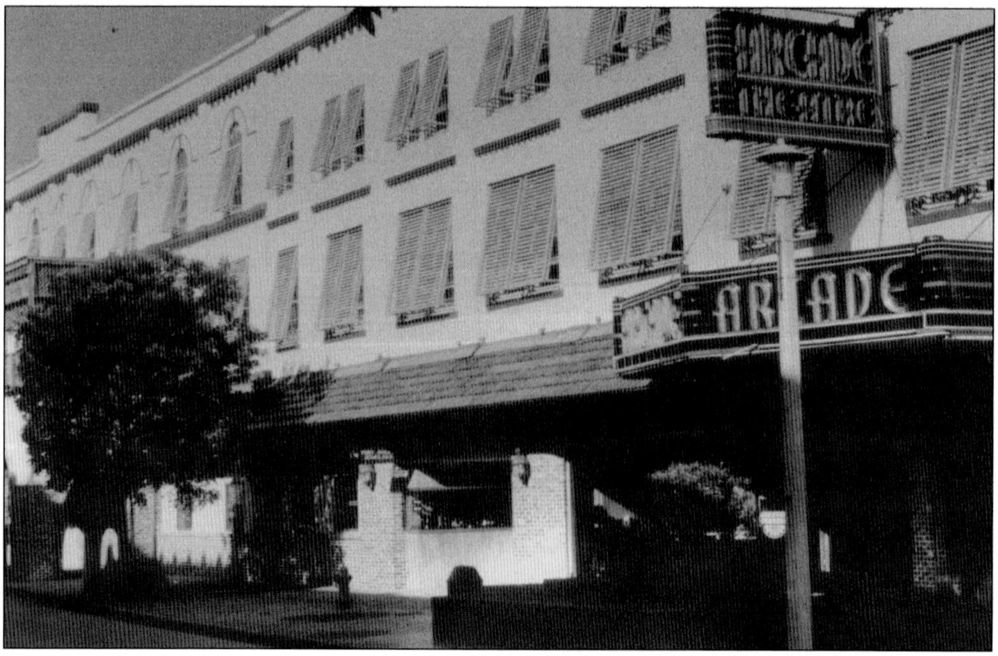

The Arcade Theatre on First Street became part of the Bradford Hotel complex in 1915. For years, silent movies and vaudeville acts were its principal attractions. Then, theatres removed from the downtown area forced the Arcade's stage closure. Today the Bradford is a superb apartment building, and the Arcade stages quality live theater productions.

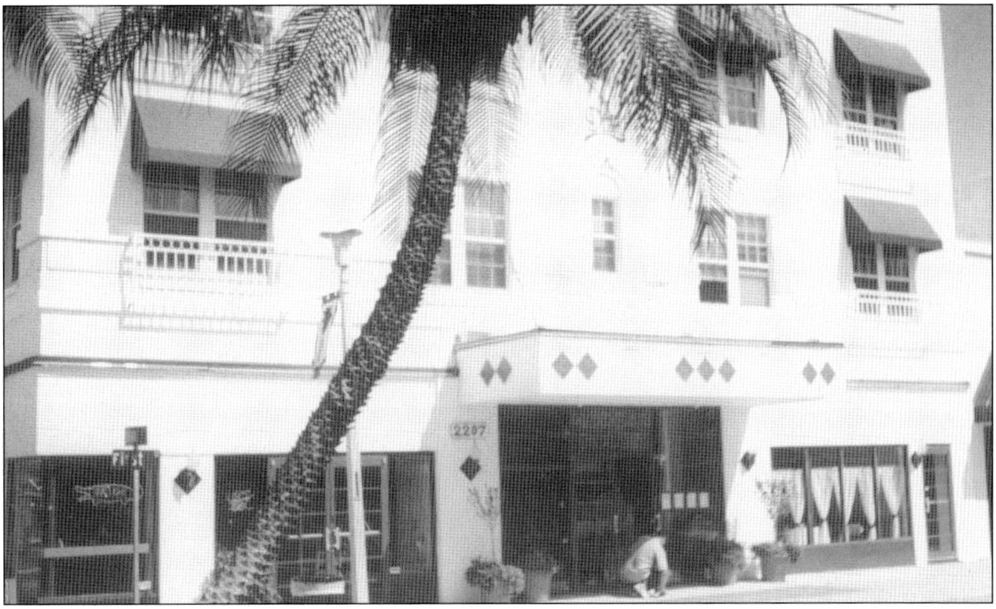

In 1924, a Rhode Island furniture merchant named John Dean, who had been investing in Fort Myers for two decades, bought the old Sanchez boardinghouse. By converting the wooden structure and wrapping it in concrete block, Dean created the 62-room Morgan Hotel. The operation, though, fell on hard times in the 1930s, closed in the 1970s, and is now a beautifully restored apartment building.

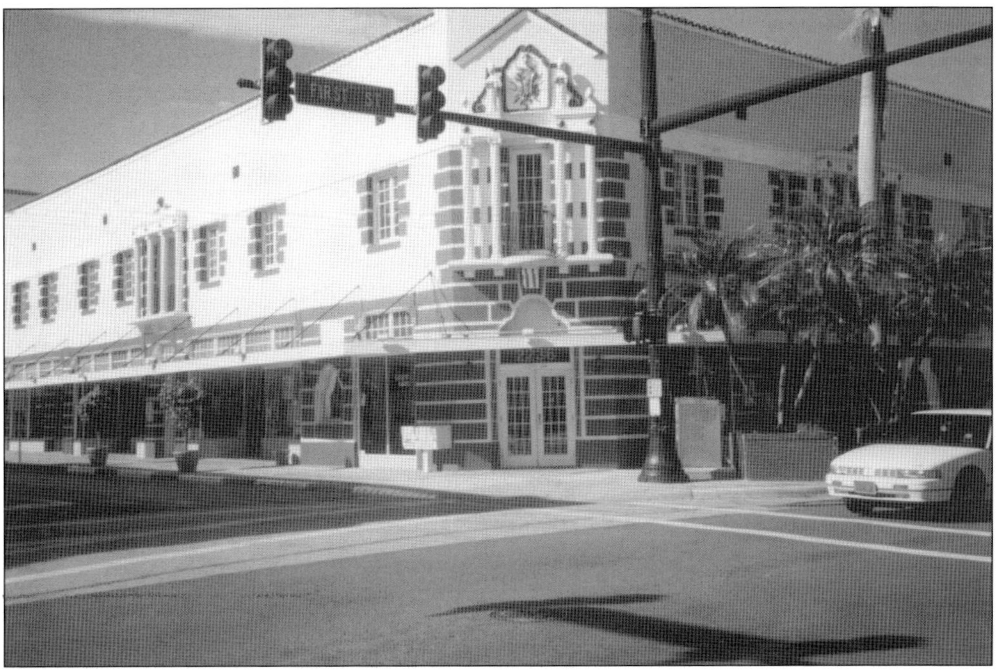

The DeLeon Building is another Fort Myers masterpiece restored to its glamour of the 1920s. It was first built in 1905 of pressed concrete stone. A number of facelifts have occurred over the years, and finally its new owner, after evaluating photographs of the building in its heyday, duplicated it in spades.

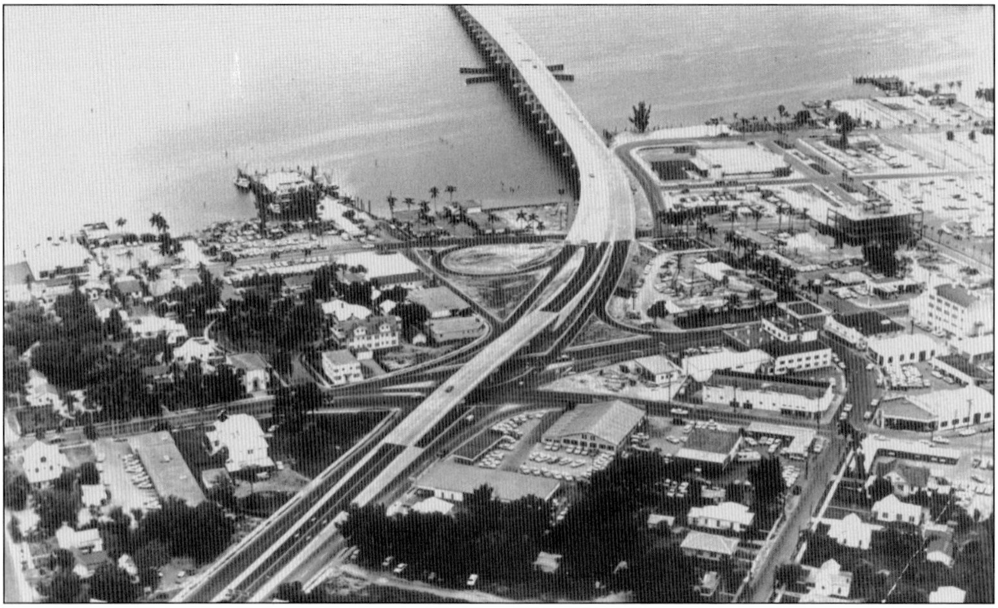

The first bridge over the Caloosahatchee into Fort Myers was built in 1924, a narrow wooden affair that brought in the Tamiami Trail. Then came the concrete Edison Bridge of 1931, but it had only two lanes and a drawspan that was forever delaying vehicular traffic. In 1964, the four-lane, 58-foot-high Caloosahatchee Bridge, seen above, opened to an eager public, and the population race was on.

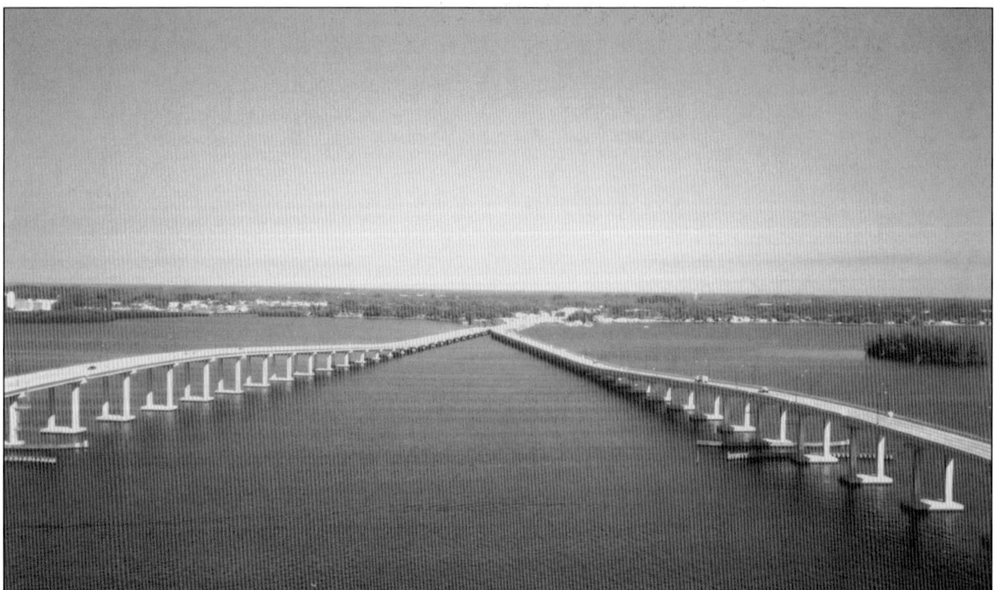

Tom Edison made a special trip to Fort Myers in 1931 to dedicate the bridge over the Caloosahatchee built in his name. Sixty-two years later the relentless surge of progress demanded the twin spans seen above—one for northbound traffic, another for southbound. Both retain the Edison name.

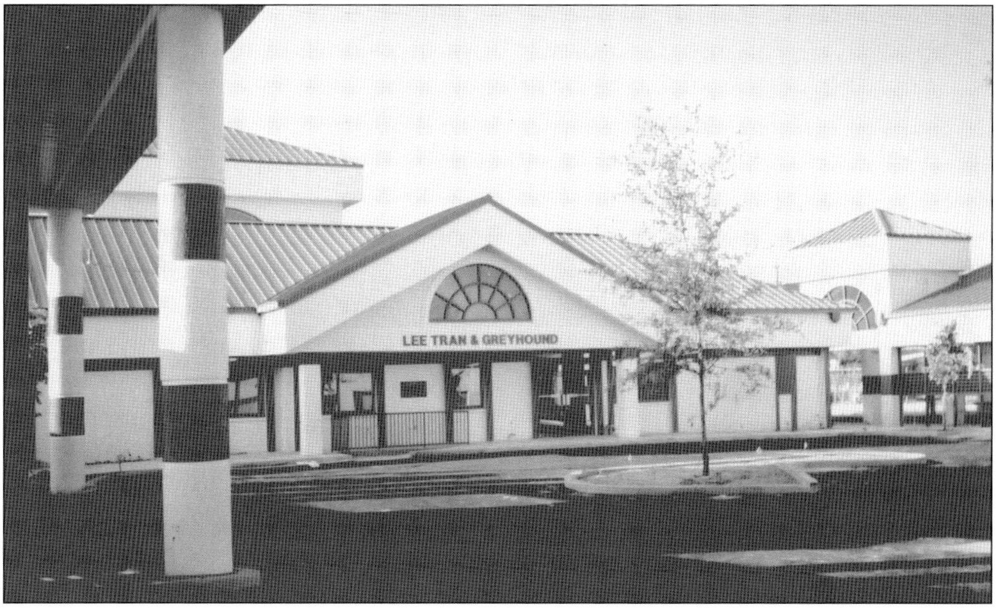

Construction has been completed on a new bus terminal in Fort Myers, which will serve both the Lee County transit system ("LeeTran") and commercial bus lines. It is located directly across from the Fort Myers Historical Museum, which served as the passenger train depot from 1924 to 1971.

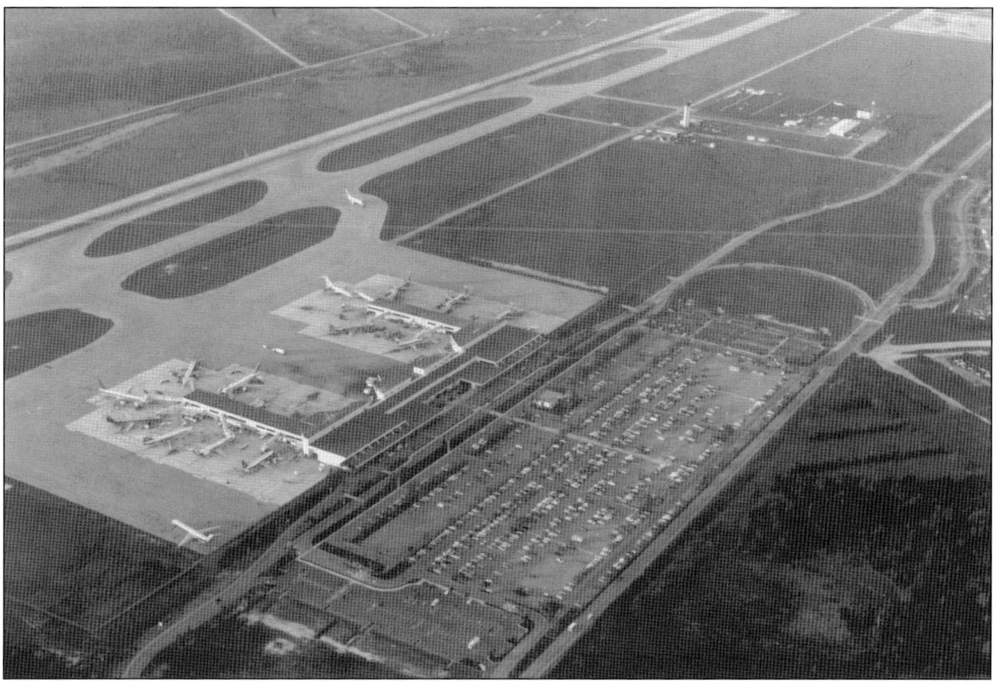

Southwest Florida International Airport opened in 1983 at a cost $90 million and instantly relieved the cramped conditions over at Page Field on Cleveland Avenue. Two years later, the new facility received port of entry status from U.S. Customs, which facilitated foreign travel. Today millions of passengers are accommodated every year and expansion is ongoing.

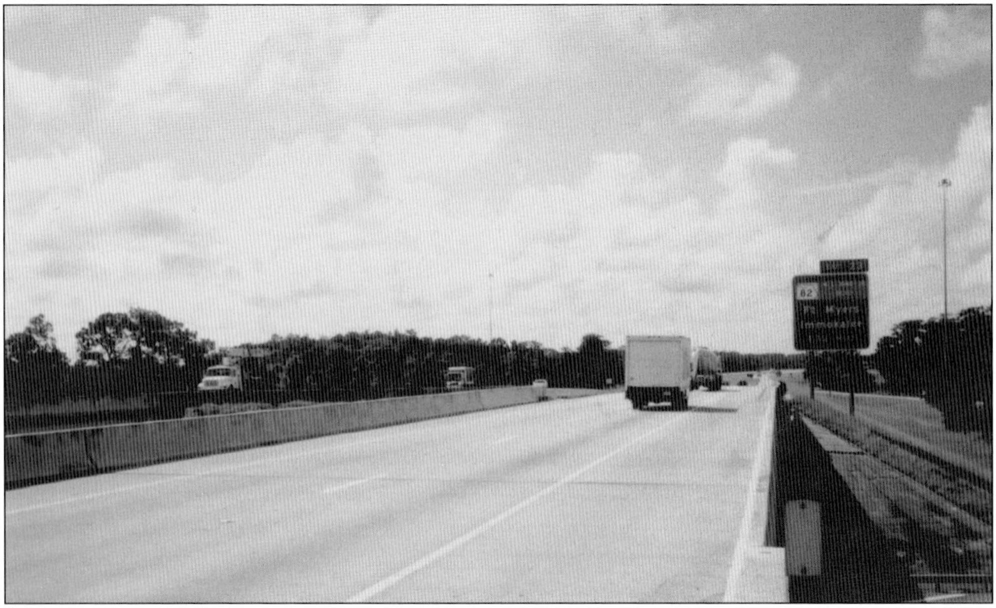

In 1928 the two-lane Tamiami Trail finally connected Tampa with Miami by way of Fort Myers. A faster trip across the Everglades became possible in 1966 when the famed "Alligator Alley" opened across the Glades. Then, in the 1980s, a real interstate highway (I-75) connected the cities of Southwest Florida, which has fueled development and growth never thought possible.

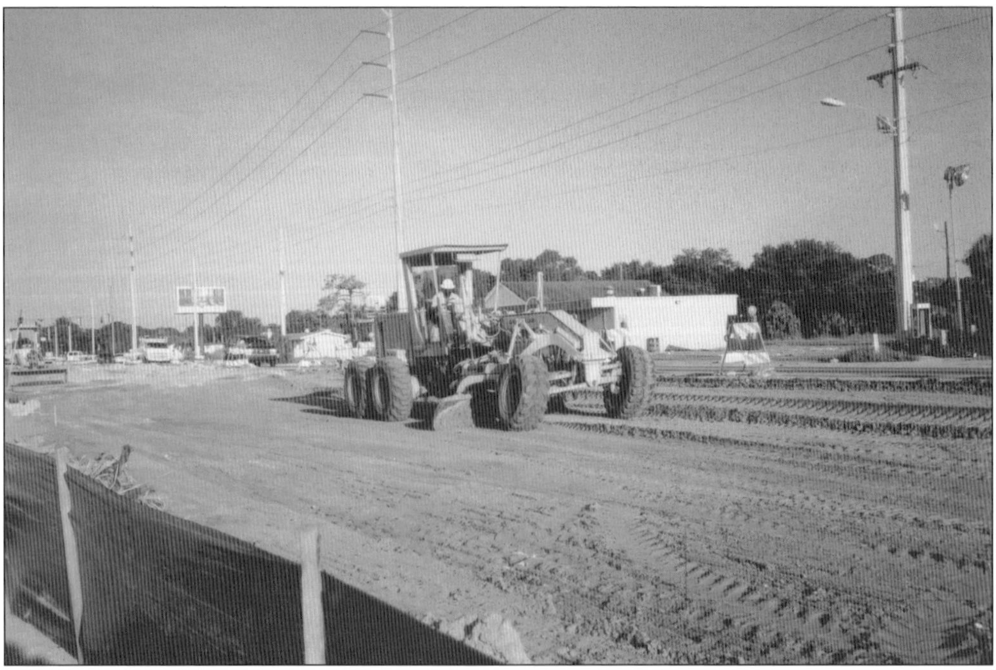

Several interchanges radiate from I-75 in the Fort Myers area. As traffic increased, several arteries into the city proper required widening, such as Palm Beach Boulevard and Colonial Avenue. In the year 2000, work continues on four-laning Martin Luther King Boulevard from the downtown area to the interchange seen in the previous photograph.

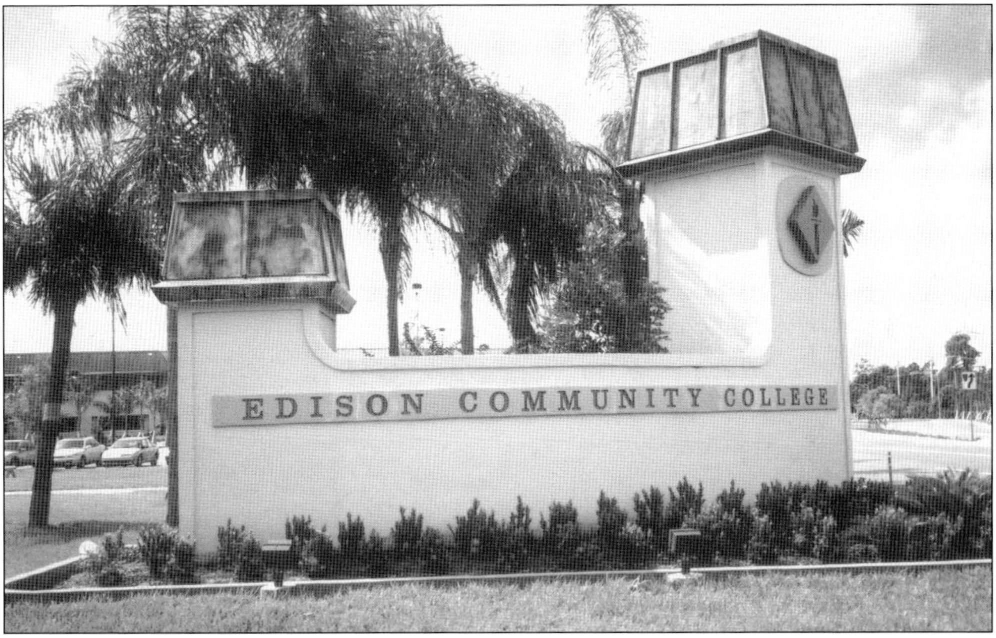

From a handful of students attending classes in the old Gwynne Institute beginning in 1962, Edison Community College has enrolled over 175,000 students. Its 140-acre south Lee County campus, located on College Parkway, opened in 1965. Today the college has 23 permanent structures, including the popular Barbara B. Mann Performing Arts Center.

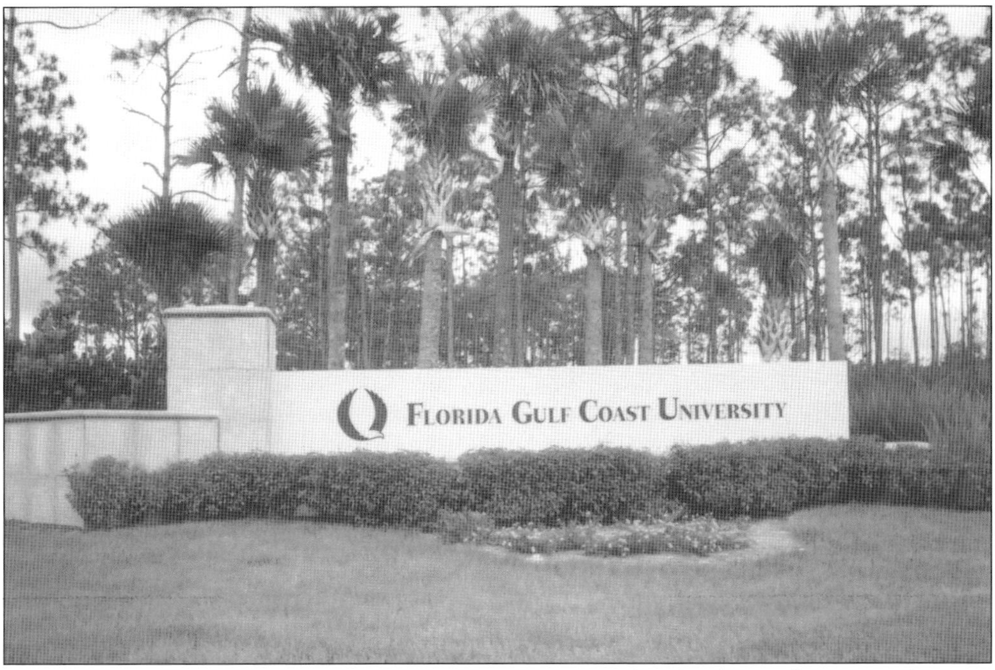

After seven years of planning and building, Southwest Florida obtained its own four-year university in 1997. Florida Gulf Coast University is the tenth and newest institution in the Florida State University System. The campus, nestled in a 760-acre tract of pine forest and wetlands, is conveniently located near Interstate 75 in South Lee County.

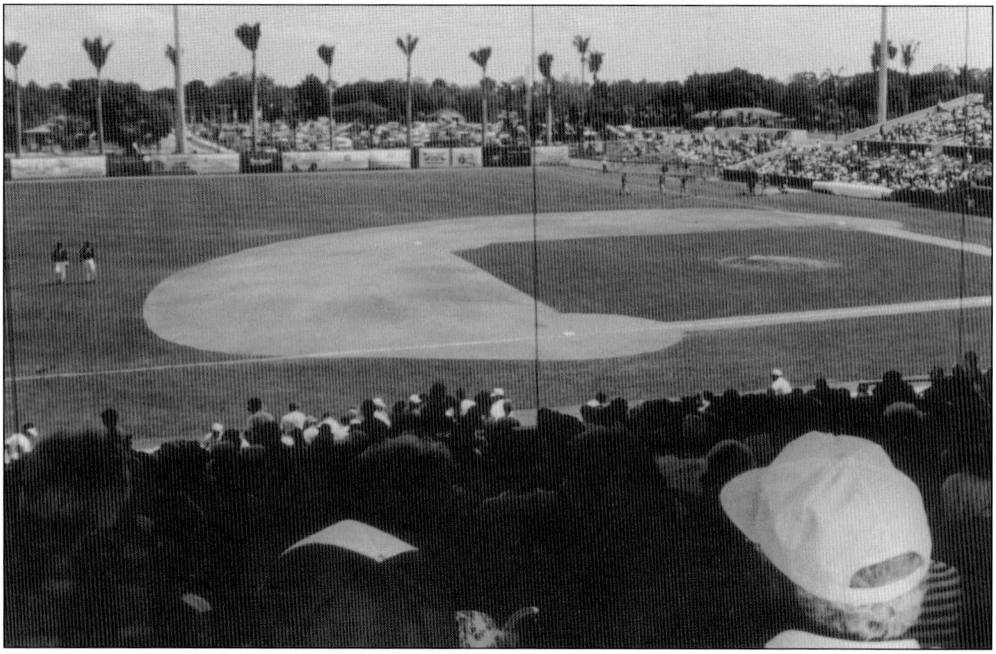

When the Boston Red Sox opened spring training at the City of Palms Park on March 5, 1993, they became the sixth team to call Fort Myers their winter home. The stadium, located on Edison Avenue near downtown, can seat some 7,000 spectators with no roof-supporting poles to mar the view.

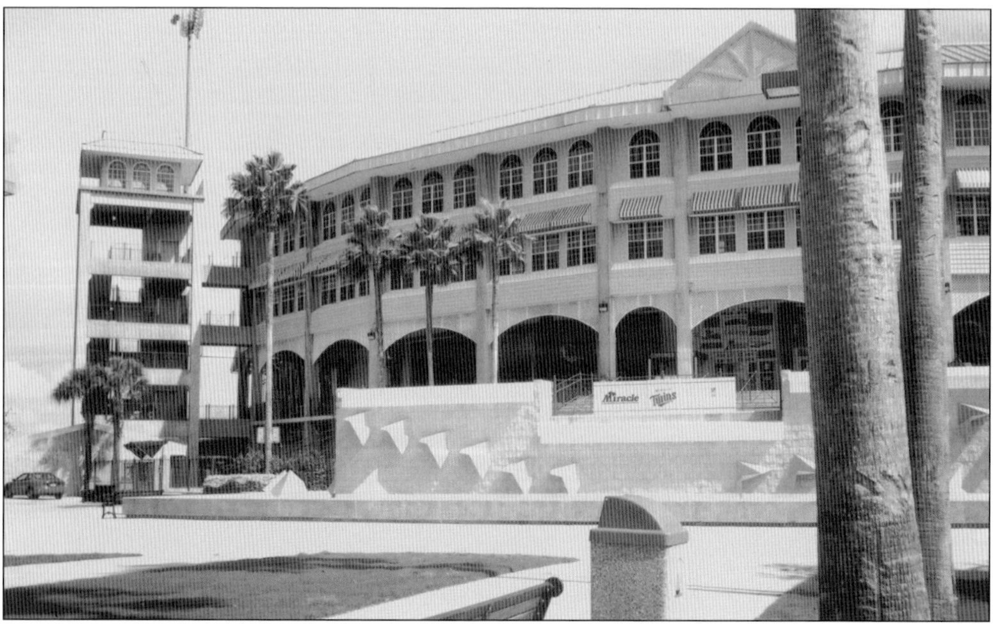

Fort Myers has had a long love affair with baseball. In 1925 the Philadelphia Athletics trained here, followed by the Cleveland Indians, the Pittsburgh Pirates, and the Kansas City Royals. When the latter could not negotiate a new stadium, they left town. Lee County then hustled another team by building the above stadium in 1991 on Six Mile Cypress Road. Today it is home to the Minnesota Twins.

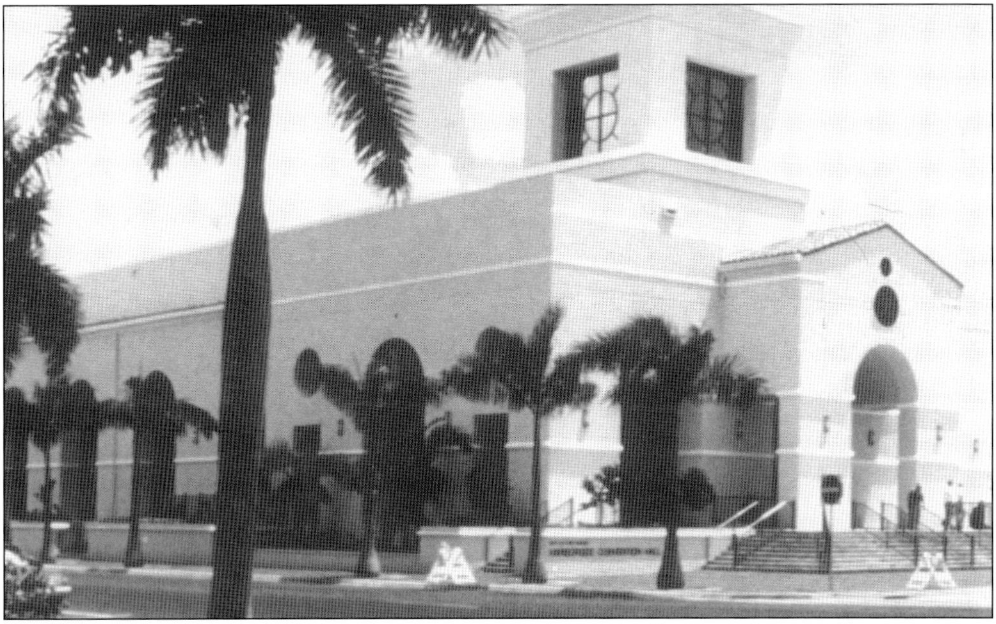

Harborside Convention Center opened in 1991 and specifically catered to small conventions. For several years the facility hosted a variety of nationally known entertainers and bands like Frank Sinatra and the Oak Ridge Boys; however, with limited seating, the payoff was negligible. Lately the space is rented for trade shows, and plans are afoot to expand the complex.

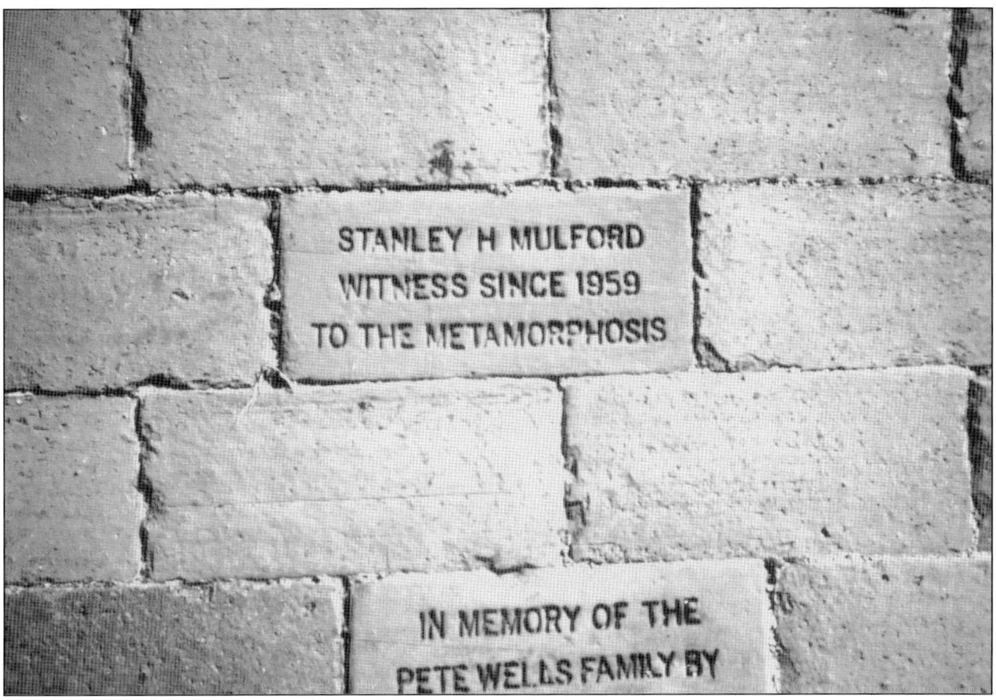

The pavement on two sides of the Harborside Convention Center, seen in the previous image, is paved with bricks paid for by people at $30 with inscriptions up to 64 letters. The messages thereon are a varied lot and numerous, including this one placed by one of your authors.

Further Reading

*Board, Prudy T. and Esther B. Colcord. *Pages From the Past: A Pictorial Retrospective of Lee County, Florida*. Virginia Beach: Donning Company, 1990.

*Board, Prudy T. and Patricia Pope Bartlett. *Lee County: A Pictorial History*. Virginia Beach: Donning Company, 1985.

Covington, James W. *The Story of Southwestern Florida*. New York: Lewis Historical Publishing Company, 1957.

———. *The Seminoles of Florida*. Gainesville: University Press of Florida, 1993.

*Godown, Marion and Alberta Rawchuck. *Yesterday's Fort Myers*. Miami: E.A. Seeman Publishers, 1975.

Gonzalez, Thomas A. *The Caloosahatchee*. Fort Myers Beach: Island Press, 1982.

*Grismer, Karl H. *The Story of Fort Myers*. Fort Myers Beach: Island Press Publishers, 1982.

Schell, Rolfe F. *History of Fort Myers Beach, Florida*. Fort Myers Beach: Island Press, 1980.

Tebeau, Charlton W. and William Marina. *A History of Florida*. Coral Gables: University of Miami Press, 1999 (3rd ed.).

*Turner, Gregg M. *Railroads of Southwest Florida*. Charleston, SC: Arcadia Publishing, 1999.

*available from Fort Myers Historical Museum bookstore
2300 Peck Street
Fort Myers, FL 33901
Tel. (941) 332-5955